THE BUDDHIST TEACHING OF TOTALITY

華嚴談舍

THE BUDDHIST
TEACHING
OF TOTALITY

The Philosophy of
Hwa Yen Buddhism

Garma C. C. Chang

**THE PENNSYLVANIA STATE
UNIVERSITY PRESS**

University Park and London

Previous Books in English by Garma C. C. Chang include:

THE PRACTICE OF ZEN
THE TEACHINGS OF TIBETAN YOGA
THE HUNDRED THOUSAND SONGS OF MILAREPA

Copyright © 1971 by The Pennsylvania State University
Printed in the United States of America
All rights reserved
Library of Congress Catalog Card Number: 70–136965
International Standard Book Number: 0–271–01142–4
Designed by Marilyn E. Shobaken

CONTENTS

PREFACE

During my thirty-five years of association with Buddhism, I have always asked this question: "Of all Buddhist Schools—Hīnayāna, Mahāyāna and Tantra alike—which one truly holds the highest teaching of Buddhism?" The answer is now a clear-cut one: it is the Hwa Yen School of China. The Hwa Yen School, or Hwa Yen Tsung, was established in the T'ang period, roughly in the 7th and 8th centuries A.D., by outstanding thinkers such as Tu Shun (557–640) and Fa Tsang (643–712). The Chinese word Hwa Yen means "the flower-decoration" or "garland," which is originally the name of a voluminous Mahāyāna text: *The Garland Sūtra* (*The Gaṇḍavyūha* or *Avataṁsaka Sūtra*). Therefore, the teaching of this School is based mainly upon this text and draws inspiration from it.

What does this scripture say and to whom are its messages addressed? The Hwa Yen Sūtra has one central concern: to reveal the Buddha-Realm of Infinity. Its messages are therefore directed to those who appreciate the awe-inspiring Infinity of Buddhahood revealed in Buddha's Enlightenment experience, which is described briefly in the first chapter. There is no other Buddhist scripture, to the best of my knowledge, that is superior to Hwa Yen in revealing the highest spiritual inspiration and the most profound mystery of Buddhahood. This opinion is shared, I believe, by the majority of Chinese and Japanese Buddhist scholars. It is small wonder that Hwa Yen has been regarded as the "crown" of all Buddhist teachings, and as representing the consummation of Buddhist insight and thought.

Inspired by the revelation of the all-embracing Totality in this Sūtra, the pioneer Hwa Yen thinkers, notably Master Tu Shun, developed what was at that time a novel approach to Buddhist thinking. They taught that the correct way of thinking is to view things through a multiple or totalistic approach. Nothing is rejected, because in the "round" Totality of Buddhahood there is not even room for contradiction; here the inconsistencies all become harmonious. This totalistic way of thinking was first introduced in Tu Shun's epoch-making essay, "On the Meditation of Dharmadhātu," which eventually became the fountainhead of all subsequent Hwa Yen works. It was mainly through Tu Shun's great insight shown in this essay that the "Hwa-Yen Round-Thinking" (Yüan Chiao Chien) first broke its ground. Two generations later, Fa Tsang systematized the doctrine through his profuse writings; therefore he is generally regarded as the founder of the Hwa Yen School.

The reader will notice that Hwa Yen is a synthesis of all major Mahāyāna thoughts, a philosophy of *totalistic organism*. The three major concepts of Mahāyāna—namely the Philosophies of Totality, of Emptiness, and of Mind-Only—are all merged into a unity. Far from being a concoction, Hwa Yen Doctrine represents an "organic whole" of all essential elements of Mahāyāna Buddhism. When one comes to Hwa Yen, he sees Buddhism in a completely new light. Even the tedious Mind-Only doctrine now becomes vivid and alive. The Ālaya Consciousness of Yogācāra is no more a dull and torpid "store-house," the tyrannical Jungian Collective Unconscious is no more an ever-evasive archetypal image-projector. In Hwa Yen the "Universal Mind" is likened to a vast Ocean-Mirror in which the infinite dramas in the universe are spontaneously and simultaneously reflected. No more is the Mind-Only doctrine a one-way projection, but it becomes a kaleidoscope of multi-dimensional, mutual projections and inter-penetrations. Even the Philosophy of Śūnyatā (Voidness) now appears to be different from what it was before. The Totalistic Voidness presented in Hwa Yen literature reveals many hidden facets of Śūnyatā which are not immediately clear in the Mādhyamika theses. Only in Hwa Yen do the far-reaching implications of the Śūnyatā doctrine laid down in the Prajñāpāramitā literature become transparently clear. The majority of intellectually inclined Zen monks all come to Hwa Yen because they could oftentimes find therein spiritual guidance in their bewildering Zen Path and discover sensible solutions to those abstruse Zen problems. Many "senseless" Zen koans become meaningful if one can appropriately apply the Hwa Yen Round-Thinking to these cases.

As any pioneer work, this book does not claim to be an exhaustive study of the stupendous Hwa Yen literature. But it is my humble opinion that the gist and the essential elements of Hwa Yen teachings, especially the philosophical aspects, are all included in this volume. I have tried to avoid meticulous annotations and excessive footnotes in order to make the reading easier for the general reader.

The Romanization of the Chinese characters is based on the most unsatisfactory but academically accepted Wade-Giles system, with one exception: instead of Hua Yen, I have used Hwa Yen for the simple reason that the former will be mispronounced by Westerners so as to mean "ashes-salt" (反 盐) in Chinese, instead of its proper meaning, "garland" (華 嚴). Certain Chinese words are now well known in their Japanese form in the West; therefore, instead of Ch'an, I have used Zen, and Koan instead of Kung An. Quotations from the Sūtras and Śāstras are mainly based on the *Taisho Tripiṭaka,* abbreviated in the notes as *Taisho.*

The most problematic matter I have encountered is which words or terms should be capitalized and which should not. To indicate respect and reverence, words such as *Buddha, Bodhisattva,* and the like are all capitalized, although, strictly speaking, these are general terms. Certain special qualities of Buddha and the Bodhisattvas are also capitalized—for example, *Wisdom*—because of their paramount importance in Buddhist doctrines. Important terms which represent the key concepts of the Doctrine are also capitalized, but not their opposites (e.g., Buddha but not men, Nirvāna but not saṁsāra, Voidness but not form, and Wisdom but not ignorance or avidya). Certain words are both capitalized and lower-cased such as *Dharma* when it indicates Buddhist teaching or truth, but *dharma* when it refers to objects or things; *Mind* when it means the Universal or Cosmic Consciousness, but *mind* when it means the ordinary individual psyche; and *Wisdom* when it implies the unique ultimate knowledge of Buddha, but *wisdom,* the relative saṁsāric intelligence. Important terms with special significance for Hwa Yen Philosophy are also capitalized, such as Non-Obstruction (Wu-Ai), Dharmadhātu (Fa Chieh) Li, Shih, Svabhāva, Śūnyatā, and so forth. A certain amount of inconsistency seems to be unavoidable because in certain places a word can apply to both cases (such as *Mind/mind* or *Dharma/dharma*), and in these contexts the word can be interpreted in either way. Finally, there are some situations where capitalizations are rather arbitrary—for example, *Ten Stages* but the *ten mysteries.* This is because of the difference in the relative importance of these two terms.

To facilitate the task of both the general reader and the specialist, a glossary and a list of special names and terms, together with their equivalent Chinese characters, are included at the end of this book.

Finally, I wish to express my deepest appreciation to the Oriental Studies Foundation, whose generous financial assistance has made this book possible.

GARMA C. C. CHANG

University Park, Pennsylvania,
September, 1970

PROLOGUE

When a human being surveys the universe, and contemplates the drama of life and his role therein, he is compelled to ask himself, "What kind of play is this? What is its meaning and purpose, and what is this all about?"

Different religions give different answers to these questions, but two approaches are outstanding: the Buddhist view and that of the Judeo-Christian tradition. The former is called by some theologians non-historical, and the latter historical. Allowing for the great differences between various interpretations, it is apparent that the historical religions, by and large, depict human drama or history as follows:

1. History has a beginning and an end.

2. It is teleological; the universe is designed and the history of humanity is directed toward an end, for a definite purpose.

3. History is imbued with meaning, even though this meaning may be incomprehensible to man. History, or the human drama, is not accidental; it has exclusive significance in the fulfillment of a Divine will or plan. Nevertheless, the ultimate how, why, and when of this grand plan are beyond human comprehension; they are known only to God, the Creator.

4. Human history, as it unfolds, resembles a drama of increasing intensity. It is produced, directed, and sponsored by God in either a direct or an indirect manner. Like every drama, it has a beginning, a climax, and an end, which are analogous to the theological concepts of Genesis, the coming of a Messiah, and an ultimate Judgment Day.

5. This *unique* human drama is played exclusively upon a stage called Earth, which is accepted as the center of the universe, insofar as this unique performance is concerned.

These convictions, once accepted by most followers of Western religions, have been gradually modified, and some have even been abandoned by contemporary theologians. Yet, by and large, this is still the orientation held by a great portion of Western religious adherents, and it has decisively affected both the history and the mentality of the West, leaving indelible marks on both.

The main criticism of this viewpoint is that it tends to foster self-centeredness, narrowness, and intolerance. Because it claims the exclusive significance of human history in relation to God, it maintains a man-centered, earth-centered orientation and is therefore a limited and a closed viewpoint.

Arnold Toynbee in his book, *A Historian's Approach to Religion,* has pointed out the errors of self-centeredness: "Self-centeredness is thus a necessity of life, but this necessity is also a sin. Self-centeredness is an intellectual error, because no living creature is in truth the center of the universe; and it is also a moral error, because no living creature has a right to act as if it were the center of the universe. It has no right to treat its fellow creatures, the universe and God or Reality as if they existed simply in order to minister to one self-centered living creature's demands." [1]

In contrast to this belief, the Buddhist tradition, especially the Mahāyāna, depicts the universe and the human drama in a completely different manner. The Buddhist view is universal and all-inclusive; it does not claim the unique significance of human history as being a single-performance drama written by God. Some scholars, notably Paul Tillich and Arnold Toynbee, label the Buddhist view a non-historical religion, but I think that this is misleading. The Buddhist concept is not *non*-historical, but rather *trans*-historical, and this may be shown as follows:

1. History has a beginning and an end but in a relative, not an absolute sense.

2. History is imbued with great significance because it is a necessary process for the realization of Perfection (Buddhahood) for all living beings.

3. *Human* history has no unique significance; there are numerous histories of other sentient beings of equal significance in other universes.

4. There are innumerable universes; earth is only one tiny spot in the vast expanse of Dharmadhātu (the infinite universes), and by no means is earth the only stage upon which a unique drama, willed by an authoritative God, is performed.

5. History, human or otherwise, is not a drama schemed and produced by God; it is brought into being by the *collective karma* of sentient beings.

6. There is no definite pattern or mold into which all histories must fall. The mold of history is dictated by the nature of the *collective karma* of living beings in that particular history.

These points may be elaborated further. History does have a beginning and an end, but in a relative, not an absolute sense. The history of a particular event can be spoken of as having a beginning and an end, but this beginning and ending are not of an absolute nature. The history of men is a good example. Estimates place its beginning at approximately 600,000 years ago. But 600,000 B.C. is not the initial beginning of history in the absolute sense. Prior to this time, other events and histories had taken place. Similarly, some day in the future, there will undoubtedly be an end to human history, but this end should not be construed as the absolute or ultimate terminating point of human existence. According to Buddhism, the histories of other species may then develop; possibly the "souls" of those members of the human race who have not attained Buddhahood will then move on to other planets and start a new chapter of another history.

In the phenomenal world, the ever-flowing chains of events continuously interweave with one another, forming an immense "rimless net" rolling forward without cessation. But man, having only limited capacity and interest, cannot comprehend this vast intermeshing of events. With self-determination, he cuts off this "ever-flowing chain" and designates one point therein as the beginning and another as the end of a *particular* incident. Gradually and unconsciously, he begins to forget the fact that the very concept of a beginning and an end were first created for the sake of expediency, and make sense only when a *particular* event is referred to. Instead, he goes on from the particular to project a concept of absolute beginning, a first cause, an unmoved mover, and the like. He then further extends these ideas and elaborates them into theological and philosophical systems, thus exaggerating their theological significance to an excessive degree.

To the best of our knowledge, no one has ever experienced an absolute beginning prior to which nothing existed. The first cause, or absolute beginning, has no logical or empirical basis. The beginning of event Y is always the simultaneous end of event X. The ending of event B is always the beginning of event C. A Martian, looking at our planet, does not see any sign of a beginning or an end; what he sees is a continuous, ever-flowing chain of events. Therefore, to say that a particular event has a beginning or end is indeed meaningful, but to say that there is an absolute beginning of all events is meaningless.

To those who are in the habit of thinking of an absolute beginning and end, the Buddhist expression, "from the very no-beginning," [2]
must present an odd, if not a perplexing, concept. Yet it is because of
this concept that many unprofitable theological problems are dis-
pensed with in Buddhism.

The importance of the Buddhist concept of "no-beginning" cannot
be over-emphasized. It is here that the distinction between Buddhism
and the historical religions becomes clear. Because of this concept,
the outstanding theological problems of "creation" and its aftermath
are easily unraveled. It is also because of this concept that many
theological problems concerning God simply do not exist in Buddhism.
Since there is no absolute beginning, there is no Creator or creation.
Since there is no omnipotent and omniscient God the Creator, the
problems of evil, Divine will, salvation, and eschatology are also either
non-existent or "exist" in a completely different context. Some people
think that to reject the concept of creation and its first cause automatically implies the rejection or abolition of the very foundation of
religion, but this is not necessarily so. The foundation of Buddhism,
for instance, does not depend on the first cause—God the Creator; it
depends rather on the ubiquitous Buddha-nature and its functions. A
spiritual life does not necessarily depend upon God, a creator and
judge, who stands above us and beyond our grasp; man's religious
aspirations can truly be fulfilled by his realization of the Buddha-
nature that lies within all sentient beings.

The original spirit of Buddhism was reflected in its radical emphasis upon achieving liberation and upon abolishing all philosophical
speculation. This spirit was vividly expressed by the Buddha's famous
silence when a set of philosophical questions was put to him.[3] Philosophical interest, however, was in ferment everywhere. A few centuries
after the death of Gautama Buddha, many philosophical schools of
Buddhism began to spring up, gradually giving rise to Mahāyāna Buddhism itself.

Although the doctrine of Mahāyāna Buddhism differs greatly
from that of Hīnayāna Buddhism, they are essentially in agreement
concerning the problem of "beginning and end." Their view of this
problem is briefly given in the following statements.

1. Saṁsāra (the phenomenal world) has no beginning, but it
   does have an end.

2. Nirvāṇa (the "state" of cessation) has a beginning but no end.

3. The Reality-of-Suchness (Bhūtatathatā) has neither beginning nor end.

The first statement says that from the very no-beginning of time, saṁsāra has been taking place throughout the vast expanse of infinite universes without interruption. No single or particular time element in the remotest past can be designated as the absolute starting point of the universe; it follows, therefore, that history, as we know it, can have no beginning. On the other hand, an individual (or group) can terminate or transcend history if he (or it) so desires and makes sufficient effort toward that end. This terminating point of saṁsāra is also the beginning of Nirvāṇa, the state of Buddhahood which can suffer neither decay nor expiration. Therefore, Nirvāṇa has a beginning but has no end. Embracing both saṁsāra and Nirvāṇa, yet not in the slightest tainted by either, is the Reality-of-Thusness (Bhūtatathatā), which transcends both purity and defilement. This is a state devoid of any designatable attributes which goes beyond all words or distinctions. It simply *is,* and remains so throughout eternity, regardless of the emergence of good or evil, ignorance or enlightenment.

The tenets of this doctrine have been simply shown in Illustration No. 1.

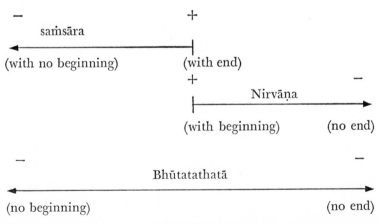

This diagram denotes that the times of saṁsara and Nirvāṇa each have a negative and a positive aspect, indicating either the presence or the absence of a beginning or end; whereas, the time of Bhūtatathatā is shown with a negative temporal sign at either end, indicating that it has no beginning and no end. In the foregoing diagram saṁsāra and Nirvāṇa are represented in two lines purely for the sake of illustration; actually there is only one continuous line, as shown in Illustration No. 2.

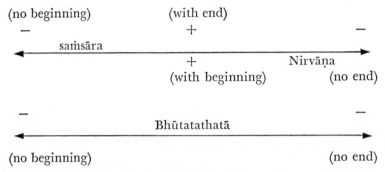

The two positive marks here testify to the simultaneous extinction of samsāra and "arising" of Nirvāṇa, implying that they are the same, and that this is only a "coalescing point." It has been suggested that when samsāra and Nirvāṇa are seen as one continuous whole they approximate the Reality-of-Suchness which has no beginning or end. Here is the point where phenomena join the noumenon and the relative coalesces with the absolute.

Now, the main criticism of the Buddhist view leveled by Western thinkers is that this order of "cyclic" orientation takes all significance out of life. To them, samsāra seems to be merely a monotonous, repetitive bore, possessing neither meaning nor purpose. Professor Toynbee remarks: "This astronomical view of history provides a radical correction of the bias towards self-centeredness that is innate in every living creature; but it corrects self-centeredness at the price of taking the significance out of history—and indeed, out of the Universe itself. From this astronomical standpoint it is impossible for an historian to believe that his own here and now has any special importance, but it is equally difficult for him to believe that any other human being's here and now has ever had, or will have, any special importance either. . . ." [4]

Here the critic seems to have forgotten that meaning and significance do not depend entirely on outside circumstances. Instead, they clearly depend upon one's *attitude toward* those circumstances. A cyclic and lasting samsāra can also become wholly meaningful and significant if the individual's attitude and commitment in life are both constructive and altruistic. Recurrent life is, then, not necessarily a repetitious state of boredom; instead, it can ensure one ample opportunity for acts of altruism and spiritual progress.

The meaning and purpose of life are envisioned by Mahāyāna Buddhism as a challenge and an opportunity for every man to gain his highest good through an approach to the state of Buddhahood. Life, therefore, is imbued with great significance in spite of cyclic recurrence. Furthermore, saṁsāra actually is not a cyclical but an upward, spiraling movement; for it is the basic faith of Mahāyāna Buddhism that all living beings are moving through progressive stages toward Buddhahood. History, therefore, is full of meaning and opportunity for achieving this goal.

When I first read this criticism of the meaninglessness of the nonhistorical viewpoint I was quite astonished. Why have Western thinkers failed to perceive these obvious facts? Then I realized that this criticism is not a philosophical evaluation, but a psychological one. Consider the situation of a man who is told by his doctor that he has only a year or so to live. Upon hearing this, the man's philosophy and outlook on life may change completely. He might give up his profession, sell his property, and begin traveling around the world seeking excitement and adventure. In other words, this man attempts to live life to its maximum in a minimum of time. To him time is not only precious but pressingly so; every second has become of the greatest significance. Understandably, his attitude towards and evaluation of his shortened life are entirely different from that of most men, who never seriously think of death as being imminent. Now, if a man is aware that his days are numbered, he will naturally seek to extract the utmost significance out of his life and to make it count for as much as possible. In this light, I think it is fair to say that Christians are much more energetic and enterprising than Buddhists. The psychological reasoning behind this enthusiasm is perhaps the belief that they have only one life to live; whereas, Buddhists believe that many lives await them. To a faithful Christian, salvation or damnation is determined in a single lifetime; he must do the right thing now, because there will be no second chance. A person who seriously believes in the tenets of Christianity will feel the "tremendously pressing significance" of obligations that he must fulfill during his one lifetime, and because of this religious conviction, he suffers under great pressures and tensions. But a Buddhist, experiencing frustration and disappointment, can always console himself by saying, "Well, why worry so much about these difficulties and frustrations? I can always try again in my next life, which certainly cannot be as bad and as disappointing as this one!"

Thus we can easily see that although the concept of saṁsāra tends to make one more sober, liberal, and tolerant, it can also make one passive, inert, and even cynical. To combat this tendency, Buddhism has many exhortations on the difficulties of obtaining a human form in the next life, on one's obligation to help his fellow man, and on aspiring for rapid spiritual progress and thereby quickly achieving the state of Buddhahood. To sum up, in the Buddhist view, life in the history of mankind does not lack significance. Instead, it is broader and has a longer range; although this is sometimes obscure and difficult for those brought up with the philosophies of the Judeo-Christian tradition to perceive and comprehend.

Now, according to Mahāyāna Buddhism, human history is not unique. There are numerous equally significant histories of other living beings now taking place in an infinite number of other universes. The vastness and infinite variety of universes are repeatedly described in various Sūtras. For example, in the *Diamond Sūtra*[5] we read:

> What do you think, Subhūti, if there were as many Ganges rivers as there are grains of sand in the river Ganges, and if there were as many world-systems as there are grains of sand in all of these innumerable rivers, would these world-systems be considered numerous?
>
> Very numerous indeed, World-Honored One!
>
> Listen, Subhūti. Within these numerous world-systems there are [to be found] every form of sentient being with all their various mentalities and conceptions, all of which are known to the Tathāgata. . . .

And in the *Hwa Yen Sūtra*[6] we read:

> Oh sons of Buddha! If a man pulverizes millions and billions of Buddhas' universes[7] and reduces them to dust-motes, each of which represents another universe, and he again pulverizes these universes and holds the total amount of dust-motes acquired thereby in his left hand and walks eastward; and after passing over the same vast number of universes, he then drops one dust-mote and continues walking eastward, and each time he passes over the same number of universes, he drops another dust-mote until he exhausts

all that he held in his hand; if he then walks south, west, and north in the four directions and upward and downward, dropping dust-motes as before, Oh, Pao Shou, what do you think? The total space in the ten directions of all these universes touched or untouched by his dust-motes, is this space of a Buddha-land not vast, broad, and beyond comprehension?

Yes, indeed, this Buddha-land is infinitely vast and broad, wonderful and incomprehensible. However, if there are men who, having heard this metaphor, can have faith in and understanding of it, it is even more rare and wondrous!

The Buddha said to Pao Shou, "Yes, yes, just as you have said. I now predict that if there are good men or good women who can have faith in this metaphor, they will attain the Supreme Enlightenment and the Peerless Wisdom of Tathāgathahood.

In another chapter of this Sūtra [8] we read:

Thereupon Bodhisattva Samantabhadra addressed the assembly: [9]

> "By the blessing of Tathāgata's magic power,
> In the ten directions I see every place
> In all the worlds and universes
> Pervading the vast expanse of space . . .
> Some worlds of pure light are [made],
> Suspended steadily in space . . .
> Some are shaped like flowers,
> Lamps adorned with jewels,
> Some are vast as the ocean,
> Spinning like a turning wheel . . .
> Some are slender, some are small,
> For they have countless forms—
> And spin in various ways . . .
> Some worlds are like a glowing wheel
> A volcano . . . lion or a sea shell . . .
> Infinitely different
> Are their forms and shapes . . .
>
> [In the vast expanse of Dharmadhātu,]
> Some worlds are round and others square,
> Some lands are pure and some defiled,
> Others joyful or distressing . . .
> All were caused by karmas
> Varied as the oceans . . .

Some world-systems remain for but one kalpa, while others
For hundreds, thousands, or an infinity of aeons.

In some world-systems there are Buddhas;
But in others they do not appear.
Some have only one,
But others many.

Unfathomable are the countless worlds
In the totality of universes.
Many worlds are new or are decaying,
While many others soon will cease to be.
Like leaves in a forest,
Some flourish others fall . . .
As different seeds give birth to different fruits,
Or magicians project conjurations with their spells,
So sentient beings by the power of [collective] karma
Make various world-systems that are incomprehensible . . .

As a painter draws many pictures,
A sentient beings's Mind can also create
Infinite variations of world-systems.

Because of bad karma, passions and desires,
Many world-systems are full of rock-torn earth,
Dangerous and distressing. Yet many worlds
Through good karma are wrought of jewels and contain
Rich places of great variety, where
Fruits of pleasure are enjoyed [by all] at will.

In the ocean-like world-systems all Buddhas
Give myriad teachings with the utmost skill,
To suit all men's needs and inclinations.

Inscrutable is Buddha's Dharma-Body—
Without form or image—
But to accommodate
Man, he manifests in a myriad forms.
For the benefit of sentient beings,
He may incarnate as a short-or-long-lived being,
Or one who lives for countless aeons.
To suit men's temperament and need,
He gives limitless teachings of many Vehicles,
Or teaches but one Vehicle with many variations.
By leading a few gifted men to tread the Path,

> He may seem without effort
> To achieve Buddhahood.
>
> Through these indescribable ingenious ways,
> The Buddhas benefit all sentient beings!"

In reading the above quotations, we can see that the Buddhist view on history is extremely flexible and all-inclusive. Since its outlook is neither god-centered nor man-centered nor earth-centered, but rather oriented upon a basis of an infinite variety of universes and sentient beings, it does not and cannot set a definite pattern which history must follow. The Buddhist view on history is, therefore, entirely fluid and open to all possibilities.

If there is one characteristic of Buddhist teaching that distinguishes it from many other religions, it is its inclusiveness. This is true from the basic doctrine of karma up to the doctrines of Śūnyāta, Bodhicitta, and the Dharmadhātu of the *Hwa Yen Sūtra*. If we compare the Buddhist teaching to that of Western religions, we sense that the tendency of the former is to adopt a pluralistic approach, whereas, the latter tends to be exclusive and holds a "singularistic" approach. There are many reasons contributing to this difference, but I believe the main one is that while the Judeo-Christian tradition preserves the exclusiveness of God and all that belongs to Him, in Buddhism this factor is entirely absent. The teaching of the Judeo-Christian tradition, regardless of its complexities and variation, is centered upon God and His relation to man. It is because of God and His overall plan that life is meaningful and that history has purpose. Behind this history and all of nature, therefore, is a consciousness and a will, that is, God's omniscient and purposeful Mind. Contrary to this belief, the Buddhist view, as we have seen above, holds that everything depends on the collective karma of sentient beings. Karma is the creator, maintainer, and destroyer of both history and the universe. Karma is a "natural" force, essentially unconscious and unplanned. So, according to Buddhism, the mold and nature of any history does not depend upon God's will or plan, but on the nature of the collective karma of the sentient beings in that particular history.

The evidence of collective karma is not lacking in our own world. For instance, the history and fate of the American Indians, of Aztecs, of Mayans, and to a certain extent, of Negroes and Jews and all those other sufferers of mankind's inhumanity cannot be regarded as having been planned or caused even *indirectly* by God. Their fate would be inexplicable in the light of the justice and benevolence attributed to Him. Even if we give generous allowance to the wistful belief that everything will be taken care of eventually, that a happy ending is definitely in order when the kingdom of God comes, the phenomena of Auschwitz, of Stalin and Mao Tse-tung, and of the other innumerable man-made and natural disasters in human history would certainly make any sensible man hesitate to accept this alleged act of creation as both benevolent and wise. All of the enormous suffering that man has gone through in history is supposedly explained away either by original sin or by the inscrutability of the ultimate will of God, but the inner voice, arising from the depths of human dignity and good sense finds it hard to echo such perplexing pre-suppositions. Sometimes even the most pious religionists cannot help wondering, during their silent hours, about the sensibleness of the whole business of life. With the doctrine of karma, however, the problem of evil or moral justice seems to be comparatively easier to explain in the Buddhist tradition. Of course, this is not to say that it has no inherent difficulties. The doctrine of karma, coupled with the absence of God might explain why the problem of evil has never become as excruciating in the Buddhist tradition as in the Judeo-Christian.

The most difficult doctrine in Buddhism is no doubt the doctrine of karma, whose complexity and elusiveness often baffles one to the point of exasperation. To make it reasonably clear, a separate book is needed. A few words about karma however might be helpful here as a preamble to our next discussion, which deals with the Hwa Yen doctrine of Totality.

Explicitly karma means action, but implicitly it also means force. Since an action always produces a certain force, and this force in turn promotes further actions, karma is essentially a doctrine of the intricate reciprocations between forces and actions that push forward the turning wheel of saṁsāra. When expressed on a cosmological scale this force-action complex is a stupendous power that propels the universe and life; when expressed in the ethical sense, it is an unfailing, impersonal law that effectuates the moral order, "dispensing" natural rewards and retributions. Metaphysically, karma is a creative energy brought forth by the collective actions of certain groups; it sustains the order and function of a particular universe in which those groups reside. Ultimately karma is a mystery, a marvel that evades

human comprehension. All the great wonders of the world, such as the
biological and astronomical mysteries are not, according to Buddhism,
due to the skillfulness of God's hand, but to the ingenuity of the power
of karma. In many ways, karma, in the Buddhist tradition, is almost
equivalent to what general expression calls the Will of God. The difference is that Buddhism views the ultimate unknown of life's mystery
from a naturalistic orientation; whereas the Judeo-Christian tradition
adopts a theistic view. The mystery of karma is as imponderable as the
mystery of the Will of God, no better and no worse. The great ignorance and limitation of man's mind is clearly exposed during his
inquiry into any deeper problem. One must make one's peace with the
ultimate unknown and commit himself to an orientation and faith that
appears to be most sensible and inspiring to him.

With this brief review of the basic perspectives of the cosmic
drama as they are seen in a trans-historical religion, we can now proceed to our next discussion on the Realm of Totality of Hwa Yen
Buddhism.

NOTES [Prologue]

1. Arnold Toynbee, *A Historian's Approach to Religion* (New York, 1956), pp. 4–5.
2. From the very no-beginning—Chinese: wu shih i lai; Tibetan: Thog.Ma.Med.
Pahi.Dus.nas.; Sanskrit: anādikālam.
3. Henry Warren, *Buddhism in Translation* (Cambridge, Mass., 1947). pp. 117–28.
4. Toynbee, op. cit., p. 10.
5. *Taisho* 235, p. 751.
6. *Taisho* 279, p. 257.
7. Buddha's universe or Buddha's Domains: according to tradition, a Buddha's Domain consists of 1,000,000,000 solar systems.
8. *Taisho* 279, p. 35.
9. Bountiful descriptions of the infinite universes in the Dharmadhātu are given
in many passages in the fourth chapter, the "Formation of the World," and in
the fifth chapter, "The World of Flower-Treasury," of the *Hwa Yen Sūtra*. But
to read them all would be wearisome and unprofitable. A selection of abridged
passages is therefore given here to present a general view to the reader. For the
sake of perspicuity, the translations are taken from various passages in the text
but not necessarily in their original order. The selections are taken from passages on pp. 35, 36, 37, 38, 42, 51, 52, and 53 of *Taisho* 279.

華嚴境眇

PART ONE

THE REALM OF TOTALITY

THE INFINITY OF BUDDHA'S REALM

What does a Buddha [1] see and hear? How does He act and think? What does He know and experience? In brief, what does it feel like to be a Buddha? These questions have been asked by all Buddhists throughout the ages, just as Jews, Christians, Moslems, and Hindus have always asked about their gods and prophets. If these questions are answerable at all, the answers must be very difficult. To raise a question is to reveal a state of mind, and to answer a question is to try to share one's experience with others. An answer cannot make sense if it is given to those who do not share the experience it implies. Let me illustrate this.

A caravan was slowly making its way through a Tibetan desert under a scorching sun. Among the travelers was an American who, under the pressure of extreme heat and thirst, exclaimed, "Oh, what wouldn't I give to have a big glass of ice-cream soda right now!" A Tibetan nearby heard this remark, and asked the American, "What is this 'ice-cream soda' you want so much?"

"Ice-cream soda is a wonderfully delicious, cold drink!"

"Does it taste like our butter-tea when it is cold?"

"No, it is not like that."

"Does it taste like cold milk?"

"No, not exactly—an ice-cream soda tastes quite different from plain, cold milk; it can have a great variety of flavors. Also, it bubbles up."

"Then, if it bubbles, does it taste like our barley-beer?"

"No, of course not!"

"What is it made of?"

"It is made of milk, cream, eggs, sugar, flavors, ice and soda-water. . . ."

The puzzled Tibetan still could not understand how such a grotesque mixture could be a good drink.

Thus, communication becomes extremely difficult without a common ground of shared experience. Einstein's world is quite different from that of the average man. If the distances that separate people's worlds are too great, nothing can help to bring them together. When

Buddha tried to describe His Experience to His audience, He foresaw this difficulty. In many of His discourses, as witnessed in the Sūtras,[2] He often accompanied His expressions with an air of resignation, implying that Buddhahood is not something to be described in words or apprehended through thought. The basic difficulty lies in the fact that we do not share the same experience as the Buddha.

To reveal the unrevealable, and to describe the indescribable realm of Buddhahood, the *Hwa Yen Sūtra*,[3] one of the greatest scriptures in Mahāyāna Buddhism, has presented us with an awe-inspiring panorama of Buddhahood for those aspirants who, despite all the inherent difficulties, are eager to have a glimpse of this great mystery.

The mystery of Buddhahood can perhaps be summed up in two words: *Totality* and *Non-Obstruction*. The former implies the all-embracing and all-aware aspects of Buddhahood; the latter, the total freedom from all clingings and bindings. Ontologically speaking, it is because of Totality that Non-Obstruction can be reached, but causally speaking, it is through a realization of Non-Obstruction—the complete annihilation of all mental and spiritual impediments and "blocks"—that the realm of Totality and Non-Obstruction is reached. In the pages to follow, we shall examine the philosophical, experiential, and instrumental implications of Totality and Non-Obstruction; but first let us read a few passages from the *Hwa Yen Sūtra* in order to get a far-reaching view of the Dharmadhātu [4]—the infinity and totality of Buddhahood.

> . . . Buddha replied to the Bodhisattva Cittarāja: [5] "In order to make the world apprehend the numbers and quantities in Buddha's experience, my good son, you have now asked me [a question about the inconceivable, unimaginable, unutterable infinity]. Listen attentively, and I shall now explain it to you.
>
> "Ten million is a koṭi; one koṭi koṭi is an ayuta; one ayuta ayuta is a niyuta; one niyuta niyuta is a binbara [a number followed by seventy-five zeros]; and one binbara is . . . [thus it goes on in geometrical progression one hundred twenty-four times more, and the number then is called] one Indescribable-Indescribable Turning. . . ." [6]

Then Buddha continued in the following stanzas: [7]

> The Indescribable-Indescribable
> Turning permeates what cannot be described . . .
> It would take eternity to count

All the Buddha's universes.
In each dust-mote of these worlds
Are countless worlds and Buddhas . . .
From the tip of each hair of Buddha's body
Are revealed the indescribable Pure Lands . . .
Indescribable are their wonders and names,
Indescribable are their glories and beauties,
Indescribable are the various Dharmas now being preached,
Indescribable are the manners in which they
    ripen sentient beings . . .
Their unobstructed Minds are indescribable,
Their transformations are indescribable,
The manners with which they observe, purify and educate
Sentient beings are indescribable . . .
The teachings they preach are indescribable.
In each of these Teachings are contained
Infinite, indescribable variations;
Each of them ripens sentient beings in indescribable
    manners.
Indescribable are their languages, miracles,
    revelations, and kalpas . . .
An excellent mathematician could not enumerate them,
But a Bodhisattva can clearly explain them all . . .

The indescribable infinite Lands
All assemble in a hair's tip [of Buddha],
Neither crowded nor pressing
Nor does this hair even slightly expand . . .
In the hair all lands remain as usual
Without altering forms or displacement . . .
Oh, unutterable are the manners they enter the hair . . .
Unutterable is the vastness of the Realm . . .
Unutterable is the purity of Buddha's body,
Unutterable is the purity of Buddha's knowledge.
Unutterable is the experience of eliminating all doubts,
Unutterable is the feeling of realizing the Truth.
Unutterable is the deep Samādhi,
Unutterable is it to know all!

Unutterable is it to know all sentient beings' dispositions,
Unutterable to know their karmas and propensities,
Unutterable to know all their minds,
Unutterable to know all their languages.

Unutterable is the great compassion of the Bodhisattvas,
Who, in unutterable ways, benefit all living beings.
Unutterable are their infinite acts,
Unutterable their vast vows,
Unutterable their skills, powers, and means . . .

Inconceivable are Bodhisattvas' thoughts, their
    vows and understanding!
Unfathomable is their grasp of all times and all Dharmas.
Their longtime spiritual practice is incomprehensible,
So is their abrupt Enlightenment in one moment.

Inconceivable is the freedom of all Buddhas,
Their miracles, revelations and compassion
Toward all men!

To explain the infinite aeons is still possible
But to praise the Bodhisattva's infinite merits
Is impossible . . . .

Thereupon, Bodhisattva Cittarāja addressed the assembly thus: [8]
   "Listen, O sons of Buddha, one kalpa (or aeon) in this Saha
world—the Land of Buddha *Śākyamuni*—is one day and one
night in the great Happy Land of Buddha *Amita;* one kalpa in
the Land of Buddha *Amita,* is one day and one night in the Land
of the Buddha *Diamond Strength,* and one kalpa in the Land of
the Buddha *Diamond Strength,* is one day and one night in. . . .
continuing in this manner, passing millions of incalculable
worlds, the last world [of this series] is reached. One kalpa there,
is again one day and one night in the Land of the Buddha *Supreme Lotus;* wherein, the Bodhisattva Samantabhadra and all
the great Bodhisattvas now assembled here, are also present *there,*
crowding the sky. . . .
   ". . . . When a Bodhisattva obtains the ten wisdoms, he can
then perform the ten universal enterings. What are they? They
are: To bring all the universes into one hair, and one hair into all
the universes; to bring all sentient beings' bodies into one body,
and one body into all sentient beings' bodies; to bring inconceivable kalpas into one moment, and one moment into inconceivable
kalpas; to bring all Buddhas' Dharmas into one Dharma, and one
Dharma into all Buddhas' Dharmas; to bring an inconceivable
number of places into one place, and one place into an inconceivable number of places; to bring an inconceivable number of
organs into one organ, and one organ into an inconceivable num-

ber of organs; to bring all organs into one non-organ, and one non-organ into all organs . . . to make all thoughts into one thought, and one thought into all thoughts; to make all voices and languages into one voice and language, and one voice and language into all voices and languages; to make all the three times [9] into one time, and one time into all the three times . . .

". . . Sons of Buddha, what is this supreme Samādhi that a Bodhisattva possesses? [10] When a Bodhisattva engages in this Samādhi, he obtains the ten non-attachments . . . the non-attachment to all lands, directions, aeons, groups, dharmas, vows, Samādhis, Buddhas, and stages. . . .

"Sons of Buddha, how does a Bodhisattva enter this Samādhi, and emerge from it? A Bodhisattva enters Samādhi in his inner body, and emerges from it in his outer body . . . he enters Samādhi in a human body and emerges from it in a dragon body . . . enters Samādhi in a deva's body, and emerges from it in a Brahmā's body . . . enters in one body, and emerges in one thousand, . . . one million, one billion bodies . . . enters in one thousand, one million, one billion . . . bodies, and emerges in one body . . . enters in a sullied, sentient being's body, and emerges in one thousand, one million . . . purified bodies; enters in one thousand, one million . . . purified bodies, and emerges in one sullied body; enters in the eyes, and emerges in the ears, in the noses, in the tongues . . . in the minds . . . enters in an atom, and emerges in infinite universes; enters in his self-body, and emerges in a Buddha's body; enters in one moment, and emerges in billions of aeons; enters in billions of aeons, and emerges in one moment . . . enters in the present, and emerges in the past . . . enters in the future, and emerges in the present; enters in the past, and emerges in the future . . . The Bodhisattva who dwells in this Samādhi can perceive infinite, immeasurable, inconceivable, incalculable, unutterable, and unutterably unutterable . . . numbers of Samādhis; each and every one of which has infinitely vast varieties of experiences—their enterings and arisings, remainings and forms, revelations and acts, natures and developments, purifications and cures . . . he sees them all, transparently clear. . . . A Bodhisattva who dwells in this supreme Samādhi,[11] sees infinite lands, beholds infinite Buddhas, delivers infinite sentient beings, realizes infinite Dharmas, accomplishes infinite actions, perfects infinite understandings, enters infinite Dhyānas, demonstrates infinite miracles, gains infinite wisdoms, remains in infinite moments and times. . . ."

Obviously, the above quotations are too short, too discursive and unsystematic to describe the Totality of Buddhahood as depicted in the *Hwa Yen Sūtra*—a voluminous scripture of more than half a million words. Nevertheless, through these quotations, we can secure a small foothold from which to analyze and study the Realm of totality and Buddhahood.

In Buddha's reply to the Bodhisattva Cittarāja we are told of the vastness of a realm which, if translated in terms of numbers, would go far beyond the remotest edge of the empirical world. The passage leaves us with an impression that the author was speaking in the language of modern astronomy. The name given to the last number, the Indescribable-Indescribable Turning, is extremly interesting and significant. It is apparently not an arbitrary name given to denote a definite and inflexible number, but a descriptive term designed to portray the experiential insight of a vast mind. What does the Indescribable-Indescribable Turning mean? Why should an emotive word like *indescribable* be used here at all to define a number or quantity?

Exceedingly large or small numbers, including infinity at the two extremes, can easily be conceptualized and expressed in terms of symbols and abstractions, but they are difficult to experience or "touch" in an intimate and direct way. We have no difficulty in understanding the *idea* of a million, a billion, a trillion, or even of infinity, but it is very difficult for us to grasp or project these larger numbers in terms of empirical events. The world of symbols and abstractions is characteristically different from that of sense experience and insight. The former is, to use the Buddhist terminology, a realm of indirect measurement, and the latter, a realm of direct realization.[12] It is said that in a Buddha's mind these two realms are not separate. The Yogācāra philosophers even go so far as to say that a Buddha's mind has only one realm, that of direct realization. A Buddha never "thinks," but always "sees." This is to say that no thinking or reasoning process ever takes place in a Buddha's Mind; he is always in the realm of direct realization, a realm that is intrinsically symbol-less. The claim that a symbol-less Buddha-Mind can convey its experience to men by means of symbols, is perhaps an eternal mystery that can never be solved by reason. But is it not also true that if such a mystery exists, it cannot be otherwise than indescribable—a term denoting the impossibility of approximating something through symbolization?

The pen of Leo Tolstoy can reproduce a living panorama of the battle of Borodino in our minds, but whose pen can reproduce the battles of Borodino, of Normandy, of Stalingrad, of Verdun, of Zama, of Okinawa . . . the one thousand and one battles, all at the same time? Is it not quite understandable, then, that Buddha had to resort to the use of this apologetic term, Indescribable-Indescribable Turning, to release the "tension" of conveying His direct experience of "seeing" the awesome panorama of Totality through such a pitiful means of communication as human language?

> The Indescribable-Indescribable
> Turning permeates what cannot be described . . .
> It would take infinity to count
> All the Buddha's universes.
> In each dust-mote of these worlds
> Are countless worlds and Buddhas . . .
> From the tip of each hair of Buddha's body
> Are revealed pure Lands that cannot be described . . .
> Nor can their wonders, glories, names and beauties.

These words remind us of Pascal's *Pensées*,[13] in which his great insight into Totality is so clearly expressed.

Let man contemplate the whole of nature in her full and grand majesty, and turn his vision from the low objects which surround him. Let him gaze on that brilliant light, set like an eternal lamp to illumine the universe; let the earth appear to him a point in comparison with the vast circle described by the sun, and let him wonder at the fact that this vast circle is itself but a very fine point in comparison with that described by the stars in their revolution round the firmament. But if our view be arrested there, let our imagination pass beyond; it will sooner exhaust the power of conception than the power of nature to supply material for conception. The whole visible world is only an imperceptible atom in the ample bosom of nature. No idea approaches it. We may enlarge our conceptions beyond all imaginable space; we only produce atoms in comparison with the reality of things. It is an infinite sphere, the center of which is everywhere, the circumference nowhere. In short it is the greatest sensible mark of the almighty power of God, that imagination loses itself in that thought.

Returning to himself, let man consider what he is in comparison with all existence; let him regard himself as lost in this remote corner of nature, and from the little cell in which he finds himself lodged . . . let him estimate at their true value the earth, kingdoms, cities, and himself. What is a man in the Infinite?

But to show him another prodigy equally astonishing, let him examine the most delicate things he knows. Let a mite be given him, with its minute body and parts incomparably more minute, limbs with their points, veins in the limbs, blood in the veins, humours in the blood, drops in the humours, vapours in the drops. Dividing these last things again, let him exhaust his powers of conception, and let the last object at which he can arrive be now that of our discourse. Perhaps he will think that here is the smallest point in nature. I will let him see therein a new abyss. I will paint for him not only the visible universe, but all that he can conceive of nature's immensity in the womb of this abridged atom. Let him see therein an infinity of the universes, each of which has its firmament, its planets, its earth, in the same proportion as in the visible world; in each earth animals, and in the last mites, in which he will find again all that the first had, finding still in these others the same thing without end and without cessation. Let him lose himself in wonders as amazing in their littleness as the others in their vastness. For who will not be astounded at the fact that our body, which a little while ago was imperceptible in the universe, itself imperceptible in the bosom of the whole, is now a colossus, a world, or rather a whole, in respect to the nothingness which we cannot reach? He who regards himself in this light will be afraid of himself, and observing himself sustained, in the body given him by nature, between these two abysses of the Infinite and Nothing, will tremble at the sight of these marvels, and I think that, as his curiosity changes into admiration, he will be more disposed to contemplate them in silence than to examine them with presumption.

For in fact what is man in nature? A Nothing in comparison with the Infinite, an All in comparison with the Nothing, a mean between nothing and everything. Since he is infinitely removed from comprehending the extremes, and the end of things and their beginning are hopelessly hidden from him in an impenetrable secret; he is equally incapable of seeing the Nothing from which he was made, and the Infinite in which he is swallowed up.

What will he do then, but perceive the appearance of the middle of things, in an eternal despair of knowing either their beginning or their end. . . .

What has been said so far about Totality, both the Pascal and the Hwa Yen versions, can perhaps be summarized as follows: as a solar system contains its planets, or a planet contains its atoms, a "larger" universe always includes the "smaller" ones, and, in turn, is included in a universe that is larger than itself. This system of higher realms embracing lower ones is envisioned in a structure consisting of "layers" extending ad infinitum in both directions. A universe can be infinitely vast or infinitely small, depending on the *scale of measurement,* or the *position from which the measurement is made.* Totality, in short, is here portrayed as realms-embracing-realms ad infinitum (chung-chung wu-chin).

Up to this point we find no difference between the Hwa Yen version of Totality and that of Pascal. But if we read further and scan more closely, we find that a great difference exists between the two.

We read in Hwa Yen:

> The infinite lands that cannot be described
> Gather in the tip of one hair [of the Buddha],
> They neither crowd nor press
> Nor does the hair tip swell . . .
> In it all Lands remain
> Just as they were before . . .
> How these Lands enter the hair . . .
> The huge vastness of the Realm . . .

And:

> . . . when a Bodhisattva obtains the ten wisdoms, he can then perform the ten universal enterings . . . to bring all the universes into one hair, and one hair into all the universes; to bring all sentient beings' bodies into one body, and one body into all sentient beings' bodies; to bring inconceivable aeons into one moment, and one moment into inconceivable aeons . . . to make all thoughts into one thought, and one thought into all thoughts . . . to make all the Three Times into one time, and one time into all the Three Times . . .

> He enters Samādhi in one moment, and emerges from it in billions of aeons, enters in billions of aeons and emerges in one moment . . . enters in the present, and emerges in the past . . . enters in the past, and emerges in the future . . .

Here we find that both time and space have lost their meaning and power as we understand and experience them. Here is not merely a realm-embracing-realm ad infinitum, but a total change-over, a thorough liberation from *all obstructions*. Here is a perfect melting and merging of all realms, the all-in-one and the one-in-all, the dissolving of being and non-being, the convergence of Voidness and existence, the "simultaneous abrupt rising" and the "perfect mutual solution."[14] All these mysteries of Totality consist, however, in one basic principle; namely, *all things of dependent-arising* (pratītya-samutpāda) *are void*. In contrast to the doctrines of various monisms and monotheisms, the Hwa Yen Doctrine holds that the wonders of Dharmadhātu are brought into play not because of the *one*, but because of the great *Void*. This is as if to say that *zero*, not one, is the foundation of all numbers. It is because of Voidness or Emptiness (Śūnyatā) that the mutual penetration and Non-Obstruction of realms become possible. It is also owing to Voidness that the all-inclusive Totality can reveal the infinite possibilities without obstruction. Śūnyatā (Emptiness or Voidness) is indeed the essence, and the mark of Buddhism, which is sometimes called non-ego (wu wo), sometimes non-clinging (wu chih), non-abiding (wu chu), Non-Obstruction (wu ai), Emptiness (k'ung hsing), penetrating-through (t'ou-t'o), and a hundred and one other names. To stress the "ego-less" aspect of this great mystery of Śūnyatā, we have Hīnayāna Buddhism; to stress the void aspect of this mystery, we have Mādhyamika Buddhism; to stress the non-clinging, non-abiding aspect we have Zen; and to stress the non-obstructing and all-embracing aspect, we have Hwa Yen.

In making a summary of what we have read in the quotations from the *Hwa Yen Sūtra*, we have found that the Totality and Non-Obstruction of Buddhahood are expressed in these terms:

1. That a universe can be infinitely vast or small depending on the scale of measurement, or the position from which a measurement is made.

2. That the "larger" universes include the "smaller" ones as a solar system contains its planets, or a planet contains its atoms. This system of higher realms embracing the lower ones is pictured in a structure extending ad infinitum in both directions to the infinitely large or the infinitely small. This is called in the Hwa Yen vocabulary the view of *realms-embracing-realms*.

3. That a "small" universe, (such as an atom) not only contains the infinite "lesser" universes within itself, but also contains the infinite "larger" universes (such as the solar system), thus establishing the genuine Totality of Non-Obstruction.

4. That "time" has lost its meaning as merely a concept for measuring the flow of events in the past, present, and future. It has now become an element of Totality which actualizes the total interpenetration and containment of all the events of past, present, and future in the eternal present.

5. Upon the grand stage of the infinite Dharmadhātu, countless various dramas of religion are being enacted in numerous dimensions of space/time throughout eternity.

A DIALOGUE CONCERNING TOTALITY

Before we discuss further the Hwa Yen doctrines of Non-Obstruction and Totality, let us first read a dialogue which may mitigate the wistful skepticism that by now must have arisen in the reader's mind concerning the "illogical" and fantastic statements he has just read in these Hwa Yen sources. This dialogue might have taken place in the classroom of any Chinese monastery where the doctrine of Hwa Yen was being preached.

The teacher is speaking: ". . . thus, the realm of Buddhahood is the Totality of Non-Obstruction—the all-fusing, interpenetrating and simultaneous arising of infinite realms perceived by an omniscient and omnipresent Mind. If one reaches this realm, he liberates himself from the binding of time and space, of purity and defilement, of Nirvāṇa and saṁsāra. . . . He can bring a chiliocosm into a dust-mote while the chiliocosm does not shrink, and the dust-mote does not expand; this is because the bonds of matter and size no longer exist for Him. He can take the past and throw it into the future, and take the future and throw it into the past; this is because the bonds of time and causality have lost their grip on Him. The realm of Hwa Yen is . . ."

At this point, the patience of a student is exhausted. He rises and interrupts the teacher. "But Master . . . how can we be convinced of these claims? One may say that all these things are beyond our comprehension, but even so, we would still like to know the *possibility of the existence* of these things. It seems insufficient merely to tell us what a Buddha is experiencing and how inscrutable these experiences are. There must be some rational ground for all these claims, as there is in every field of Buddhist study. Could you please give me some illustrations, or parables, to dispel the darkness in my mind?"

The teacher listens with a sympathetic smile. He remembers that these were the exact words he spoke to his Master when he first attended classes in Hwa Yen.

"So, you think it is impossible to put a bigger thing into a smaller one without compressing the former or inflating the latter?"

"It seems to be so, sir."

"Now close your eyes," commands the teacher, "and visualize a begging bowl in your mind." After a few seconds he continues, "Now visualize a buffalo in your mind . . . now visualize the whole monastery . . . now the huge mountain that stands before the monastery."

He then asks, "Did you find any difficulty in visualizing a buffalo, a monastery, or a huge mountain in your mind?"

"No difficulty at all, sir."

"Your head is smaller than the image of a buffalo, and much smaller than an image of the monastery or of a mountain, but you can visualize them without any difficulty. Does not this suggest the possibility that a smaller thing can contain a larger thing, without expanding itself or compressing the other? This is a simple illustration of the Non-Obstruction of 'sizes' or 'spaces.' Now I shall give you an illustration of the Non-Obstruction of 'times': If a man dreamed that his father, who had long been dead, visited a house into which he had not yet moved—a not improbable case—he would bear witness to the possibility of taking events in the past and throwing them into the future, or vice versa. If even in the case of men, the bindings of time and space can sometimes be broken it would become very understandable in the case of the Buddhas—those Enlightened ones who have gained freedom from every bondage!"

These arguments silence the student, but he is only half convinced. After a whole day's contemplation, he raises new objections in class the next morning.

"Sir, after carefully thinking over your arguments, I still say that they are not completely convincing. One may think of a big mountain in his head without inflating it to the size of the mountain, but he does not actually put the real mountain into his real head; If he tried, I am sure his head would be crushed to pieces. Nor does the dreamer *actually* bring his dead father into his future home. All he did in his dream was to project a thing of the past, with a thing in the future, at the present moment."

The teacher replies, "I think you have missed the point. Your original question yesterday was, 'What is the rational ground for the claims made by Hwa Yen? And what examples or illustrations can be given to validate them?' I gave you an illustration of the fact that it is not impossible for a larger thing to exist in a smaller one; that is, the image of a vast mountain can exist within the small area of the brain. I did not say that we can *actually* put a vast mountain into our head *while we are dwelling in this particular realm*. It is extremely important to remember that the doctrine of Hwa Yen violates the laws of neither our empirical world nor our rational world, as long as we confine the subject matter under discussion to the realm of men. But if we speak about something from the viewpoint of Buddhahood, it becomes another matter. This is clearly stated in the Sūtra:

> . . . The infinite Lands that cannot be described
> Gather in the tip of one hair [of the Buddha]
> They neither crowd nor press,
> Nor does the hair tip swell . . .
> In it all Lands remain
> Just as they were before. . . .

and in the statement:

> '. . . Buddha threw this chiliocosm upward and downward, in the Western, Eastern, Southern, and Northern directions . . . passing it through millions, billions . . . infinite universes therein . . . and then He threw it back, passing it through the same number of universes to its original position. . . . The sentient beings living in this chiliocosm were not aware of this great movement; they lived in their respective realms as if nothing had happened. . . .' "

The teacher continues. "Giving a little thought to these two quotations, we find nothing unusual about them. They simply say, first, that an experience may take place in one realm without hindering an experience in the same category in another realm, though these two realms are interconnected, interfused, and even 'interidentical' with each other. And second, that a principle or experience which is accepted as true in one realm may not necessarily be so in another; this contradiction, however, does not negate or invalidate either of the two; they co-exist harmoniously without impeding each other. To understand this fully you should follow carefully the ten mysteries,[15] especially the first and the third.

"Before I go further, let me first ask you what do you mean by saying that we cannot actually put a real mountain into our heads? Specifically, what do you mean by *actual* and *real?*"

"By actual, or real, I mean the encountering of an experience shared by myself and others. If I say I am actually drinking a cup of water, I mean that I and others, that is, the spectators, are undergoing an experience of a kind that provides a common background for both myself *and* the spectators to refer to *it* as, 'Mr. So-and-so has just drunk a cup of water.' "

The teacher: "In other words, what you mean by *actual* is something that both you and others have been experiencing together. Now, do you think the experience you were having and the experience these spectators were having are identical—or are they different? Furthermore, what do you mean by 'refer to *it*'? Are you sure you should say *it,* and not *them*?"

The student: "Well, the experience I was having and the experience the spectators were having may not be exactly the same, but the common ground from which these experiences are derived is the same. *It* exactly refers to this common ground."

The teacher: "Are you sure of that? I think the problem is much more complicated than you think it to be. For the sake of convenience, let me now grant that all you have said is true. Your understanding of the *real* is based on a combination of subjective and objective grounds . . . this is to say, not only you, but also the spectators, can share a similar experience, thus ruling out the purely subjective ground which, in your opinion, is not always reliable. I will also accept this proposition for the time being. But the important thing to note here is that to share a common, or similar experience, the participants referred to must be in the same realm. A blind man cannot share the experience of observing a scene as other spectators do, even though he is physically present among them. His physical presence does not grant him the ability to enjoy the experience of seeing. *Existence or non-existence is only meaningful when a definite realm is predetermined or implied.* This very act of confining oneself to a particular realm in order to make something meaningful is the fundamental difference between the orientation of men and that of Hwa Yen. Men judge and view things from a definite, thus limiting, realm, but Hwa Yen views things from the standpoint of Totality—thus repudiating the very essence of 'defining,' or binding of any kind. To conclude my answer to your question of the 'rational ground' for the claims of Hwa Yen, I would say that the validity of Hwa Yen is based upon the knowledge and realization of *realms,* their relationships and self-sufficiency, genuiness and illusoriness, obstacles and 'reduction,' liberations and bindings, existence and non-existence, and so forth. To elucidate these points is the main concern of Hwa Yen philosophy—the task so successfully undertaken by the five Patriarchs [16] and their successors."

NON-OBSTRUCTION—
THE PIVOT OF TOTALITY

The dialogue in the preceding chapter clearly shows that the central theme of Hwa Yen philosophy hinges upon the concept of *realms*. Totality and Non-Obstruction would become meaningless without realms, for the very meaning of Totality is defined here as the embracing of all realms, and Non-Obstruction as the infinite possibilities of their interpenetrations.

But what *is* a realm? A realm, as generally understood, is an area, or sphere within which certain activities, thoughts, or influences take place; hence, a realm always implies a territory with definite boundaries. Here is a simple illustration: a cup of water is seen by ordinary people as merely a liquid with which to quench one's thirst; it is seen by a chemist as a compound of hydrogen and oxygen; by a physicist as the complex result of electronic movements; by a philosopher as something expressing relationship or causation, *by a Buddha as the manifestation or outflow of divine Buddhahood*. . . .

From this simple example we may deduce some arguments which in turn can be utilized to depict the interpenetration of realms.

Converging within this simple object—a cup of water—are numerous realms; they co-exist with one another in a very mysterious manner. On the one hand, they "live quietly," each within its own sphere, without jumping out of bounds; and on the other hand, they "live harmoniously together" without creating the slightest hindrance or interference with other realms. The fact that water can be used as a means to quench one's thirst does not prevent it from also being H_2O, a complex of electronic movements, a revelation of causation and relationship, and all the rest. On one level, or in one realm, water is a means with which one can extinguish fire, but on another level, it is a means from which one can draw fuel (hydrogen) to set a fire. Thus the orientations and evaluations of the same object can diametrically oppose one another when the frame of reference is set in different ways, or when it is viewed from different angles.

The fact that different realms can co-exist with each other within the same object is referred to by the Hwa Yen philosophers as the truth of "simultaneous arising" (t'ung-shih chü-ch'i), and the fact that these different realms, while simultaneously existing, do not impede or undermine each other, but mutually penetrate one another in a harmonious way is referred to as the truth of "simultaneous Non-Obstruction" (t'ung-shih wu-ai).

Simultaneous-arising and simultaneous Non-Obstruction are two important terms frequently used in the Hwa Yen literature; we shall discuss them more fully later, but here they remind us of an important point, that intrinsically the human mind is not simultaneously arising or non-obstructive. At the moment when we think of water as a means to quench thirst, we cannot think of it as H_2O, electronic movements, and so forth, and we must shift realms in sequence in order to apprehend them. This shows that the human way of thinking follows the "one-at-a-time" and "shifting-realm" approach which is characteristically *anti-* or *non*-simultaneous-arising. Here is an illustration: An extremely capable but hard-pressed executive has six telephones sitting on his desk, and each one of them is specifically connected to a department of his firm. He can usually handle two calls at the same time, and occasionally even three. He can "shift realms" so quickly and so smoothly that he almost reaches the point of "simultaneously dealing," but sometimes even he is helplessly thrown out of gear when all six phones ring together.

In contrast to this shifting-realm and one-at-a-time approach adopted by man's mind, the omniscient Mind of Buddhahood "adopts" *an entirely different approach* in its functionings. A mind that sees all must not, and cannot follow the shifting-realm, and one-at-a-time approach; it must see things in numerous realms, one penetrating another, all simultaneously arising on an enormous scale!

If for a moment, we step out of our perfunctory and automatic way of acting and scan the things surrounding us, what a vast and awe-inspiring mystery we will discover! Just look at any object that stands before your eyes—a cup of water, a table, a pencil, a vase of flowers, or a trace of wavering smoke rising from a stick of burning incense—in each and every object in a small room, what innumerable things of infinite realms now exist right before you, and yet you cannot see them! But this is only the picture of a room, greater still will be the total-realm picture of the house, of the block, of the city, of the country, of the earth, of the solar system, of the cosmos, and of the entire Dharmadhātu. . . .

What a stupendous panorama an omniscient Mind must see! But to see this panorama of simultaneous total-arising is not possible without a realization of the simultaneous Non-Obstruction. The former savors of the "outer appearance," or revelation of Totality; whereas, the latter implies the "inner relationship" or "construct" between different realms as seen from the standpoint of Totality. Ontologically speaking, simultaneous Non-Obstruction is even more important than simultaneous arising; it is through a realization of Non-Obstruction that the revelation of Totality is made possible. Non-Obstruction is, therefore, the core of Hwa Yen philosophy. But what is *obstruction?* As understood by common sense, obstruction is something that blocks or stands in the way of some matter or act. Yet obstruction (Chinese: Ai) as understood in Hwa Yen has a wider sense than this; it implicitly refers to the "boundary-walls" that stand between the different realms. To explain this, let us return to our example of a cup of water. In it we find many different realms. Although these different realms simultaneously exist and interpenetrate in a most harmonious way, between them stand definite "boundary-walls." These boundary-walls may be "tangible" or "elusive," "concrete" or "abstract," "impregnable" or "breachable," "unyielding" or "submissive," but they all have a definite restricting or limiting function. We can use an illustration to make this point clear: a man with no training in science can drink a thousand cups of water, or dive into the deep ocean a hundred times, but this will not make him understand the chemical or physical structure of water. He is confined within the boundaries of a certain realm and is unable to break through them. To understand the chemical structure, he must break through the boundary-walls that have hitherto confined him in the realm of ignorance. What he needs is not the repetition of experiments leading to that which he already knows, but a new approach and a new orientation that will lead him to break through these boundary-walls. The phrase, *breaking through,* has been heard so often that we tend to forget its significance and implications. To break through means not only to tear apart the "boundary-wall" standing between the old and the new realms, but it also implies the enlargement and integration of the two. A revolutionary break-through always involves great patience, effort, and insight—a clear indication of the uncompromising restrictive function of the boundary-walls. These "walls" should not, of course, be treated as something concrete in the external world. They are merely abstractions denoting the limiting or restricting functions of a realm. Using the Hwa Yen expression, they are "blocks" standing in the way of Totality. A complete removal of these "blocking walls" will enable one to reach the realm of Non-Obstruction, which again is the aim and core of Hwa Yen.

Here one may ask, "Since the obstructions or 'boundary-walls' are innumerable as the infinite realms themselves, how then is it possible for one to demolish all of them?" The answer is that, although the obstructions are innumerable, they are all derived from one basic, obstructing block, that is, the idea of *being*. Once this bedrock of being is crushed, all the constructions built upon it will also be demolished. The *idea of being,* that primordial root from which all other ideas sprout, is therefore the source of all obstructions. This inveterate, stubborn, and all-pervasive idea of being is the prime obstruction that stands in the way of Totality and our liberation. Instead of glorifying and deifying it as many philosophers and theologians of both the Western and Eastern traditions have done, Buddhism stresses the unsatisfactory and illusory aspects of being and the importance of destroying it. A Zen proverb has made this point very clear: "All things are reducible to the One; but to what is this One reducible?" The greatest break-through that can ever be achieved by man is the pulverizing of the block of "being" and of "one," which, psychologically speaking, is but a deep-rooted tendency to grasp things, a form of clinging manifested in a manner of arbitrary assertion. Totality is inaccessible without a thorough annihilation of this basic clinging, and Non-Obstruction cannot be realized without an understanding of the truth of "Non-being," which is śūnyatā (Voidness) —the core and essence of Buddhism.

Non-Obstruction as depicted by Hwa Yen is therefore pivoted on the doctrine of Voidness, for only the Void, that which is without boundary or obstruction itself, can "dissolve" all obstructions.

We shall elaborate the principle of Voidness and Non-Obstruction in more detail later, but first let us read a famous story about Master Fa Tsang's (643–712) ingenious way of illustrating the realm of Totality to the Empress Wu, or Wu Tsê-T'ien of the T'ang Dynasty,[17] who ruled from 684 to 704 A.D.

FA TSANG'S HALL OF MIRRORS

In the glorious age of T'ang, when Chinese people in all walks of life enjoyed the prosperity and progress of the times, and when cultural and spiritual inspiration were heightened in an atmosphere of afflu- ence and success, the Empress Wu Tsê-T'ien took a special interest in patronizing Buddhism. She was so intrigued by the fascinating teaching of this foreign religion that for some years (before becoming the em- press) she had even lived the life of a nun in a convent. Later, Wu Tsê-T'ien withdrew from the convent and joined the Emperor Kao Tsung in the palace as his imperial concubine. When Kao Tsung died, she usurped the throne and became the first—and also the last— empress in Chinese history. She then successfully governed the Empire for twenty years. She was hated and loved, denounced and admired, both by her contemporaries and by posterity, and she has been a con- troversial figure for many centuries. But no one could deny the fact that this extraordinary woman was one of the greatest statesmen ever to appear in Chinese history.

The Empress Wu Tsê-T'ien was not only a great patroness of Buddhism, but, in my opinion, a quite remarkable Buddhist scholar. Her famous "Prayer Before Opening the Holy Scripture" [18] was so excellent that it has been recited by all Buddhists in China throughout the centuries. Her deep interest in Hwa Yen led her to send an envoy to the country known as Yü Tien (Chinese Turkestan) for a more complete text of the *Hwa Yen Sūtra*.[19] Under her sponsorship, the eighty-volume version of this Sūtra was translated through the joint efforts of Chinese and foreign scholar-monks under the leadership of the famous Sanskritist, Śikṣānanda. It has been said that during the translation the Empress often went to the monastery herself to offer food to the monks. In the tenth month of the year A.D. 699, the transla- tion was completed, and an excellent preface for the book was written by the Empress herself in honor of this monumental task.

At that time she invited Master Fa Tsang to the capital to preach Hwa Yen in the light of this new translation. When he began to preach on the chapter of "The Lotus-Treasury World," the earth shook for a whole hour as an auspicious sign for the occasion. The Empress Wu was greatly pleased.

On this same day she summoned Fa Tsang to the royal palace and questioned him on the Hwa Yen doctrines of the ten mysteries, of Indra's Net, the Ocean Seal Samādhi, the principle of six forms, and so forth. With prodigious learning and insight, Fa Tsang expounded them easily and well—but these doctrines were too profound to be comprehended at once, even for a mind as brilliant as that of Wu Tsê-T'ien. In the first round she was at a loss. Surprised and fascinated by Fa Tsang's talk, she questioned him again and again. Fa Tsang then looked around (for an illustration) and saw a golden lion standing in a corner of the hall. He walked over to the lion, called her attention to it, and then delivered his celebrated discourse *On the Golden Lion,* in which he illustrated the essentials of Hwa Yen philosophy by using the lion as a metaphor, and thus brought the Empress to a quick understanding of the Doctrine.

One day Empress Wu asked Fa Tsang the following question:

Reverend Master, I understand that man's knowledge is acquired through two approaches: one is by experience, the direct approach, and the other by inference, the indirect approach. I also understand that the first five consciousnesses and the Ālaya only take the direct approach; whereas, the mind, or the sixth consciousness, can take both. Therefore, the findings of the conscious mind are not always trustworthy. The superiority and reliability of direct experience over indirect inference is taught in many scriptures. You have explained the Hwa Yen Doctrine to me with great clarity and ingenuity; sometimes I can almost see the vast Dharmadhātu in my mind's eye, and touch a few spots here and there in the great Totality. But all this, I realize, is merely indirect conjecture or guesswork. One cannot really understand Totality in an immediate sense before reaching Enlightenment. With your genius, however, I wonder whether you can give me a demonstration that will reveal the mystery of the Dharmadhātu— including such wonders as the "all in one" and the "one in all," the simultaneous arising of all realms, the interpenetration and containment of all dharmas, the Non-Obstruction of space and time, and the like?

After taking thought for a while, Fa Tsang said, "I shall try, your Majesty. The demonstration will be prepared very soon."

A few days later Fa Tsang came to the Empress and said, "Your Majesty, I am now ready. Please come with me to a place where the demonstration will be given." He then led the Empress into a room lined with mirrors. On the ceiling and floor, on all four walls, and even in the four corners of the room were fixed huge mirrors—all facing one another. Then Fa Tsang produced an image of Buddha and placed it in the center of the room with a burning torch beside it. "Oh, how fantastic! How marvelous!" cried the Empress as she gazed at this awe-inspiring panorama of infinite interreflections. Slowly and calmly Fa Tsang addressed her:

> Your Majesty, this is a demonstration of Totality in the Dharmad-hātu. In each and every mirror within this room you will find the reflections of all the other mirrors with the Buddha's image in them. And in each and every reflection of any mirror you will find all the reflections of all the other mirrors, together with the specific Buddha image in each, without omission or misplacement. The principle of interpenetration and containment is clearly shown by this demonstration. Right here we see an example of one in all and all in one—the mystery of *realm embracing realm ad infinitum* is thus revealed. The principle of the *simultaneous arising of different realms* is so obvious here that no explanation is necessary. These infinite reflections of different realms now simultaneously arise without the slightest effort; they just naturally do so in a perfectly harmonious way. . . .
>
> As for the principle of the non-obstruction of space, it can be demonstrated in this manner . . . (saying which, he took a crystal ball from his sleeve and placed it in the palm of his hand). Your Majesty, now we see all the mirrors and their reflections within this small crystal ball. Here we have an example of the small containing the large as well as of the large containing the small. This is a demonstration of the non-obstruction of "sizes," or space.
>
> As for the non-obstruction of times, the past entering the future and the future entering the past cannot be shown in this demonstration, because this is, after all, a static one, lacking the dynamic quality of the temporal elements. A demonstration of the non-obstruction of times, and of time and space, is indeed difficult to arrange by ordinary means. One must reach a different level to be capable of witnessing a "demonstration" such as that. But in any case, your Majesty, I hope this simple demonstration has served its purpose to your satisfaction.

THE CAUSES OF TOTALITY

At this point some questions shoud be raised: What are the causes of this all-merging Dharmadhātu? Who can realize it? How and why is this realm of Totality realizable? Ch'eng Kuan (738–839), the celebrated Hwa Yen Master, proposed ten reasons for the answer. In his famous work, *A Prologue to Hwa Yen,* we read:

> Question: What are the causes that enable all dharmas [or things] to merge, through and through, in such a manner?
>
> Answer: The reasons are many; it is difficult to discuss them all, but ten of them can be briefly given here:
>
> 1. Because [all things (dharmas)] are merely manifestations of the mind.
> 2. Because nothing has a definite nature.
> 3. Because [all things] are causes relative to one another . . . that is to say, they arise because of the principle of dependent-arising [pratītya-samutpāda].
> 4. Because the Dharma nature itself is completely merging and free.
> 5. Because [all things] are like phantoms and dreams.
> 6. Because [all things] are like reflections or images.
> 7. Because the infinite seeds [of virtue] were planted.
> 8. Because Buddha has exhausted all Realizations.
> 9. Because the power of deep Samādhi makes it so.
> 10. Because Buddha's miraculous power and inscrutable liberation make it so.
>
> *Any* of these reasons will enable the dharmas to merge through and through without obstruction.

Among these ten reasons, the first six can be said to describe the dharma-nature, and it is owing to them that the virtue and glory of Buddhahood are made possible. The seventh reason stresses the spiritual practice that brings about Buddhahood; the eighth stresses its merit, and the ninth and tenth its function and play.[20]

It is clear that the first six arguments are of a philosophical nature, given to explain the why of Dharmadhātu, and the remaining four are of a religious nature for the how and the who. But to expound these ten reasons in their original sequence is not very helpful, so we will reverse the order and discuss the last four reasons first.

Question: What makes Buddha realize this unfathomable all-merging Totality? [Reasons seven, eight, nine, and ten say:]
7. Because the infinite seeds [of virtue] were planted by Buddha.
8. Because Buddha has exhausted all Realizations.
9. Because the power of deep Samādhi makes it so.
10. Because Buddha's power is wondrously free.

If, in the final analysis, the realm of Totality is only realizable by direct experience, but not by reasoning, as Hwa Yen stresses, then the necessity of taking some steps to dissolve the barriers or obstacles that block the viewing of Dharmadhātu becomes obvious. Among the many obstacles that stand in the way to the Dharmadhātu, the fundamental one is the clinging-to-ego (wo chih), which is a persistent tendency to cling to a small, enclosed self and its interests. Its essence is to *exclude,* its function is to *separate.* The result of ego-clinging, as men have witnessed, is the birth of conflicts, pains and vices. Since the clinging-to-ego is by nature exclusive not inclusive, rejecting not embracing, conflicting not harmonious, it is something diametrically opposed to the all-inclusive and all-embracing harmony of Dharmadhātu. It is therefore easy to see that ego-clinging hinders rather than helps the realization of Dharmadhātu. What then can be regarded as leading to the realization of Dharmadhātu? Dharmadhātu is the whole, the boundless, the loving and good. It is on this basis that the seventh reason has made its claim. Why? Because virtue and goodness, in whatever form conceived, always imply some relinquishment of the "little self," and an affirmation of harmony and unity. They are intrinsically of the nature of Dharmadhātu. It is thus said in the *Hwa Yen Sūtra* that in His long-past lives, while He was still a Bodhisattva striving for Enlightenment, Buddha planted the virtuous seeds of:

A great compassionate heart, which longs to protect
all;
A great loving heart, which longs to benefit all
beings;
An understanding heart, which breeds sympathy and
tolerance;

A free heart, which longs to remove obstructions
 from others;
A heart, which fills the universe;
A heart endless and vast as space;
A pure heart, which conforms to the wisdom and the
 merit of the past, the present and the future. . . .

So it is through the cultivation of these benevolent wills and deeds that the obstacles to Dharmadhātu are removed and the Totality is seen. For virtue and benevolence not only deny the clinging-to-ego, but affirm the identity of one's interest in others which, in the vocabulary of Hwa Yen, is called the seeds of mutual-entering (hu ju) and the mutual-identity (hu chi) of Dharmadhātu.

THE TEN STAGES OF THE
BODHISATTVA'S ENLIGHTENMENT

We shall now turn our attention to *Reason eight:*

Because Buddha Has Exhausted All Realizations

Realization (Chêng) denotes the direct experience of seeing Reality; it is practically interchangeable with the frequently used Buddhist term, Enlightenment (Chüeh). Although Realization is a universal experience and does not, in essence, vary from one person to another, it has a great many strata, or degrees, of depth. This variation, in turn, expresses itself in the vast difference found between a "preliminarily enlightened Bodhisattva" and a "perfectly enlightened Buddha." Enlightenment, therefore, cannot be said to be universally identical, for it can vary greatly—from a shallow glimpse of the "Suchness" (Tathatā), to the complete unfolding of the Dharmadhātu. A tyro in music can "play the piano," and so can a concert pianist, but there is a big difference between the two. The initial Enlightenment often seems to come in an abrupt manner, but to deepen and consummate this realization, a long period of "fostering" and cultivation is required. Reality is like a bottomless pit or a roofless sky—the more you explore, the deeper it becomes. The pursuit of enlightenment is endless; the further you go, the longer the road, and the end seems never to come in sight. But, on the other hand, once the initial Realization is won, the rest of the journey will be much easier than before. Although the powers and functions vary greatly between the initial and advanced stages, the essence of the realization always remains the same. In this sense, Buddhist Enlightenment can be regarded as one and also many.

In the beginning stages of Enlightenment, a Bodhisattva often has a high opinion of his mystic experience. He is quite confident that even the perfect Buddha cannot have a deeper insight than his! This is why the great Zen masters often try to beat off the disciple's Realizations as shown in many Zen Koans. This is why Tê Shan said, "If you cannot answer my question, I will give you thirty blows; if you can, I shall also give you thirty blows." To awaken the Bodhi-seekers from ignorance and pride and to demonstrate the boundless vista of Dharmadhātu, the *Hwa Yen Sūtra* has elaborated on the famous Ten Stages of the Path. A study of them will soon make one aware of the infinite vastness of Buddhist Enlightenment, which in my opinion, has dwarfed many claims of celebrated mystics in both Eastern and Western religions. Since an extensive survey of these progressive stages is beyond the scope of this book, we shall quote some essential passages from the *Hwa Yen Sūtra* concerning the famous Ten Stages of Enlightenment: [21]

> All the Buddhas in the ten directions then stretched out their hands to touch the head of the Bodhisattva Diamond Treasury; whereupon, he arose from Samādhi and addressed the great assembly:
>
> "Oh Buddha's sons, the good vows of all Bodhisattvas cannot be changed, defiled or fathomed. They are as vast as the universe, as ultimate as the Void, and they pervade the universes to protect sentient beings. . . . [With these great vows, a Bodhisattva is able to] enter the Wisdom-Realm of all Buddhas. . . . What then is the Bodhisattva's Wisdom-Realm and its stages? . . . There are, all together, ten successive Stages preached by the Enlightened Ones in the past, present, and future:
>
> 1. The Stage of Great Joy
> 2. The Stage of Spotless Purity
> 3. The Stage of Illumination
> 4. The Stage of Intense Wisdom
> 5. The Stage of Invincible Strength
> 6. The Stage of Direct Presence
> 7. The Stage of Far-reaching
> 8. The Stage of Immovable Steadfastness
> 9. The Stage of Meritorious Wisdom
> 10. The Stage of the Assembling Clouds of the Dharma."
>
> He continued:
>
> "I do not see a single Buddha in the whole universe who fails to preach these Ten Stages. Why? Because this is the path through which all Bodhisattvas proceed toward ultimate Enlightenment. . . ."
>
> The Bodhisattva Diamond Treasury suddenly stopped and fell silent [as if unwilling to expound this difficult and profound matter further]. All the Bodhisattvas in the assembly were perplexed at this. They thought, "Why does he list the names of the

Ten Stages but give no explanations?" Whereupon, the Bodhisattva Liberation Moon, knowing the thought of the assembly,
asked Diamond Treasury:

> Why, though wise and full of merit,
> Do you name but not explain these Stages?
> Why, though strong and full of courage,
> Do you list them without explanations?

> All of us long to hear
> The wonders of these Stages.
> Pray explain them to us,
> Who, a fearless audience,
> Long to hear the Truth.

To please all Bodhisattvas in the assembly, Diamond Treasury,
the great and fearless sage, sang in reply:

> Supreme Buddhahood depends upon
> The Bodhisattvas' acts and Stages.
> Hard to explain, they are unique and superb.
> Difficult to see, they are deep and subtle.
> They give birth to Buddha's realm.
> Men will be perplexed, confused,
> When they hear of these wonders.

> Only those with adamantine minds
> Who have realized egolessness,
> And believe in the omniscience
> Of Buddha can receive his teaching.
> Like a painting in the sky, or wind
> In space, the Wisdom of the Buddha
> Is hard to know if you make distinctions.

> This realm is deep, inscrutable,
> And hard for the world to take.
> Thinking thus, I hold my tongue
> And so remain in silence.

. . . [Finally, after repeated entreaties from many Bodhisattvas,]
He observed the ten directions and resumed his address in order
to strengthen the faith of the assembly:

> Hard to conceive, subtle and wondrous
> Is the Way of the Tathāgatas!
> No arising and no extinction—
> Forever pure, forever peaceful. . . .

It is a realm that can be reached
Only by the wise and pure. . . .
Without duality and limit,
It is beyond all words and pointings.
The Stages of a Bodhisattva,
His love, compassion, and his Vows,
Are hard to tell and to believe . . .
Mind and thought can never reach them,
Only Wisdom can behold them.
The track a bird makes in the sky
Is hard to trace and to define;
Hard is it to describe
What the Ten Stages mean.
It is a realm that can be known,
But cannot be expressed [in words].

An ocean drop can be explained
If you rely on Buddha's blessings,
But since the meanings of *this* truth are infinite,
They can never be exhausted down the aeons. . . .

The Bodhisattva Diamond Treasury continued:[22]
"If a man cultivates a deep root-of-merit, practices innumerable virtues, and assembles all favorable conditions for the Path
. . . if with faith, compassion, and a vast mind he aspires to attain Buddha's Wisdom, the Thought-of-Enlightenment [Bo-
dhicitta], can then arise in him. He arouses this Bodhi-Mind (or
Thought-of-Enlightenment) so that he may seek the all-embracing
Wisdom, attain the ten powers of a Tathāgata, secure the great
fearlessness . . . and strive for the salvation of all sentient beings.
. . . This is why the Bodhi-Mind is aroused. Oh sons of Buddha,
this Mind is deep, sincere, and straight; great compassion domi-
nates it, great wisdom nourishes it, and skillfulness protects it. It
is as vast as the Buddha's power, which enters into the Wisdom
of Non-Obstruction, accomodates the insight into nature, and
embraces all teachings of the Tathāgatas. This Mind is [by itself]
the great Wisdom, with which the Bodhisattva can teach and
guide all sentient beings. It is vast as the universe, ultimate as
the Void, and everlasting as the endless future. . . . Oh sons of
Buddha, the very moment this Mind has arisen within a Bodhisattva, he passes beyond the state of an ordinary man . . . he
is born into the family of Buddhas. He surpasses all the dharmas
of the world and yet he enters the world. . . . Surely and posi-

tively he will consummate the Perfect Enlightenment of Buddha-hood. When a Bodhisattva reaches this Stage, he is said to have attained the Stage of Great Joy . . . [From his heart] overflows abundant delight, abundant faith, purity, and enthusiasm, abundant modesty and tolerance. He eschews argument and strife; he does not trouble others, nor is he prone to anger. His joy is boundless when he thinks of the Bodhisattvas . . . their altruistic deeds, their superiority and invincible strength. . . . He often thinks, 'My heart is so full of joy that it transcends all earthly imagination! [Why is this so?] It is because I have entered the realm of the great equality of all Buddhas, because I have gone far from the state of ordinary men, because I am close to Wisdom and the Tathāgatas, because I can share wondrous experiences with Buddhas, and can protect and deliver all sentient beings. . . .' When a Bodhisattva reaches this Stage of Great Joy, he is forever freed from all fears. No more will he fear insecurity, loss of reputation, or death. . . . Why? Because, from him, all ego-clinging has forever been removed since he cherishes not even his own body, let alone other things. . . .

"Oh sons of Buddha, with great compassion and a vast mind this Bodhisattva will practice even more virtuous deeds than before. Increased will be his faith, his pure thoughts, his understanding . . . modesty, tolerance, love, and compassion. . . . He will then take upon himself these ten great vows:

1. I will render inexhaustible offerings and services to all the Buddhas in the infinite universes . . . vast as the universe, ultimate as the Void, everlasting as the endless future. . . .

2. I will learn, keep, protect, and follow all the teachings and Sūtras given by all the Buddhas . . . vast as the universe, ultimate as the Void, everlasting as the endless future. . . .

3. I will beseech all the Buddhas to set in motion their "descent" into the world . . . vast as the universe, ultimate as the Void, everlasting as the endless future . . .

4. I will teach, guide, and ripen all sentient beings with the immense, profound, and far-reaching Dharmas and Pāramitās of Bodhisattvas . . . vast as the universe, ultimate as the Void, everlasting as the endless future. . . .

5. I will behold and enter all the universes, the large, small, flat, round, square, upright, and upside down ones; realm embracing realm, all appear in the ten directions like Indra's net.

. . . I will see and know them all . . . vast as the universe, ultimate as the Void, everlasting as the endless future. . . .

6. I will bring all Buddha's Lands into one Land and one Land into all Buddha's Lands, with infinite light and glory and without the slightest flaw or defilement . . . vast as the universe, ultimate as the Void, everlasting as the endless future. . . .

7. I will attain Buddha's Wisdom and superb powers to work miracles for the fulfillment of sentient beings' wishes and needs . . . vast as the universe, ultimate as the Void, everlasting as the endless future. . . .

8. I will stand shoulder-to-shoulder with other Bodhisattvas to further our common goal [of benefit to all sentient beings]. In harmony and with devotion, I will study and work with them without jealousy or grudge. . . . With a thorough understanding of Buddha's teachings, powers, and Wisdoms, I shall perform miracles, journey in all lands, and attend all Buddha's congregations in infinite bodily forms. . . . With this great, unfathomable insight, a Bodhisattva raises his vows aloft, and sets himself to work . . . vast as the universe, ultimate as the Void, everlasting as the endless future. . . .

9. I will accommodate all sentient beings by providing them with various teachings according to their dispositions and needs, deliver them from desires and pains, make them aware that all dharmas are illusory, make them realize that all things bear the stamp of Nirvāṇa, show them wisdoms and great miracles . . . vast as the universe, ultimate as the Void, everlasting as the endless future. . . .

"Oh sons of Buddha, when a Bodhisattva reaches the Stage of Great Joy, he accentuates the ten vows, which again give birth to thousands, millions, billions, and an infinity of other vows. . . . With great diligence he strives to fulfill them with the ten inexhaustible Dharmas:

1. Inexhaustible are sentient beings.
2. Inexhaustible are the worlds.
3. Inexhaustible is space.
4. Inexhaustible is the dharma-nature [dharmatā].
5. Inexhaustible is Nirvāṇa.
6. Inexhaustible are Buddhas who appear in the worlds.

7. Inexhaustible is Buddha's Wisdom.
8. Inexhaustible are the games of Mind.
9. Inexhaustible are the arisings of Wisdom.
10. Inexhaustible are the seeds of the paths of the world, of Dharma and of Wisdom. . . .
    "With resolution this Bodhisattva will make a final Vow:

10. If sentient beings are exhaustible, so will be my vow; if the worlds, space, dharma-nature, Nirvāṇa, Buddha's Wisdom . . . are exhaustible, so will be my vow; but since they are not exhaustible, neither shall be my vows . . . [vast as the universe, ultimate as the Void, everlasting as the endless future] . . . ."

In the above quotations, we notice that Enlightenment is produced not merely from the cultivation of "insight," but also from virtues and good will; it consists not only in the so-called "mystic experience," but in the presence of a solemn vow and a vast mind. In other words, Enlightenment is a realization of both truth and love, a merging of both the compassion and the Void. The first stage, the *Stage of Great Joy*, marks the important beginning of a Bodhisattva who, after having conquered innate-ego clinging and desires through the realization of the unborn Void, will strive to deepen his insight of Śūnyatā and increase his meritorious and altruistic deeds in the Path of Bodhi till the day he reaches Buddhahood. In the aeons of kalpas to come, he will practice all the Bodhisattvas' acts and fulfill their Vows by progressively passing through the ten stages till he attains the perfect Enlightenment of Buddhahood.

Because of a lack of space, I cannot quote the complete text describing each of the ten stages as given in the *Hwa Yen Sūtra*. A brief survey of those stages is therefore given below: [23]

The First Stage—The Stage of Great Joy

The individual who reaches this stage is said to behold, for the first time, the holy nature (shên hsin) through his pure Wisdom of nondistinction. Having eradicated the dichotomy of subject and object, he is able in great measure to benefit himself and others in various ways. A Bodhisattva of this stage is said to be extremely joyful at all times; he is unusually generous, and nothing pleases him more than to be

asked for charity. Hence he is capable of consummating the practice
of the first Pāramitā—the Perfection of Charity.

The Second Stage—The Stage of Spotless Purity

The individual who reaches this stage is said to be able to keep perfectly the Bodhisattva's discipline. He is immune from the slightest
transgression of the precepts. He is by nature free from hatred, malice,
grudges, and impatience, and he is always gentle, kind, forgiving, and
benevolent. He practices all the ten Pāramitās, but stresses and consummates the second one—the Perfection of Discipline.

The Third Stage—The Stage of Illumination

One who reaches this stage is said to master many Samādhis, to perform
many miracles, and to acquire heavenly vision; whereby, he sees
clearly the karmas and incarnations of many sentient beings. He develops a superb intelligence and memory, which enable him to recollect all the things he has ever experienced, including those in his remote past lives. He practices all the ten Pāramitās, but stresses and
consummates the third one—the Perfection of Patience.

The Fourth Stage—The Stage of Glowing (Intense) Wisdom

One who reaches this stage will be able to eradicate the clinging of
body, of self, of "I" and "mine." A glowing Wisdom arises in him with
which he burns away all desires and passions. He practices all the ten
Pāramitās, but stresses and consummates the fourth one—the Perfection of Diligence.

The Fifth Stage—The Stage of Great Triumph (Invincible Strength)

The individual who reaches this stage can achieve the most formidable
task ever confronting a Bodhisattva, for he conquers the "cleavage between insight and concept." He thus unifies the mundane intellect of
distinction with the transcendental Wisdom of non-distinction, and
causes both of them to arise simultaneously without obstruction. This
implies that he can now bridge the gulf hitherto separating the "this"

and "that" sides of duality. He practices all the ten Pāramitās, but stresses and consummates the fifth one—the Perfection of Dhyāna.

The Sixth Stage—The Stage of Direct Presence

When a Bodhisattva of the previous stage, in deep contemplation, observes that all things are devoid of substance, are immanently pure, transcending all "playwords," and are like phantoms, dreams, reflections . . . he comes to the realization of the great equality, and reaches the Sixth Stage. The Prajñā truth, otherwise called the "Non-Obstructing Wisdom Light," will then appear nakedly before him. He practices all the ten Pāramitās, but stresses and consummates the sixth one—the Perfection of Wisdom.

The Seventh Stage—The Stage of Far-Reaching

In the *Hwa Yen Sūtra* [24] we read:

> When a Bodhisattva reaches the Seventh Stage, he can then enter the infinite realms of sentient beings; enter infinite Buddhas' Lands and Wisdoms; enter infinite varieties of dharmas, kalpas, and sentient beings' faiths, understandings, desires, and temperaments; enter infinite Buddhas' words and languages . . . enter the Buddhas' vast and profound Wisdom and their ingenious ways of ripening sentient beings. . . .
>
> This Bodhisattva then thought: "The infinite realms of Tathāgatas cannot be known [by means of thought] even in thousands and millions of kalpas, so I shall rely on the effortless and non-distinguishing mind to realize them in full." With profound insight this Bodhisattva contemplates, observes, and practices the Wisdom of ingenuity [Fang Pien Hui], and the superior Dharma in a most steadfast manner. In all activities—whether walking, standing, sitting, or lying—his mind is always absorbed in the Dharma, and not for a single moment, *even during sleep or dream,* could his mind ever become veiled by ignorance or obstructions. . . .
>
> Thereupon the Bodhisattva Liberation Moon asked the Bodhisattva Diamond Treasury, "Is this Seventh Stage the only stage wherein a Bodhisattva can accomplish all the virtuous deeds leading to Buddhahood?" Diamond Treasury replied:
>
> "A Bodhisattva in any of the Ten Stages can accomplish them,

but the Seventh Stage is the superior one. Why? Because the Bodhisattvas of this stage have completed all spiritual preparations,
so they can enter the realm of Wisdom and free acts. Oh son of
Buddha, a Bodhisattva of the First Stage fulfills the Enlightened
Acts [Bodhyaṅgas] by vowing to practice all Buddha's teachings;
a Bodhisattva of the Second Stage fulfills the Enlightened Acts
by purifying the defilements of the mind; a Bodhisattva of the
Third Stage, by augmenting the vows and illumination; of the
Fourth Stage, by entering the Tao; of the Fifth Stage, by accommo-
dating the world; of the Sixth, by penetrating the most profound
Prajñāparamitā; and of the Seventh, by accomplishing all the
Dharmas of Buddhas. . . . The Bodhisattva of the First Stage,
of the Second Stage, and on up to the Seventh Stage, cannot fully
overcome the desire-passions in his acts . . . only when he enters
the Eighth Stage from the Seventh, will he be able to transcend
all desire-passions. . . . A Bodhisattva who has reached the Sixth
and Seventh Stages can enter the Dhyāna-of-Cessation [saṁjñā-
vedayita-nirodha] at any moment, but because of his compassionate vows [to help all sentient beings], he will never enter the
Dhyāna-of-Cessation. . . . The Bodhisattvas of the Seventh Stage,
however, have attained the treasury of Buddhahood; they always
appear in the abode of devils, though they have forever transcended the path of devils; they always appear to follow the devil's
ways, and yet, although their actions are similar to those of
heretics, they never withdraw from the Dharma. . . . Although
they appear to be engaging in worldly activities, they always
practice the world-beyond-teachings. . . .

"The Bodhisattva of this Seventh Stage practices all the Ten
Pāramitās, but stresses and consummates the seventh—the Perfection of Contrivance."

The Eighth Stage—The Stage of Steadfastness [25]

The Bodhisattva Diamond Treasury continued:

When a Bodhisattva of the Seventh Stage has thoroughly practiced both the Dharma of Wisdom and the Dharma of ingenuity,
stored with spiritual provisions, equipped with the great vows,
blessed by the power of the Tathāgatas . . . he, with great compassion and kindness, will never abandon a single sentient being.
. . . Entering the realm of infinite Wisdom, he sees that all
dharmas are from the beginning unborn and unproduced, devoid

of form, substance, or extinction. . . . He sees that all things are of Suchness, equal in the past, present, and future. He realizes that this is a realm of non-distinctive Wisdom, unreachable by the mind and its acts. He is then detached from all thoughts and discriminations. Without any clinging he enters the Void-like nature of all dharmas. . . . When he comes to this state he is said to have accomplished the "thorough realization of the unborn reality" [anutpattika-dharma-kṣānti] and to have reached the Eighth Stage, the Stage of Steadfastness, which is the inner abode of Bodhisattvas, difficult to describe and to comprehend, transcending discriminations, forms, thoughts, and attachments. It goes beyond all calculations, limitations, and disturbances, and surpasses the sphere of great sages. . . .

As a monk, furnished with miraculous power and freedom of mind can gradually enter the Samādhi of Cessation, thus halting all wavering thoughts, memories, and discriminations, the Bodhisattva of the Eighth Stage also abandons all works-of-effort and reaches a state of effortlessness; wherein, all mental, verbal, and physical strivings come to an end. . . . This is like a man who, in a dream, finding himself falling into a great river, strives to reach the other shore by exerting all his strength so hard that he suddenly awakens from the dream, thus setting at rest all his strivings. So, in a like manner, a Bodhisattva, when seeing all sentient beings drowning in the stream of the four pains,[26] exerts himself to save them with vigor, courage, and fortitude. He eventually reaches the Stage of Steadfastness, and thus all efforts spontaneously stop. He is forever freed from all activities, forms, dualisms, and all undertakings of a contrived consciousness. In his mind there is no conscious discrimination of Bodhisattva, of Buddha, of Enlightenment, or of Nirvāṇa, let alone the thought of worldly things.

But ah, son of Buddha, because of the original vows made by the Bodhisattva himself [in his previous lives], all the Buddhas in the universe will appear before him in order to confer upon him the Wisdom of Tathāgatahood. . . . All the Buddhas will then declare:

"Well done, well done, oh son of a good family! This is the thorough realization of the first order, which is in accordance with the teachings of all Buddhas. But, son of a good family, you have not yet acquired the ten powers, the fourfold fearlessness, and the eighteen special qualities of Tathāgatas;[27] you should still strive further to achieve them. Though you have now established serenity and emancipation, there are ignorant beings who have not yet done so and are being enslaved by desires and distinctions. Now is the time for you to show your compassion for them. Oh, son of a good family, you should now recall your original vows and set yourself once more to the task of benefiting all sentient beings, bringing them all to the realization of the inconceivable Wisdom of Buddhahood. Oh, son of a good family, what you have now realized is the dharma-nature [dharmatā], which is eternally so, regardless of the appearance or disappearance of Buddhas. But it is not because of this realization that Tathāgatas are so named, for all Śravakas and Pratyeka Buddhas, too, can realize it. . . .

"Again, son of Buddha, you should now look up to the beyond-measure Buddha's Body, Wisdom, Land, halo of illumination, skillfulness . . . and try to attain them all [without omission]. You have now attained only one light of Dharma—the light that sees into the real nature of all things, unborn and beyond discrimination. But the innumerable lights of Dharmas possessed by Tathāgatas, and their enterings, functions, and changes, are inconceivable and immeasurable even through millions and billions of aeons. . . . It is this great Dharma you should strive to attain. Oh behold, son of Buddha! Behold how numberless are sentient beings, how boundless are the universes, how infinitely different are divided things. . . . You should know clearly all these infinite variances in infinite realms of infinite universes, without the slightest effort or error."

So in this manner all the Buddhas inculcate in the Bodhisattva of the Eighth Stage the desire to strive for the infinite *Wisdom of distinction*.[28] Oh son of Buddha, without this urge [from all Buddhas] this Bodhisattva would enter Parinirvāna and abandon all altruistic deeds. But since an exhortation was given to him by all Buddhas, this Bodhisattva, in a brief moment, can produce Wisdoms and works incomparably greater than before. . . . Why is this so? Because, prior to his arrival at this Stage, he had only one body with which to act like a Bodhisattva; but now, having arrived, he attains infinite bodies, voices, insights and miraculous powers . . . so he can teach and guide infinite Dharmas. . . . All this is possible because he has now attained the Dharma of the immovable. . . . Metaphorically, it is like a man in a boat who must exert great strength to keep his boat moving before he reaches the sea; but once he reaches it, he can, without effort, sail the boat a much greater distance than before. By the same token, when a Bodhisattva enters the course of Mahāyāna and sets out on a Bodhisattva's actions, he can then, with the Wisdom of "effort-lessness," enter the realm of omniscience in a much more effective form than ever before.

Oh sons of Buddha, with the effortless awareness produced by the great Wisdom of Skillfulness, the Bodhisattva of this Eighth Stage can observe the sphere of the omniscience of Buddhahood. He sees clearly when and how a world is established and destroyed, and through what karma it is made and destroyed. His knowledge of these things is crystal clear, without the slightest error. He also knows the elements of earth, of fire, of water . . . and of atoms (specks of dust) —their small, large, infinite and different forms . . . in each and every world in the universe. He knows the subtle, the different, the infinitely different forms of atoms. . . . He knows clearly the total sum, though infinite in number, of atoms of the lands and of sentient beings' bodies. He knows the exact number of the atoms that make up small and large bodies, or those of a hungry-ghost, an asura, a man or a deva. . . .

Oh son of Buddha, this stage of the Bodhisattva is called the Stage of Steadfastness. Why? Because nothing can corrupt it; it is called Irremovable, because his Wisdom never regresses; it is called Inaccessible, because all of the world cannot fathom it; it is called the Stage of the Innocent Child, because it is so far from vices; it is called the Stage of Birth, because it is spontaneous and free. It is the Stage of Accomplishment, because there is no more effort to be made . . . of Transformation, because it can fulfill all wishes . . . of No-Effort, because everything has been accomplished. Thus, Oh son of Buddha, this Bodhisattva enters the Realm of Buddhahood and illumines the merits of the Enlightened Ones. . . . He has great miraculous power, gives out great light, enters the Totality of Non-Obstruction, displays all the great merits, and discerns the nuances between all worlds. With spontaneity and freedom, he thoroughly knows things in the past, present, and future; he conquers all devils and vices, and enters deeply the sphere of Tathāgatahood. Because he has attained the Dharma of non-regression, he can practice the Bodhisattva's actions in infinite lands . . . with the power of Samādhi he sees infinite Buddhas in infinite Lands; serves, worships, and offers to them through thousands, millions, and billions of kalpas. . . . This Bodhisattva attains the Buddha's treasury of profound Dharmas. . . . If one asks him about the differences between the various worlds, he can describe them all without the slightest difficulty. . . .

Oh son of Buddha, the above is a very brief account of the Stage of Steadfastness; it would take aeons of kalpas to elaborate it, but even within this vast duration of time, one could not fully exhaust it. . . .

This Bodhisattva practices all the Ten Pāramitās, but stresses and consummates the eighth—the Perfection of Vows.

The Ninth Stage—The Stage of Meritorious Wisdom

Again in the Sūtra we read:

He who reaches this stage clearly and unmistakably knows all the good, bad, and neutral acts . . . the pure and the defiled acts, the worldly and the transcendental acts, and those of the Śravakas, of the Bodhisattvas, and of the Tathāgatas. . . . With such great Wisdom, this Bodhisattva discerns the difficulties of sentient beings' minds, of the desire-passions and of karma; the difficulties of organs, concepts, temperaments and inclinations; of drowsiness, of incarnations, of the continuance of habitual thoughts, and of the distinct differences between the three groups.[29] This Bodhisattva sees clearly, without error, the numerous forms and functions of sentient beings' minds . . . the forms of hetero-arising, of speedy-transforming, of extinction and of shapelessness and of nonentity, of infinity, of purity, of defilement and nondefilement, of binding and nonbinding, and of magic-creation. . . . This Bodhisattva knows crystal clear all these different forms and functions which add up to thousands, millions, and billions, and to infinity. . . .

Again, this Bodhisattva knows distinctly the numerous modes of sentient beings' desires—the numerous modes of deeply rooted desires established through long kalpas, the infinite ways in which the desire-passions are aroused, the way sentient beings adhere to the desire-passions from birth to death, the innumerable ways they show their ignorance and in which the desire-passions arise in both conscious and unconscious states.

Again, this Bodhisattva knows, crystal clear, karma's numerous forms and manifestations; the good, bad, and neutral forms; the symbolic and symbol-less forms; and also the concomitants arising with the mind. He knows the mystery of karma's momentary extinctions and yet its unfailing production of effects. He also knows the karma that produces effects and the one that does not produce them . . . the karma that, like a field, contains infinite forms, the karma that distinguishes a common from a holy person, that ripens in this life or in after-lives, that leads one to the various Paths. . . . If a Bodhisattva can follow this Wisdom, he reaches the Stage of Meritorious Wisdom. *He is then said to be able to know sentient beings. He can then teach, guide, and lead them to Liberation.*[30]

Oh sons of Buddha, a Bodhisattva who reaches this Stage of Meritorious Wisdom can be a great teacher of Dharma, can perform all the functions of a teacher, and can protect and preserve the Tathāgatas' Dharma-treasury without fail. With infinite, ingenious Wisdoms he can bring forth the four unimpeded eloquences . . . and follow at all times the four unimpeded Wisdoms. . . . What are they? They are the unimpeded Wisdoms of dharma, of meaning, of words, and of eloquence. With the unimpeded Wisdom of dharma, he knows the self-form of all things; with the unimpeded Wisdom of words, he preaches without mistake, and with the unimpeded Wisdom of eloquence, he preaches without cessation.

Again, with the unimpeded Wisdom of dharma, he knows that all things are devoid of a self-being; with the unimpeded Wisdom of meaning, he knows the arising and extinction of all things; with the unimpeded Wisdom of words, he knows the illusory nature of all words, and yet he abandons them not; with the unimpeded Wisdom of eloquence, he uses illusory words to deliver infinite discourses.

Again, with the unimpeded Wisdom of dharma, he knows the differences and distinctions between all things at the present moment; with the unimpeded Wisdom of meaning, he knows the differences and distinctions between all things in the past and future; with the unimpeded Wisdom of words, he preaches all things in the past, present, and future without error; and with the unimpeded Wisdom of eloquence, he preaches the infinite Dharmas of all times with great clarity. Again, with these Wisdoms . . . he adopts sentient beings' words and languages to preach in accordance with their interests and aspirations. . . .

Son of Buddha, if all the sentient beings in the infinite universes came before this Bodhisattva, and every one of them asked him a different question in an infinite number of languages, in a split second he would comprehend them all and give proper answers with full explanations in one voice, and thus make all questioners fully satisfied and pleased. . . .

This Bodhisattva practices all the Ten Pāramitās, but stresses and consummates the ninth Pāramitā—the Perfection of Power.

The Tenth Stage—
The Stage of Assembling the Dharma Clouds

Thereupon the Bodhisattva Diamond Treasury said to the Bodhisattva Liberation Moon:

> From the First Stage to the Ninth Stage, a Bodhisattva observes, practices, and completes all meritorious deeds through his infinite Wisdoms . . . he develops great merits, virtues, and insight, and practices altruistic deeds in fullest measure; he knows the differences between all the worlds; he enters the "jungle" of the desire-passions of men; he probes into the sphere of Tathāgatahood . . . then he is said to have reached the Stage of being a Candidate for Buddhahood. . . . He then attains the Samādhi of entering the differences of Dharmadhātu . . . the Samādhi of the Ocean Mirror . . . of the vast Void . . . of knowing all sentient beings' Minds . . . of the presence of all Buddhas. . . . Then . . . sitting upon a great lotus seat as large as billions of universes, from his feet he gives out infinite beams of light to illumine all the hells in the ten directions, and thus relieves all the sufferings therein . . . from his knees . . . his navel . . . his armpits, he gives out infinite beams of light to relieve the pains and sorrows of the realms of animals . . . of asuras . . . of men . . . and of heavens. From his face flow infinite beams of light to bless all Bodhisattvas—from the First up to the Ninth Stage; from his head he gives out infinite lights to illumine all the Dharma congregations in the infinite universes. . . .
>
> Thereupon all the Buddhas and Bodhisattvas become aware that in such-and-such a world, a certain Bodhisattva, after having practiced vast meritorious deeds, has now reached the Stage of being a Candidate for Buddhahood. Infinite Bodhisattvas, including those of the Ninth Stage, will come to serve, to worship, and to observe him; and as they do so, they will all attain thousands and millions of Samādhis . . . and thereupon boundless, inscrutable miracles will be performed. . . .
>
> Oh son of Buddha, a Bodhisattva who has reached this Stage of Assembling the Dharma Clouds knows clearly and exactly the change of sentient beings' desires and of their views, and the

change of the great Dharmadhātu. . . . He enters the secret of Tathāgatahood . . . the secret of body, words and mind, of taming sentient beings, and of demonstrating different paths. . . . This Bodhisattva attains the inscrutable and unobstructed liberation, the pure-insight and the all-illuminating liberation, the Buddha-treasury liberations . . . and the Ultimate-Realm liberations. . . . The Bodhisattvas, including those of the Ninth Stage, cannot know this Bodhisattva's acts, wonders, glories . . . and Wisdoms, nor can these wonders be exhausted by description through aeons of kalpas. . . .

The Bodhisattva of this stage knows truly and accurately the entering into the subtle Wisdom of all Buddha Tathāgatas, such as: the subtle Wisdom of spiritual practice, the subtle Wisdom at the time of death,[31] the subtle Wisdom of rebirth, of priesthood, of performing miracles . . . of setting in motion the wheel of Dharma, of Parinirvāṇa, of maintaining the Doctrine. . . . He knows exactly and truly such Wisdom of all Buddhas. The Bodhisattva of this stage also enter into the secrecy of Tathāgatas, such as: His secrecy of body, of words and of mind . . . His secrecy of making predictions to Bodhisattvas. His secrecy of collecting sentient beings, of providing various vehicles, of [knowing] the wide differences of all sentient beings' capacities and actions. . . . He also knows all Buddhas' Wisdom of entering into all kalpas, such as: with one kalpa, they enter into the innumerable kalpas, with infinite kalpas, they enter one kalpa . . . with one moment, they enter into kalpas . . . with kalpas in the past and future, they enter the present, and with the present kalpas, they enter into the past and future . . . with long kalpas, they enter the short and with short, the long kalpas. He knows all these facts accurately as they truly are. . . . A Bodhisattva of this Stage attains the inscrutable liberation of pure observation, of universal illumination, of knowing the three times, . . . of exhausting all realms and experiences. . . .

Oh sons of Buddha, this Bodhisattva fully realizes the great Wisdoms [of Tathāgata] . . . and [all] that which is possessed by the infinite Buddhas, such as: the infinite great Dharma-illuminations, great Dharma-reflections, the great Dharma-rains. In a fraction of a second, this Bodhisattva can receive and hold them all with ease. This is just like the great ocean which alone can receive and hold the great rain sent by Sāgara, the naga-king in the sea; no other water body has the capacity to receive and hold it. Likewise, the Tathāgata's store of secrecy, His great Dharma-illumination, great Dharma-reflection, and Dharma-rain can only be received and held by the Bodhisattva of the Tenth Stage. All sentient beings, disciples, Pratyeka Buddhas, and even the Bodhisattvas of all nine stages cannot receive and hold them. . . . Because of the vast and infinite capacity with which this Bodhisattva is endowed, he can receive and hold with ease the Dharma-illumination and Dharma-reflection of one Buddha, of two, three, and infinite Buddhas. He can express them all in a single moment. This is why it is called the Stage of Assembling the Dharma Clouds. . . .

Oh son of Buddha, the Bodhisattva of this stage, is endowed with the illumination and penetrating Wisdom. He can perform all sorts of miracles. At will, he can make a small world into a large world, a defiled world into a pure world, and a pure one into a defiled one. He can place the [different world systems] in an anomalous order . . . reverse order, or regular order. He can place a whole world system into a small dust-mote, with all the mountains and rivers therein remaining as usual; neither the dust-mote changes its form, nor the world system reduces its size. . . . By expelling a single breath, this Bodhisattva can move the infinite universe in the ten directions, and yet the sentient beings living therein will not be even slightly stirred or frightened. He can also manifest the hurricanes, floods and fires in the ten directions; or in accordance with the desires and wishes of beings, he can reveal glorious bodies-of-forms. The Bodhisattvas including the Bodhisattvas of the Ninth Stage, cannot know this Bodhisattva's acts, Wisdoms, glories and wonders; nor can these wonders be exhausted by description through aeons of kalpas. . . . This Bodhisattva practices all the Ten Pāramitās, but stresses and consummates the tenth—the Perfection of Wisdom.

In concluding our summation of the Ten Stages, let us read another passage from the same Sūtra: [32]

All the Ten Stages of Bodhisattvas have their roots in the great ocean of supreme Wisdom of Tathāgatahood; it is also on this basis that they differ from one another. Oh son of Buddha, the great ocean is so called because of its ten exclusive qualities. What are they? They are:

1. Step by step it becomes deeper.
2. It rejects dead bodies.
3. The rivers and waters, when they enter the ocean, all lose their names and identity.

4. Everywhere it tastes the same.
5. It has infinite treasures hidden beneath.
6. It is difficult to reach its bottom.
7. It is vast and limitless.
8. It houses the giants.
9. Its ebbs and flows of tide are always on time.
10. It receives all the rain without showing the slightest strain of overflowing.

Even so, are the Bodhisattva's actions. Because of the ten unsurpassed, distinctive qualities, they are called the Bodhisattva's actions:

1. In the First Stage of Joy, the great vows of a Bodhisattva are brought forth, and step by step they become deeper.
2. In the Second Stage of Spotless Purity, the Bodhisattva rejects the dead body of transgressions.
3. In the Third Stage of Illumination, the Bodhisattva discards all that which pertains to words and letters in this world.
4. In the Fourth Stage of Intensive Wisdom, the Bodhisattva's merit corresponds to that of the Buddhas.
5. In the Fifth Stage of Invincible Strength, the Bodhisattva acquires infinite magic power and ingenuity which [enable] him to accomplish all undertakings in the world; therefore, he is as valuable as jewels.
6. In the Sixth Stage of Direct Presence, the Bodhisattva observes the dependent-origination, reaching the profound depth of reality.
7. In the Seventh Stage of Far-Reaching, the Bodhisattva's wisdom is immense, capable of making great observations.
8. In the Eighth Stage of Immovable Steadfastness, the Bodhisattva is able to make infinite glorious revelations.
9. In the Ninth Stage of Meritorious Wisdom, the Bodhisattva attains the deep liberation. He lives in the world, but never acts in an extreme fashion.
10. In the Tenth Stage of Assembling the Dharma Clouds, the Bodhisattva can receive and hold all the great rain of Dharma from all Tathāgatas without satiation. . . .

The full description of the Ten Stages as given in the *Hwa Yen Sūtra* totals more than 35,000 words. The brief account given in the foregoing pages naturally cannot present the whole picture of the Ten Stages as seen in the original Sūtra. Selecting for translation is extremely difficult in this case; omission and deficits are therefore unavoidable. But with this brief account, the reader may glimpse some of the vastness of the Bodhisattva's spiritual endeavors and the inexhaustible depth of their Enlightenment insight.

THE INCONCEIVABLE
DHARMAS OF BUDDHAS

Now, if the Bodhisattvas are said to possess these immense spiritual qualities, as described in the Ten Stages, what about their admired exemplars, the Buddha-Tathāgatas? It is said that the aim of the entire *Hwa Yen Sūtra* is to reveal the realm of Buddhahood, and the elaborate description of the Bodhisattva's merits is given to reflect the more august and inconceivable state of the Tathāgatas. In the *Hwa Yen Sūtra* there is one whole chapter entitled, "The Chapter of the Inconceivable Dharmas of Buddhas." [33]

At that time in the great assembly, many Bodhisattvas had these thoughts in mind: "In what way are the Buddha's Lands inconceivable? In what way are the original vows and revelations of Buddhas inconceivable? In what way are the body, voice and Mind of Buddha, His freedom, liberation and Non-Obstructions inconceivable?"

In reply, Bodhisattva Blue Lotus Treasure [guided by Buddha's blessing] addressed the Bodhisattva Lotus Treasure:

"All the Buddhas, the World-Honored Ones, have ten Dharmas pervading the infinite and illimitable universes: They all have infinite bodies with pure forms, pervading all walks of life [in saṃsāra], without being contaminated. They all have infinite non-obstructive eyes, perceiving all things in the universe as being transparently clear; infinite non-obstructive ears, able to hear and understand all voices; infinite non-obstructive noses, reaching the other shore of freedom; infinite broad and long tongues, issuing pleasing voices resounding throughout the entire Dharmadhātu; infinite bodies, appearing before all beings in accordance with their visions; infinite consciousness ever abiding in the all-equal and non-obstructive Body-of-Truth [Dharmakāya]. . . .

"All the Buddhas have infinite pure Lands, with inconceivable glories and beauty, revealing the Buddha's domain in conformity with sentient beings' wishes, without attachment. All the Buddhas have infinite Bodhisattva's Pāramitās and perfect insight; they sport in all fields with complete freedom. . . .

"Oh son of Buddha, all the World-Honored Buddhas have
the merit of never-missing-the-appropriate-time in ten different
ways: They never miss the appropriate time to attain the supreme
Enlightenment. They never miss the appropriate time to ripen
sentient beings, or miss the opportune time to make predictions
upon Bodhisattvas. Never do they miss the right time to reveal
Buddha's Bodies in accordance with beings' understandings. Nor
would the Tathāgatas ever miss the appropriate time to perform
great charities, to enter villages and towns, to sustain devoted
followers, to tame and subdue the wicked or to demonstrate the
inconceivable miracles. . . .

"Oh son of Buddha, all the World-Honored Buddhas have ten
inscrutable peerless capacities: Sitting cross-legged, they can manifest themselves everywhere in the universe; with one sentence
with one meaning, they can illucidate the infinite Buddha's
doctrines; emanating one beam of light, they illuminate the entire
cosmos; within one body, they reveal all bodies; at one place,
they disclose all world systems; in one insight, they perceive all
dharmas without obstruction. In one moment, they can reveal the
unfathomable holiness, travel all the worlds in the ten directions
and perceive the minds of all sentient beings and all Buddhas in
the three times. At all times, they remain identical in essence with
all Tathāgatas in the past, present, and future.

"Oh son of Buddha . . . all the Buddhas know that all
dharmas are *not two* from the beginning, yet they can bring forth
the Wisdom of Observation . . . all Buddhas know that all
dharmas have no selfhood and no existence, yet they can produce
the Wisdom of taming sentient beings; all the Buddhas know that
all dharmas have no marks in the first place, yet they can generate
the Wisdom of knowing all forms. . . . Oh son of Buddha, all the
Tathāgatas are endowed with the indiscriminative great compassion; never will they renounce all sentient beings. They have all
obtained the profoundest Dhyānas; they ever observe and care
for all creatures. With good roots of altruism, they will teach and
ripen beings without rest. . . .

"Oh son of Buddha, all the World-Honored Buddhas have
ten supreme Dharmas: Firm, steadfast and indestructible are their
great vows. They practice whatever they say and whatever they
say, they never change or withdraw. . . . All the Buddhas, for
the sake of ripening one being, travel through countless universes.
In this manner, they serve all sentient beings without cessation.
With great compassion and universal consideration, they treat

every man alike, whether he is devoted or blasphemous. . . . All the Buddhas can use their eyes to engage in the dharma-activities of smelling; [34] they can use their noses to taste, their tongues to touch, their bodies to think, their minds to abide in all experiences, of all fields, in all infinite universes. . . .

"All the Tathāgatas abide in the Realm-of-Dharma, but not in the past, the present or the future, because in the essence of Suchness, there is no sign of past, present or future. Even so, they can expound the infinite teachings of all Buddhas in the past, present and future, enabling the hearer to perceive the sphere of the Enlightened Ones. . . . Thus, in silence and alone, the Buddhas carry out the inconceivable Dharma-activities. . . ."

SAMĀDHI, MIRACLE, AND DHARMADHĀTU

Let us now discuss very briefly the last two of the ten Reasons why all dharmas are able to merge in the great Dharmadhātu. *Reason nine: Because the power of deep Samādhi makes it so. Reason ten: Because the Buddha's miraculous power and their inscrutable liberation make it so.*

We often read in the Sūtras that Buddha enters a certain Samādhi, and then some miracles are performed; this sequence shows a definite connection between Samādhis and miracles. An important point to note here is that Samādhi as conceived of by Mahāyāna Buddhism, especially by Hwa Yen, is quite different from the Hīnayāna version; it also differs drastically from that of the Yoga system of Hinduism. Despite its varieties and nuances, Samādhi as conceived of by the Yoga system is mainly a state of unification and "enstasis," a state of union or joining together of the subject and the object and all its physical, mental and spiritual concomitants, but Samādhi as conceived of by Hwa Yen is infinitely fluid, creative, and dynamic. This is shown in chapter sixty-one of the *Hwa Yen Sūtra*.[35]

> Thereupon, the Lord of the World, in order to enable many Bo-dhisattvas to [enter] and abide in the Lion-Awe-Inspiring-Vast-Samādhi-of-Tathāgatahood, gave out from his eyebrows a great light called the "illumination of Dharmadhātu in the three times" . . . thus illuminating the infinite Buddhas' Lands in the infinite universes, and revealing this great scene to all the attendants in the assembly. They saw great Bodhisattvas become Buddhas in each and every Buddha's Land in the infinite universes. . . . With beautiful voices sounding in the whole Dharmadhātu, these Buddhas preach infinite Dharmas. . . . Some appear in the palace of heaven, some in the palace of the asuras . . . some in the vil-lages, towns, and capitals of men's worlds. They appear in all races, with all varieties of names, forms, and customs. . . . They enter all kinds of Samādhis, demonstrate all kinds of miracles, and speak in all tongues . . . for they have now witnessed the great miraculous power of the deep Samādhi of Tathāgatahood . . . and because of their long-cultivated roots of merits, they can all

enter the inscrutable, profound Samādhi of Tathāgatahood . . .
and gain the great, miraculous powers . . .

They attain innumerable understandings, follow innumerable
Paths . . . acquire innumerable Wisdoms, accommodate innumerable sentient beings, and possess innumerable Samādhis. . . .
What are these Samādhis? They are the Samādhi of universal-
glory Dharmadhātu, of illuminating the Non-Obstruction Realm
of all times, of the all-embracing, non-differentiating Wisdom
light . . . the Samādhi of entering the Tathāgatas' Power . . .
of demonstrating bodily forms in all Worlds . . . of the compassionate Treasury . . . of observing all sentient beings' realms
. . . of mastering infinite languages and sounds . . . of demonstrating all Tathāgatas' glories. . . .

Judging by the names of these Samādhis, we see that they are of a quite
different nature from those of the Yoga and Hīnayāna systems. Here
Samādhi neither implies an "enstasis," nor the union of subject and
object, nor the cessation of all skandhas, nor the mere realization of
the Universal Brahman or Godhead, and so forth. We are not even
certain of the exact meaning of the word Samādhi as used here; does it
mean a supramundane conscious state within which all dynamic activities can take place without obstruction? Or is it simply a fanciful name
to denote an unwavering mental state within which all activities are
carried out? We do not know. Among the ten reasons, the last two are
those of which we have the least knowledge. They do not provide us
with much information, but they do indicate clearly the idea that the
all-merging Totality is realizable, not through reason or discursive
thoughts, but through direct insight by the power of Samādhi.

The tenth reason, *Because the Buddha's miraculous power and
their inscrutable liberation make it so*, is so self-explanatory that not
much comment is needed. If a miracle is understood as an event that
transcends men's knowledge of the natural laws, the wonders of
Dharmadhātu may also be regarded as Buddha's "performances of
miracles," which are, nevertheless, vastly different from miracles as
they are ordinarily understood, such as: a man walking on water, a
blind person being enabled to see, a leper being healed by a single
touch, and so forth as we find in religious literature. When these are
compared with the miracles of Dharmadhātu, they seem immeasurably
insignificant. The two are fundamentally different in scale, form and
nature. The question here is, of course, do these wonders of Dharma-

dhātu truly exist? Are they not someone's imaginations or fantasies? This problem we must leave to the perennial struggle between faith and doubt that entraps each individual in his own particular realm of experience and conviction.

The second half of the sentence, ". . . the inscrutable liberation makes it so," is rather significant. Because Buddha is no longer space-bound, He can bring the large into the small and the small into the large. Because He is no longer time-bound, He can throw the past into the future and the future into the past. Having liberated Himself from an enclosed "small ego," He asserts His identity with all beings and their ultimate interests; because He has demolished all clingings and "Svabhāva-barriers," He brings the Dharmadhātu of Non-Obstruction into play. In brief, the miracle of Dharmadhātu is the total result of liberation from the bondage of time, space, ego, desires and clingings.

NOTES   [Part I, *The Realm of Totality*]

1. Here the word *Buddha* does not imply the historical Buddha, Gautama Śākyamuni; it refers to the divine Buddha *Vairocana*. According to the tradition of Tibetan Buddhism, the Buddhas referred to in the *Avataṁsaka Sūtra* are mainly Sambhogakāyas, or more accurately, the Realm of Avataṁsaka is that of Sambhogakāyas.
2. Here *Sūtras* refers to Mahāyāna Sūtras mainly.
3. *Hwa Yen Sūtra* (Sanskrit: *Avataṁsaka or Gaṇḍavyūha Sūtra*) : there are various Chinese translations of this text. The selections made for this book are taken from the translation of Śikṣānanda's version, *Taisho* 279.
4. Dharmadhātu (Chinese: Fa Chieh) : the realm of dharmas. Here, Dharmadhātu refers to the realm of Totality or Infinity in the light of the highest insight and spiritual perspective of Buddhahood. Also see the explanation in the Glossary.
5. *Taisho* 279, pp. 237–38.
6. Since it makes no sense to include any of the endings or inflexions of the Sanskrit words here, *koṭi*, instead of *kotih*; *ayuta* instead of *ayutam*, etc. are given. Indescribable-Indescribable-Turning—Chinese: pu k'o shuo pu k'o shuo chuan; Sanskrit: anabhilāpyānabhilāpyaparivartaḥ.
7. *Taisho* 279, pp. 238–41.
8. *Taisho* 279, p. 241.
9. Three times: past, present, and future.
10. *Taisho* 279, "The Chapter of the Ten Samādhis."
11. Obviously the word "Samādhi" used here is quite different from that of the Yoga and Vedānta systems.
12. According to the Yogācāra system, there are only two sources from which human knowledge is drawn: that of direct perceptions (pratyakṣa pramāṇa), and that of intellection or inference (anumāna pramāṇa). The former is that of direct experience, containing no symbols. It can operate without the aid of any symbols; whereas, the latter must undertake its operation with the aid of symbol manipulations. The five senses and Ālaya Consciousness (the un-

conscious) said to be invariably of pratyakṣa pramāṇa, the Sixth Consciousness, or the "mind" can be of both. It is said that in the omniscient Buddha's Mind, no inference or anumāna pramāṇa functions could ever take place, because inference is always indirect and subject to mistakes and the limitations of symbol-manipulations. Buddha's Mind is therefore always symbol-less and operates through direct perceptions alone.

13. W. F. Trotter, trans., *Pascal's Pensées* (New York, 1943), pp. 16–18.

14. Simultaneous abrupt rising—Chinese: tung-shih tun-ch'i; perfect mutual solution—Chinese: hu-jung.

15. See the discussion of Shih-shih Wu-ai in the second part, and the text of *On the Golden Lion* in the third part of this book.

16. The five Patriarchs of the Hwa Yen School: Tu Shun, Chih Yen, Fa Tsang, Ch'êng Kuan and Tsung Mi. See Part Three.

17. The story told below is not a direct translation from any source book. To enliven the story, the author has dramatized it in several places. The original brief account of Fa Tsang's demonstration of Dharmadhātu to the Empress Wu through the interreflections of contrasting mirrors was given in the *Sung Kao Seng Chuan*, Taisho 2061, p. 732.

18. Prayer Before Opening the Holy Scripture—Chinese: K'ai Ching Chieh.

19. This is Śikṣānanda's "new" translation of the eighty-chapter version of the *Hwa Yen Sūtra*.

20. Quoted from *A Prologue to Hwa Yen (Hwa Yen Hsüan T'an)* chapter 5, pp. 63–64, (Shanghai, 1936; reprinted in Taipei, 1966). *Hwa Yen Hsüan T'an* is perhaps one of the most important works in Hwa Yen Buddhism; it is a survey of the essence of the entire Hwa Yen teachings and is the first chapter of the voluminous *Hwa Yen Su Ch'ao: The Exegesis of Hwa Yen Sūtra;* it is widely studied by Hwa Yen students.

21. *Taisho* 279, p. 179.

22. *Taisho* 279, p. 181.

23. The descriptions of the six bhūmis or stages, are quoted from *An Outline of (Fa) Hsiang Tsung* by Mei Kuang Hsi, pp. 78–79.

24. *Taisho* 279, p. 196.

25. *Taisho* 279, p. 199.

26. *Taisho* 279, p. 199. Literally: ". . . when seeing sentient beings' bodies being drowned in the four currents." The four currents probably imply the four pains of saṁsāra, i.e., the pain of birth, of old age, of illness, and of death.

27. The Tathāgata's ten powers are:

1. He knows wisely, as it really is, what can be as what can be, and what cannot be as what cannot be.

2. He knows wisely, as they really are, the karmic results of past, future and present actions and undertakings of actions, as to place and cause.

3. He knows wisely, as they really are, the various elements in the world.

4. He knows wisely, as they really are, the various dispositions of other beings and persons.

5. He knows wisely, as they really are, the higher and lower faculties of other beings and persons.

6. He knows wisely, as it really is, the Way that leads everywhere.

7. He knows wisely, as they really are, the four trances, the eight deliverances, the three concentrations, and the nine meditational attainments, as well as their defilement, their purification, and the condition in which they are well established in their purity.

8. He recollects his various previous lives.

9. With his heavenly eye, he knows the decease and rebirth of beings as they really are.

10. Through extinction of the outflows, he dwells in the attainment of that

emancipation of his heart and wisdom, which is without outflows, and which he has, in this very life, well known and realized by himself.

The Tathāgata's fourfold fearlessness—the self-confidence or fearlessness of the Tathāgata comes from:

1. Having fully known all dharmas.
2. Having dried up all outflows.
3. Having correctly described the impediments to emancipation.
4. Having shown how one must enter on the path which leads to deliverance.

The Tathāgata's eighteen special qualities—the Tathāgata:

1. Does not trip up.
2. Is not rash or noisy in his speech.
3. Is never robbed of his mindfulness.
4. Has no perception of difference.
5. His thought is never unconcentrated.
6. His evenmindedness is not due to lack of consideration.
7. His zeal never fails.
8. His vigor never fails.
9. His memory never fails.
10. His concentration never fails.
11. His wisdom never fails.
12. His deliverance never fails.
13. All the deeds of his body,
14. His voice,
15. His mind are proceeded by cognition, and continue to conform to cognition; his cognition and vision proceed unobstructed and freely with regard to:
16. The past,
17. The future,
18. And the present.

28. *Taisho* 279, p. 199. This paragraph is highly significant in that it indicates that a passive Nirvāṇa and the wisdom of non-distinction, are *not* the ultimate goals for which a Bodhisattva should strive. He should go beyond the realm of non-distinction in order to reach the dynamic realm of the Hwa Yen Totality of Buddhahood. This paragraph also testifies the fact that only in such an extremely advanced Stage (the Ninth Stage, only two Stages behind Buddhahood) can a Bodhisattva rise above the realm-of-non-distinction and enter the Totality of Dharmadhātu.

29. *Taisho* 279, p. 202. The "three groups" probably refer to:
1. Those sentient beings who will definitely reach Enlightenment,
2. Those sentient beings who will not reach Enlightenment,
3. And those who are indefinite, i.e., whose attainment of Enlightenment will depend on external or internal conditions.

30. Here we see a demonstration of the profundity of the mystery of karma. Only when one reaches the Ninth Stage of Enlightenment can he discern an individual's karma without mistake and thus be truly qualified to teach and guide sentient beings.

31. See the discussion of the Light-of-Death of the Chikhai Bardo in Evans-Wentz's *The Tibetan Book of the Dead*.

32. *Taisho* 279, p. 209.

33. *Taisho* 279, pp. 242–51.

34. This is also stated in chapter ten of the *Vimalakīrti Sūtra*.

35. *Taisho* 279, p. 327.

華嚴相學

PART TWO

THE PHILOSOPHICAL
FOUNDATIONS OF
HWA YEN BUDDHISM

INTRODUCTION TO PART TWO

In the preceding pages we have read short quotations from the *Hwa Yen Sūtra* and some brief comments on them in hopes that readers could grasp a general picture of the realm of Totality. But to get a better and more complete view of the subject, one must read the entire text of the *Sūtra* itself. Unfortunately, this is hardly possible at the present time because the voluminous text of the *Hwa Yen Sūtra* has not been translated into any European language. To remedy the situation as circumstances allow, one of the most important chapters of the *Sūtra*, "The Great Vows of Samantabhadra" (*Taisho* 293, pp. 844–46), is given here in translation. In my opinion, this chapter may well be regarded as the spiritual core of Hwa Yen Buddhism, and readers are advised to refer to it on page 187.

We shall now turn our attention to the philosophical arguments given by the Hwa Yen Masters to support this doctrine of the all-merging Totality. The readers will notice that the first six of the ten reasons for Dharmadhātu given previously by Fa Tsang and Ch'eng Kuan can be said to represent the three main philosophical doctrines of Mahāyāna Buddhism—the Philosophies of *Emptiness*, of *Totality*, and of *Mind Only*. In sequence, we shall examine them not as three disjointed doctrines but as elements of an integral organic whole which constitute the philosophical foundation of this school.

Section One
The Philosophy of Emptiness

ŚŪNYATĀ—THE CORE OF BUDDHISM

If there is one teaching that is peculiar to Buddhism alone among all the world's religions, I would say it is the principle of Śūnyatā (Voidness or Emptiness). If I were to choose the one doctrine among others that best represents the core of Buddhism, I would also choose the principle of Śūnyatā. If someone were further to ask me what is the Buddhist doctrine that is most difficult to explain and comprehend, most misunderstood and misrepresented, I would again say it is the principle of Śūnyatā. The importance of Śūnyatā in every field of Mahāyāna Buddhism cannot be overstressed, and in the Doctrine of Totality of the Hwa Yen School, it is especially significant.

To begin our discussion on the philosophy of Śūnyatā, let us first look into the etymological elements of the word. Śūnyatā is a combination of the stem *śūnya*, "void or empty," and a participle suffix, *tā*, here rendered as "ness." Śūnyatā is therefore translated as "Voidness or Emptiness." It is believed that *śūnya* was originally derived from the root *svi*, "to swell," and *śūnya* implies "relating to the swollen." [1] As the proverb says, "A swollen head is an empty head," so something which looks swollen or inflated outside is usually hollow or empty inside. Śūnyatā suggests therefore that although things in the phenomenal world appear to be real and substantial outside, they are actually tenuous and empty within. They are not real but only appear to be real. Śūnyatā as a spiritual term denotes the total liberation from change, impermanence, effort and longing. As a philosophical term, Śūnyatā denotes the absence of any kind of self, or selfhood. All things are empty in that they lack a subsisting entity or self-being (Svabhāva) .

Śūnya also means "cipher or zero" in Sanskrit. If one can remember that śūnya means exactly zero, then Śūnyatā must imply a *philosophy of zero,* and he cannot go too far wrong in his comprehension of the Buddhist doctrine of Voidness. Zero itself contains nothing, yet it cannot be said to be absolutely or nihilistically empty. As a mathematical concept and symbol zero has a great many functions and utilities without which it would be practically impossible to execute business and scientific activities in this modern age. If someone asked you, "Is zero nothingness?" you would be hard pressed to give an appropriate reply. Zero is both nothing and the possibility of everything. It is definitely not something nihilistically empty, but rather it is dynamic and vital to all manifestations. In the same way, śūnyatā does not mean complete nothingness; being "serenely vibrant," it has both negative and positive facets.

To study the philosophy of Voidness, the first sensible thing to do is to comprehend the inherent difficulties involved in this undertaking. Since never in our lives have we ever had an existential experience of Voidness, even for a single moment, our attempt to apprehend śūnyatā resembles trying to grasp an unknown object in pitch darkness in an unfamiliar room without a clue or a thread to guide us. It is very much like the Indian fable of the blind man trying to comprehend color. You can use snow, paper, and the fur of an albino rabbit to explain the "meaning" of *white* to the blind man, but all he will get from the examples is the cold-dampness of snow, the rustling flatness of paper, and the fluffy softness of fur. From the first moment of birth till the moment we enter the grave, we are thoroughly enwrapped in the realm of beings (bhāva). We think, act, live and dream in terms of beings. Non-being is not only unknown to us but it is even repulsive and fearful. We cannot even truly *think* about Voidness, let alone *experience* it. For instance, a synonym of Voidness is nothingness. But notice the construction of the word: no-thing-ness. It consists of three parts—*no, thing,* and *ness.* The central part of the word is "thing," so it is only through the concept of "thing" that we can reflect the concept of "nothing." It is only by way of being that non-being can be approached. Thus we have no way of comprehending Voidness in a direct manner, let alone realizing it! Because we are so helplessly entrapped by the net-of-beings, our attempts to grasp Voidness are frustrating and fruitless. Do we know what we are talking about here in the first place? Can we then find a sensible definition of Voidness? The answer here is, regrettably, *no.* To define is to mark the limits or boundaries of something. But how can one define Voidness if it has neither limit nor boundary and is, indeed, not "something" at all? Then, if Voidness cannot be defined, can it be described? Yes, this is perhaps possible, but it is said that all enlightened beings feel frustrated when they try to communicate their experience of Voidness to men. There seems to be no easy way to communicate Voidness in a positive and direct manner, for no experience of ours corresponds to it. It has often been noted that we can say a great deal about what Voidness or Emptiness is not, but very little about what it is. These characterizations of what Emptiness is not generally fall into two main categories:

1. Emptiness is not absence, and

2. Emptiness is not annihilation.

Sometimes in casual speech we say, "That house is empty." What we mean is: There is no one residing in that house at this time. Or, "That shelf is empty," and what we mean is: There are no books on that shelf right now. In both cases, we do not mean that either the house or the shelf itself is empty or non-existent. This kind of emptiness is what we called the *emptiness of absence*. It is a pseudo or indirect emptiness, implying something is absent from something else. Certain Mahāyāna thinkers have given it an appropriate name: the doctrine of Other Emptiness (Tibetan: gShan. sToṅ. Pa). A typical example of this doctrine is Śankara's Advaita-Vedānta. It claims that the manifold phenomena in the world are empty; they are upādhi or delusions superimposed upon Brahman by men's ignorance; whereas, *Brahman, the substratum of all manifestations is not empty* but truly and eternally existent. What is empty, therefore, is not the substratum Brahman, but its "shadow" in the shape of this delusory world. This view is therefore a typical example of the emptiness of absence—something is absent from something else, or the idea of other-emptiness—something is empty not in the sense that it does not exist itself, but in the sense that something extraneous to it does not exist. To a certain extent, even the Abhidharma and the Yogācāra Schools of Buddhism are considered to be advocates of the emptiness of absence. We shall discuss this more fully later.

The second misunderstanding of Emptiness is to treat it as annihilation. Sometimes we say, "That block is empty." What we mean is: That block which previously held many houses is now devoid of houses. Formerly, the block was not empty; it was full of houses, but now it is empty; there are no more houses. This kind of emptiness implies that something exists for a certain period and then vanishes from the scene. It is a notion that something existent *becomes* non-existent, implying a process of "from being to non-being." The common sense notion of death is a typical example of emptiness of annihilation: life exists for a period, then it is annihilated by external or natural causes and is reduced to nothingness. Things from the past do not continue to exist in the present. They have disappeared, or been annihilated; they have passed from existence into non-existence. This notion, held by common sense to be the only understandable emptiness, is called here the *emptiness of annihilation*. But Buddhist Śūnyatā does not mean annihilation.

Generally speaking, there are three different ways to describe a thing. The *first* is to describe through paraphrasing; for example, "U.S.A." means "the United States of America." No new information or explanation is added here. The *second* is to describe by relating different concepts in an organized sentence construction, thus creating an appropriate reflection on the subject. For instance, what is a man? A man is a rational animal who can laugh and cry. Here, man is described in a variety of terms, such as: "rational," "animal," "laugh," and "cry" which together provide a reflection of concepts pointing to the reality in question. The *third* way is to describe through direct "pointing-out" or demonstration. A foreign student asked the English teacher, "What is a table?" Instead of saying that a table is a piece of furniture consisting of a flat board fixed on legs, the teacher pounded the table in front of him forcefully with his fist and said aloud, "This is a table!" Here is a direct demonstration. No explanation or concept is needed here. The best and in fact the only genuine way to describe Emptiness is the third way. It is this approach which is frequently applied in Zen Buddhism. The following is an example.

A monk called Hung Chou came to visit Master Ma Tsu and asked, "What is the meaning of Bodhidharma's coming from the West? (What is Śūnyatā)" Ma Tsu said, "Bow down to me first." As the monk was prostrating himself, Ma Tsu gave him a vigorous kick in the chest. The monk was at once enlightened. He stood up, clapped his hands and laughing loudly, cried, "O, how wonderful this is, how marvelous this is! Hundreds and thousands of Samādhis and infinite wonders of the truth are now easily realized on the tip of a single hair!" He then made obeisance to Ma Tsu. Afterwards he said to people, "Since I received that kick from Ma Tsu I have always been cheerful and laughing."

Obviously, in our discussion of Śūnyatā here, we must rely on the second rather than on the third approach, and the limitations of this conceptual method should always be borne in mind.

THE GIST OF THE HEART SŪTRA

So far, we have only mentioned what Śūnyatā is not, and the difficulties of discussing it. We shall now examine the Śūnyatā doctrine directly by studying a pithy but representative text of Śūnyatā literature, namely the *Heart Sūtra of the Perfection of Wisdom*. The importance of this remarkable Buddhist classic and its wide influence on Buddhist thought cannot be overstressed. This Sūtra comprises only 262 words in the Chinese translation and can easily be printed on a single page. It is said, however, that the essence of the entire Mahāyāna teaching is contained therein. The text is both incredibly compact and pithy, and the reader should be alerted to its profuse and far-reaching implications.

To make this text a little easier to understand we shall first review its general contents by paraphrasing it in simple language as follows:

When the great Bodhisattva, Avalokiteśvara, the embodiment of the compassion and Wisdom of all Buddhas, was absorbed in deep meditation of the transcendental Wisdom, He perceived that all things in the phenomenal world, including both matter and mind and all that belongs to them, are empty. Because of this realization, he was able to overcome all sufferings and ills for himself and for all other sentient beings in the universe. He then said to Śāriputra, the most intelligent disciple of Gautama Buddha:

"O Śāriputra, all things are not different from the Emptiness, and the Emptiness is not different from all things. Never should one regard things and Emptiness as separate entities. In fact, all things are exactly the Emptiness, and the Emptiness is exactly all things. There is no difference whatsoever between them. This is also true in the case of mind and all its functions including such functions as feelings, thoughts, emotions and consciousness itself." To expound this principle further, Avalokiteśvara again said to Śāriputra:

"O Śāriputra, in what way can we describe the characteristics of this Emptiness? The characteristics of the Emptiness of all things can be described as not arising, not ceasing, not pure, not defiled, not increasing and not decreasing. Because of this, in the Emptiness we do not find any form, feeling, thoughts, emotions or consciousness, nor do we find the six organs, six objects or the six senses. In the Emptiness there is no blindness, the cause of rebirth, nor its consequences: sickness, old age and death; neither is there any *ending* of blindness, nor *ending* of old age and death. There is no Truth of Pain, which is the fact of life; no Truth of Craving, which is the cause of pains; no Nirvāṇa, which is the cessation of pains; and no Path, which is the way that leads to the cessation of pains. There is no Wisdom of Buddhahood, and no attainment whatsoever. Because there is nothing to be obtained, a Bodhisattva by relying on the Perfection of Wisdom has no obstruction in his mind. Because there is no obstruction, he has no fear, and he passes far beyond all confusions and imaginings and finally reaches the ultimate Nirvāṇa. . . ."

Now we shall read the text itself.

PRAJÑĀPĀRAMITĀ HRIDAYA SŪTRA
(THE HEART SŪTRA)

When the Bodhisattva Avalokiteśvara was coursing in the deep Prajñāpāramitā, He saw that all the five skandhas are empty; thus He overcame all sufferings and ills.

"O Śāriputra, form is not different from Emptiness, and Emptiness is not different from form. Form is Emptiness and Emptiness is form; likewise, the feelings, conceptions, impulses, and consciousnesses.

"O Śāriputra, the characteristics of the Emptiness of all dharmas are that it is not arising, not ceasing, not defiled, not pure, not increasing, not decreasing. Therefore in the Emptiness there are no forms, no feelings, conceptions, impulses, or consciousnesses; no eye, ear, nose, tongue, body, or mind; no form, sound, smell, taste, touch, or mind-object; no eye-elements until we come to no elements of consciousness; no ignorance and no ending of ignorance; no old age or death, and no ending of old age and death; no Truth of Suffering, no Truth of the Causes of Suffering, of the Cessation of Suffering, or of the Path. There is no Wisdom, and there is no attainment whatsover. Because there is nothing to be attained, a Bodhisattva relying on Prajñāpāramitā has no obstructions in his mind. Because there is no obstruction he has no fear, and he passes far beyond all confusions and imaginations and [finally] reaches the Ultimate Nirvāṇa. The Buddhas in the past, present, and future, also by relying on the Prajñāpāramitā, have attained the Supreme Enlightenment. Therefore, the Prajñāpāramitā is the great magic spell, is the unequaled spell which can truly protect one from all sufferings without fail. Therefore he uttered the spell of Prajñāpāramitā: *Gate, gate, pāragate, pārasaṁgate, bodhi svāhā.*

The Prologue

TEXT: When the Bodhisattva Avalokiteśvara was coursing in the deep Prajñāpāramitā, He *saw* that all the five skandhas are empty; thus He overcame all sufferings and ills.

COMMENT: The most significant word in this paragraph is *saw.* When Avalokiteśvara was absorbed in the deep meditation of Prajñā-pāramitā (the Perfection of Wisdom), He *beheld* that all the five skandhas were empty. This signifies that Prajñāpāramitā is not known through thoughts or ratiocinations, but through *direct seeing*—an experience of immediate presence which is basically different from all forms of philosophical thought and reasoning. The fountainhead of Prajñāpāramitā teaching consists therefore in an intuitive experience intrinsically beyond words and symbols. To communicate this experience to men, however, Avalokiteśvara had no other choice but to use words and concepts. The dilemma is that whatever statement he made, he had to repudiate at once. It is said that the multitude of contradicting statements found in the literature of Prajñāpāramitā is a reflection of the limitations and inadequacies of the human way of thinking rather than an indication of the absurdity of the Prajñā truth. The reasons for this will be discussed later.

Buddhism asserts that words are not the only means by which communication is made possible. They are in fact a very poor means insofar as communicating the Prajñā insight is concerned. In the *Vimalakīrti Sūtra,* there is the story about nine million Bodhisattvas from another universe who, while paying a visit to Vimalakīrti, were asked how *their* Buddha preached the Dharma in their own land. The leader of the visitors said: "In our land, the Tathāgata never preaches with words and letters. He just uses various scents to make all men and gods enter the discipline. Each Bodhisattva sits under a fragrant tree, and as he smells the fine fragrance, he will immediately attain the Samādhi of Virtue-Store, and whosoever attains this Samādhi will automatically attain *all* the merits of a Bodhisattva." [2] The visitors were in fact very much surprised that words and speech could be so important for Dharma preaching as on this planet!

A few decades ago, this statement about scents and cognition would have been treated as pure fantasy, but in this age we know that such occurrences are not entirely impossible. For we know that a man under drugs can hear music through his eyes, see things through his tactile sense and so forth. The point being stressed here is the inadequacy of thoughts and concepts as a means of approaching Śūnyatā. The highly cherished talent of symbol manipulation, that which makes Homo sapiens the conqueror of his fellow creatures, is here devalued to an inefficient tool for tackling the problem of the Prajñā truth. Śūnyatā can be grasped by seeing, hearing, and even smelling, but never by thinking! This is because seeing, hearing and smelling have the nature of direct contact or perception (pratyakṣa pramāṇa); whereas, thinking is basically an indirect symbol-manipulating process (anumāna pramāṇa), hence it often contradicts and misleads our penetrating intuitions which are also a kind of pratyakṣa pramāṇa.[3]

The next important sentence in the prologue is: "Thus, he overcame all sufferings and ills." The realization of Emptiness is therefore not merely an awakening to an ontological reality, but a soteriological step that releases man from all his frustrations and iniquities. Here the basic spirit of Buddhism again emerges to affirm that salvation is not a favor bestowed on man by God, but a natural result earned by one's cultivation of the insight of the Prajñā truth. Although in every practical sense Avalokiteśvara is regarded as a god (or, in some forms, as a goddess) and savior by the Mahāyāna Buddhists, the Sūtra here points out that even He must have Śūnyatā as the root of His divine supremacy. He is a savior not because He is born so or designated so, but because He has meditated deeply in the Prajñāpāramitā and has realized its full truth.

Illustration of the True Voidness

TEXT: "O Śāriputra, form[4] is not different from Emptiness, and Emptiness is not different from form. Form is Emptiness and Emptiness is form; likewise, the feelings, conceptions, impulses, and consciousnesses."

COMMENT: This is the key paragraph of the entire Sūtra. The sentence "Form is Emptiness and Emptiness is form" has become almost a proverb and has been widely discussed and debated in the Buddhist world; it is tantamount to saying that being is non-being and non-being is being. To understand the meaning and rationale of this statement, we must first examine the preceding sentence: "Form is *not different* from Emptiness, and Emptiness is *not different* from form." This statement clearly indicates that Emptiness is not something outside of form, nor is it in any manner isolated or different from form. Form and Emptiness should not be treated as two different entities. Under no circumstances therefore should we accept the *emptiness of absence* as the true Śūnyatā. The statement also indicates that Śūnyatā is not the *emptiness of annihilation,* for if Voidness is not different from matter, how could it be a state of nothingness or extinction? This statement implies that one should not try to locate Emptiness outside of form, because in truth the two are not different from each other. Buddhist Emptiness is therefore not static, null or dead; it is dynamic and full of vitality.

Some commentators also suggest that this statement refers to the doctrine of Māyā—that all things in the world are not truly existent but only existent in an illusory sense like dreams and visions. The Advaita-Vedānta also claims Māyā, but a Māyā supported by the eternally existent Being, the absolute Brahman. Māyā and the Absolute in Vedānta are therefore two different things regardless of how some of the Vedāntins try to state it differently.[5] But here, the *Heart Sūtra* claims that *form and Emptiness, or Māyā and the Absolute, are not at all different.* Here we see the basic difference between the Buddhist Māyā and that of the Advaita-Vedānta. The former holds that Māyā and the ultimate reality have no difference whatsoever, and whoever sees this will be enlightened. Form is Voidness and Voidness is form; Saṁsāra and Nirvāṇa are not two different entities, but one organic whole. The Advaita-Vedānta holds that the phenomenal world is Māyā, a product of nescience; it is ultimately unreal and "bad." It is forever separated from the real Being, Brahman, who alone is real and eternal. Māyā is to be annihilated completely before one attains Mokṣa. In contrast, Buddhism holds that Māyā is *not to be destroyed* or gotten rid of, since the very realization of the identity of Māyā and Śūnyatā will bring forth liberation and Enlightenment.

To further clarify the implication of the statement that form is not different from Emptiness, the Sūtra goes further and asserts that form *is* Emptiness, and Emptiness *is* form, a sentence that compresses the entire Śūnyatā doctrine into a nutshell. The critical part of this statement is presumably its second half; i.e., *Emptiness is form.* Discussions of the doctrine of Śūnyatā usually focus on the why and how of the first part: form is Emptiness; seldom is the deeper aspect of the second part: Emptiness is form, thoroughly examined. It is possible to reason out that form is Emptiness, though very difficult, but to reason out that Emptiness is form is a wellnigh impossible task. We simply have no way of starting from non-being to approach being. Our feet are helplessly fastened, either by beings or by Being! So we shall try the easier way first and see why form is Emptiness, that is, approaching non-being from being.

The Rationale of "form is Emptiness"

There are three main arguments for "form is Emptiness." First: When we observe the momentary and constant changes of all things in the phenomenal world, we can conclude that all beings (i.e., forms or rūpa) are empty. Second: When we contemplate the fact that all things are produced through the principle of dependent-arising (pratītya-samutpāda) and are, therefore, devoid of selfhood or own-being (Svabhāva), we can conclude that all things are empty. A parallel argument to this can be phrased in a slightly different manner. When we consider the fact that things do not have definite natures but change into different forms and characteristics when the frame of reference or the constructural factors are altered, we can conclude that forms are empty. Third: Since the external world is a sum total of the collective karma and the projection of one's own mind, subject to change and extinction, we can conclude that all things are empty.

Comments on the First Argument

Because things are constantly changing, they are all empty.

This is the basic principle of Buddhism accepted by both Hīna-yāna and Mahāyāna and all their secondary schools. We constantly witness the indisputable fact that things in the phenomenal world are changing all the time. Observation of change will bring us to the realization that things are not only constantly changing but momentarily so; they are not at all durable but instantaneous. With this fundamental thesis of "instantaneous being," the Buddhists believe that they can repudiate at one single stroke the God of the theist, the eternal matter (prakṛti) of Sāmkhya and all other philosophical doctrines that uphold a permanent and unchanging Being of some sort.[6] Because things change from instant to instant there is no continuous and steadfast substratum such as the Brahman of the Upanishads underlying them. Hence, things only exist discreetly in the shortest moment (kṣana) . There is no reality other than separate, instantaneous bits of existence. The universal flux we experience in the phenomenal world is nothing more than strings of momentary events. Further reflection tells us that even this shortest moment (kṣana) can again be divided into smaller units ad-infinitum. Therefore, *things have no duration whatsoever; they disappear as soon as they appear*. The durable existence of things is an illusion; just as in the cinema, the chain of many individual pictures, which appears to be a continuous whole, is an illusion; or like the flame in a lantern which, though it appears to be one, is actually a collection of discreet, momentary fire-sparks. Man sees the outstanding changes such as days changing into nights, and seeds into crops, but seldom does he bother to notice the smallest momentary change of things. Only physicists are fascinated by observations of this sort. The Buddhist philosopher Śāntirakṣita gave a succinct dictum: *"The momentary thing represents its own annihilation."* [7] This is to say that every momentary thing is annihilated as soon as it appears; it does not survive into the next moment. Since things have no duration whatsoever, disappearing as soon as they appear, they cannot be said to have true existence. But how is it possible that an existent thing has no duration at all? *That which has no duration whatsoever cannot be said to exist in any manner.* This is the rationale for the claim that if things change from instant to instant, they are said to be empty or non-existent.

This same principle is expressed in a slightly different manner in the *Diamond Sūtra*. In expounding the Emptiness of things, Buddha says, "O Subhūti, the mind of the past is not obtainable; the mind of the present and the future are also not obtainable." Based on the same reasoning, anything that is in time is said to be empty. Things of the past are forever gone, they are no longer obtainable or existent. Things of the present never abide, they have no duration, hence they cannot be grasped or even referred to. Things of the future have not yet arrived, they are unobtainable or non-existent at this moment. Hence, anything that is in time cannot be said to be truly existent, it has only illusory existence and is, in truth, empty.

A different argument for the verification of śūnyatā through an inquiry into impermanence is given in the *Vimalakīrti Sūtra*.[8]

> Kātyāyana addressed the Buddha, saying, "World-Honored One, I am not fit to call and enquire about Vimalakīrti's sickness. For what reason? I remember that once the Buddha had preached concisely the gist of Dharma, and afterwards I was expounding its meaning, telling the import of impermanence, the import of suffering, of emptiness, of no-self, and of calm cessation when Vimalakīrti came and said to me, 'O Kātyāyana, do not use arising and ceasing mental processes to explain the doctrine of Reality. Kātyāyana, *the dharmas do not arise and do not cease. This is the meaning of impermanence.*'"

The last sentences here are tantamount to saying: *The meaning of impermanence is neither arising nor ceasing.* This is diametrically opposed to the common-sense understanding of impermanence which regards impermanence as the fact of changing—a transition from arising to ceasing and vice versa. So what does this statement mean, and what are its justifications? The rationale of this statement can be given in the following six steps.

1. Impermanence means change, which can be defined as *momentarily non-remaining, or non-abiding.*

2. We have no reason to consider a particular moment as remaining and all other moments as non-remaining. If any particular moment can be regarded as remaining, all other moments should then be so regarded. If this is the case, things will remain steadfast all the time and no change is possible. Change, therefore, must be continuous and momentary.

3. The concept of being or existence is inseparable from the concept of remaining. That which exists must have some kind of duration or "remaining substance." No remaining implies no existence; therefore, if things are momentary they must be empty.

4. What actually happens in the changing world is that the moment of the so-called remaining is also the very moment of non-remaining. Only thus is extinction possible, and only with extinction is the subsequent arising made possible.

5. This *remaining-of-no-remaining* is the reality of impermanence

which is the same as the simultaneity of appearing and disappearing.

6. Our original proposition is now made intelligible: *the meaning of impermanence is neither arising* (extinction) *nor ceasing* (appearing). This is to say that the simultaneity of no-arising (disappearing) and no-ceasing (appearing) is the true meaning of impermanence.

The celebrated translator-philosopher Kumārajīva (344–413 A.D.) made the same observation in the following argument.[9]

> In expounding the doctrine of Emptiness, one usually begins with a discussion of impermanence. Impermanence is therefore a stepping stone to Emptiness. In the beginning, the problem of impermanence is examined and this will eventually lead to the conclusion of Thorough-Emptiness [Pi Chin K'ung]. The tenets of both [that is, impermanence and Emptiness] are actually the same; the difference lies in the degree of depth and profundity. Why is this so? The so-called "impermanence" means that from moment to moment something does not abide. . . . What is negated here is the abiding over a prolonged period, but abiding itself has not been negated completely. Therefore, this is only an "unrefined" impermanence. . . . The [refined or] true impermanence should signify the fact that the very abiding is the non-abiding. Now, existence is understood as that which abides; if there is no abiding, naturally there will be no existence. No-existence is a synonym for Thorough-Emptiness which is again the subtle and wondrous doctrine of impermanence.

In diametrical opposition to the Buddhist doctrine of impermanence and Emptiness are the various kinds of "eternalism" or "realism" (śāśvata-vāda or śatkāya-dṛṣṭi). The philosophy of Parmenides is a good example. Parmenides was fully convinced that to think at all, we must postulate something which *is*. That which is not (or void) cannot even be thought of; how then can it ever be a part of reality? Non-being is therefore impossible. The corollary of this conviction is the impossibility of change, because change implies both being and non-being; for instance, when A changes into B, it no longer exists. But how can anyone think such a contradiction? A quality cannot change into another quality; to say it can is to say something both is and is not. Furthermore, if being has become, it must have come from either being or non-being. If it came from non-being, it is impossible. How can something come out of nothing? If it comes from being, then it has come from itself, which is tantamount to saying that it is identical with itself, and thus has always been. If this is the case, it is then not a case of becoming.

Parmenides was forced to conclude that from being only being can come, that nothing can become something else, that whatever is, always has been and always will be, and that everything remains what it is. Hence, there can be only one eternal, undivided and unchanging Being.[10]

The contrast between the philosophy of the Eternal Being postulated by Parmenides and the Buddhist doctrine of impermanence and Śūnyatā is so sharp that to compare them side by side will make both doctrines, the radical "eternalism" of Parmenides and the radical "momentarilism" of Buddhism crystal clear.

Comments on the Second Argument

Because all things are produced by the principle of dependent-arising (pratītya-samutpāda), they are devoid of selfhood or own-being (Svabhāva); therefore, they are all empty.

This is perhaps the most important and comprehensible argument of Śūnyatā doctrine, propounded by the great philosopher Nāgārjuna, and no doubt it is the keynote of his Middle-Way (Mādhyamika) Philosophy. This argument contains two major points.

1. Since all things are produced by a combination of various causes or factors, they are mostly a structural complex, having no self-subsisting entity. They do not have an independent own-being, but owe their existence to other things.

2. In close examination, we find that nothing in this world has a definitive nature; things are such and such only in relation to so and so, or in terms of certain conditions. When the frame of reference is changed, the things in question will also change, or they may even vanish from the scene. Therefore, nothing has a self-existing own-being or selfhood. This lack of determinateness in things indicates that their existence is only relative, not absolute.

Śūnyatā is also understood as the "Emptiness of Selfhood" (Svabhāva Śūnyatā or niḥsvabhāva). But what is this selfhood? How should we define it? The different definitions given of Selfhood

(Svabhāva) have caused great controversies and schisms among the Mahāyāna Schools.[11] To simplify the matter we will not propose a strict definition of "Selfhood" here, but give a general description of it which is tacitly accepted by most schools.

Selfhood (Svabhāva) denotes a self-sufficient and self-subsistent entity; it suggests qualities of *independence, determinateness,* and *indivisibility*. Is there anything in the world we know of possessing these qualities? Do we know anything that is self-existing, not produced by other causes? Is there anything that is self-sufficient without relying on other things, that is truly independent, self-subsisting and indivisible? Buddhism gives a negative answer to all the above questions. The denial of selfhood is actually a rejection of these "being-ness bound," fallacious ideas.

THE NO-SELF DOCTRINE AND SVABHĀVA-ŚŪNYATĀ

The Emptiness of Selfhood (Svabhāva-śūnyatā) in the teaching of Prajñāpāramitā is actually an extension, or evolved principle, of the No-Self doctrine (anātman) of early Buddhism, a doctrine originally propounded by Buddha Himself. To make this point clear let us first review the essentials of the No-Self doctrine.

The Buddhist doctrine of No-Self has been a controversial topic both inside and outside of Buddhism since the day it was set forth by Buddha. It has caused perhaps more confusion, bitterness and schism than anything else in Buddhist history. As far as I can see, this is perhaps a very simple problem. Philosophers both inside and outside of Buddhism have fought bitterly over anātman mainly because they have treated it as a philosophical concept or doctrine. Actually, anātman or No-Self, is only a *meditational device,* a practical instruction to be applied in yogic contemplation for the purpose of liberation, as is clearly shown in the meditation technique of the Four Mindfulnesses (smṛti-upasthāna).[12] No wonder most of the debatants on anātman have missed the point by a wide margin! Buddha was never a philosopher; His primary concern was to point out the way to liberation—liberation from the deep-rooted attachment to a delusory self which is the source of all passion-desires and their resultant pains and frustrations. Philosophical speculations were persistently rejected and denounced by Buddha as useless, foolish and unsalutary. Actually, in Buddha's teachings we do not find a *philosophy* of No-Self; what we find is a significant *therapeutic device,* the instruction on how to get rid of the deep ego-clinging attitude. On the common sense level, however, Buddha never rejected the idea of self, for He himself used the first-person pronoun "I" all the time, nor did he deny the continuation of a changing-self-series stretching from the infinite past lives to the future rebirths, in order to uphold the doctrine of karma and the validity of spiritual endeavors. This is clearly indicated in the Jātaka stories and other sources. If this is the case, what then was that "self" Buddha tried to reject and demolish? To the faithful followers of Buddha this was not a significant problem at all, for they knew exactly what anātman meant when they reached Enlightenment. To philosophically inclined Buddhists, however, this did become a great problem. They had to decide what was that "self" which the anātman doctrine tried to demolish, and what "self," if any, was to be preserved for certain purposes. After long years of deliberation, a rather cogent definition of self was proposed as follows: *that which is perpetual, unchanging, unitary and autonomous is the so-called self.*[13]

What we generally mean by the word *self* is, in the first place, a perpetual and unchanging identity. For instance, an applicant, Mr. Lee, was required to pass three successive examinations to secure a position in a firm. He passed the first examination on the first day and went to the firm again the second day. The examiner, upon seeing him, asked, "Are you Mr. Lee?" "Yes, I am," he replied. The examiner led him in to take the second test. At this moment there was a tacit understanding between the applicant and the examiner; they both considered the examinee to be the same person who had come the day before. He remained Mr. Lee; the person was not changed, and the identity was not changed. This unchanging and subsisting element is the first and most important constituent of the alleged self. A brief scrutiny will immediately expose the falsity of this belief. In twenty-four hours, so many things have been changed: Mr. Lee's hair, eyebrows, fingernails, and so on are all slightly longer than they were the day before; he is one day older . . . his mental capacity and physical condition are both changed to a certain degree, though the changes are very slight and insignificant from a practical point of view. Nevertheless, it is a vast change from the viewpoint of, for example, a germ residing in his intestines.

A nineteen-year-old, tempestuous youngster murdered five people and escaped abroad. Forty years later he returned home. By then he had lost a leg, an arm, and also an eye. He was bald and had albino-colored skin because of a disease contracted somewhere abroad. His mental state and entire personality had also changed. He had become a very stable, wise and even kind person. If we put the reckless nineteen-year-old murderer and this pitiful old cripple side by side, no one would say the two are the same person. But he was then caught by the law, and after a prolonged and difficult investigation, he was identified as the true murderer and was sentenced to death, regardless of the thorough physical and mental changes which had taken place in a period of forty years. The law is not interested in locating an unchanging self in the strictest ontological sense; its primary concern is legality in a pragmatical and social sense. But Buddhism will not let this matter be settled in this loosely-oriented, common-sense manner. In so far as Buddhism is concerned, the problem of truly identifying the unchanging self remains unsolved, because we cannot find a single element that can be strictly considered as remaining unchanged. Even this man's fingerprints have changed somewhat. A newborn baby's fingerprints are much smaller in size than those of the adult he will later become, although the basic pattern "apparently" remains the same. So Buddhism argues that self does not, in truth, exist; the so-called self, that allegedly unchanging and perpetual element within us, is only a delusion projected by a confused mind.

Some readers will immediately raise an objection and say that it may be true that there is no such thing as an unchanging self, but how about a *changing self?* It would seem that the concept of a changing self, accepted by common sense, would solve all the problems just mentioned. But a changing self is a contradiction in terms, for we have no valid argument to confine this change to definite periods; that is, it remains unchanged for a stretch of time and then changes. This would also imply that we have two kinds of self, one changes and the other does not. Besides, by definition, change means the arising of something new in place of something old that has disappeared. *The inherent meaning of change implies the loss of identity, which is incompatible with the concept of self.* In practical life we ignore the changing part, but stress the unchanging part of the mutating self-series in order to uphold the notion of an unchanging and unitary self. In reality, this self-series not only changes constantly, but also momentarily, and no fixed selfhood is to be found therein.

The second element that constitutes our definition of self is the notion of self as an *indivisible unit.* In other words, self must be unitary—a single, pure and unblended unit. *If there were many selves, the sense of self would be lost.* You simply cannot have many selves, can you? Think of a man who has been wrongly accused of murder and is sentenced to death for the crime. Suppose that he manages to escape and searches everywhere in the country for the true murderer. As a fugitive convict he has to change names and occupations frequently, and the law is relentless in its pursuit. Although he assumes hundreds of names, his true self and identity is still the same. He simply cannot have many selves! He might change his name, occupation, appearance and sometimes even manners and personality, but all these will not alter the fact that he is still the original man. He thinks so and everyone else knows this, for there is *one* single, pure and unblended element that remains unchanged despite any superficial alterations. Self, therefore, must be a singular entity and not plural. Buddhism admits that this is perfectly true on the common-sense level, and has no argument against it. But on a higher level, when we seriously delve into this idea of self, we find that the common-sense self is a delusion, a clinging to a confused idea, and the source of all troubles and sufferings.

Viewing the self as a unitary entity either implies that it is an indivisible and elementary monad containing no constituent parts within, or it implies an integral whole which includes constituent components. In the case of amnesia or split personality, the psychopath no longer maintains his "true" self as an integral whole. He undergoes a process of "dis-integration." Normal people believe that even in condition of schizophrenia, the true integral self is still there, only temporarily blotted out. When the mental disorder is cured, the patient regains his own self. Buddhism contends that either self is an elementary monad, or it is an integral whole. The difficulty of momentary change and of structural and environmental conditioning is still insurmountable to effect an unchanging and unitary self.

To shatter this delusion of a subsisting-entity, Buddhism offers an assiduous analysis of the elements that constitute the so-called self. The unitary self is broken down into the five aggregates, twelve spheres, eighteen elements and even some ninety-four dharmas.[14] All these painstaking observations, which make certain Buddhist literature (for example, the Abhidharma series) extremely dreary and uninspiring, were directed to one aim, that is, to disintegrate the integrated whole of the cherished self. In much the same way, the smashing of atoms, which were formerly considered to be indivisible units, is now a routine operation. We know that stupendous energy is required to hold the particles together within the atom, and without this immense *binding force* no atom can subsist. Analogous to this is the case of the self; it is not indivisible or monadic, but an integral complex of various elements. To maintain this integrated self, enormous *binding force,* or *clinging,* is also required. Setting loose the binding force of ego-clinging thus releases the tremendous potential energy within, and this constitutes what Buddhism calls Enlightenment and liberation.

The third essential element in our definition of self is that it be *autonomous,* which implies freedom, independence, and volition. It is evident that the concept of self must include the quality of autonomy; for instance, if one did something unkind to his friend when he was intoxicated, he could apologize to his friend and say, "I am truly sorry, but I *was not myself* that day." If one commits a misconduct under the influence of shock or mental disturbance he is liable to receive more lenient consideration than usual, because he is regarded as *not having been truly himself*—meaning he was deprived of autonomy, hence free from moral or legal responsibilities.

Consider the scene at induction, of a haughty sergeant addressing the new draftees. The youngsters have been ordered to take off all their civilian clothes, cut their hair short, and put on their new uniforms. When all these things have been done they are led to an open court, and the lordly sergeant, filled with pride and confidence, says aloud to the youngsters, "Now you're all mine!" Anyone who wears or has worn a military uniform will deeply appreciate the autonomous facets of ātman. Strictly speaking, a soldier cannot be considered as having a complete "self," because he is no longer completely autonomous.

If Buddhism rejects the existence of self, does this mean that it also denies the existential, autonomous decision-maker which we generally call self or will? This question, like others, must be answered from two different standpoints. On the common-sense level, Buddhism has no quarrel with the existential conviction of self, which of course includes the autonomous decision-maker. It is from the viewpoint of higher truth (Paramārtha-satya) and liberation that ātman is denied. Now, if we go one step further and ask: "If from the viewpoint of higher truth, (Paramārtha-satya) , Buddhism has rejected the idea of a permanent and unitary self; does this automatically imply that it also rejects self—the autonomous decision-maker?" The answer seems to be affirmative. But to my best knowledge, Buddhism, both Hīnayāna and Mahāyāna, does not elaborate this point to a clear and satisfactory conclusion. The problem of autonomous self is exactly the problem of free will, and it necessarily involves the problem of causation and determinism. In the Western tradition, the problem of free will has been a controversial and well-studied topic. Philosophers have puzzled over this problem at great length, and it seems that no conclusive judgment has been made at present. It is indeed astonishing to note that such high-caliber Buddhist philosophers as Nāgārjuna, Vasubandu, Chandrakīrti, and Fa Tsang have all ignored this important problem. It seems that they have just followed the common-sense judgment and taken it for granted that from the conventional viewpoint (samvṛti-satya), we do have free will. No exhaustive discussions on the problem of determinism and free will have been pursued. That this problem has been neglected is perhaps due to the fact that the Buddhist philosophers were preoccupied with other interests and problems. After all, as a wise Taoist once said, *"One creates his own problem by digging into something he can ignore."*

It is not my intention to delve into the baffling problem of free will here. It is safe to say, however, that Buddhism does affirm the fact of free will, since we all witness it to be a direct and immediate experience. Total free will is, however, an extreme rarity. In the great majority of cases, our actions and judgments are predetermined. Free will is only a small spark of fire in the darkness of fate, yet this tiny spark, which often manifests itself in the exclamation of a rebellious "No" to anything that blocks its flow, is the germinal seed that will eventually revolutionize one's life and his world.

After this brief review of the No-Self doctrine of basic Buddhism, we can now return to our discussion of the Emptiness of Self-being or Selfhood. Selfhood (Svabhāva), as we mentioned before, denotes a self-sufficient and self-subsisting entity; it suggests the qualities of *independence, determinateness,* and *indivisibility.* Except for the element of autonomy this definition is almost identical with the definition we gave to ātman. The difference between the Mahāyāna Emptiness-of-Selfhood (Svabhāva-Śūnyatā) and the Hīnayāna Emptiness-of-Self (anātman) lies in the fact that the former implies a larger area—all things are devoid of selfhood; whereas the latter narrows it down to the Emptiness of individual ego.

The central thought of Śūnyatā philosophy is that all things are produced under the principle of dependent-arising, hence they are devoid of a selfhood. Take marriage as an example: it takes at least two people to bring this relationship into existence; it is, therefore, a product of *dependent-arising*, which implies that everything in the world is a relative structure and an operational complex. There are no independent and irreducible entities whatsoever. The so-called single object, such as a house, a man, a pebble, a molecule or even an atom, is only an expedient way of expressing something for some practical purpose. In reality, each and every one of these things is an operational complex and a relative structure brought into being by the coordination and mutual dependence of various factors. *Things do not exist; only events exist momentarily under relative conditions.* An indivisible and self-subsisting entity, or Selfhood, simply does not exist.

Throughout our lives we experience the fact that a thing or event can be brought into existence only when *all* the required conditions or factors are complete. A deficit of any single factor will necessarily arrest this production. The shortage of a screw or cog will keep a watch from running; the lack of physical aptitude, sound training, combative initiative or mental equilibrium will keep one from being a *top* athlete. This explains another facet of the principle of dependent-arising which says that *A is A, not because A has an own-being or self-hood, but because B, C, D, E etc. make it so.*

It was not because Hitler had extraordinary talent or intelligence that the German people in the nineteen-thirties fell into his hands and were plunged into his self-destructive enterprises. This occurred because of many factors; an economic crisis in postwar Germany, the injustice of the Versailles Treaty, the disillusionment and despondency of the German people, and still other factors all contributed to Hitler's rise. This principle: A is A, not because A has a selfhood, but because a combination of different factors makes it so, is applicable to everything in the phenomenal world.

By definition Selfhood (*Svabhāva*) denotes a self-subsisting entity, but in reality there are no entities, only structures and events. This principle seems to have been verified for some time now in both the natural and social sciences. Here are some simple examples. The strength of a combat army does not necessarily depend on its constituent entities (or materials). The deployment of various fighting elements, mobility, timing, coordination, and so on are all vital. The true strength of an army, therefore, consists in structural set-ups, not in material entities alone. A beautiful nose and mouth and a pair of attractive eyes, if improperly placed or "mis-structured," can make a face extremely ugly. This illustrates our principle that without a proper structure, elements alone would not be consequentially significant. The seven musical notes constitute the basic elements of all melodies; but what makes the melodies different are not these seven notes but their arrangements or structures.

The clearest way to show that all things are devoid of Selfhood is to indicate that they have no definitive nature, or no determinateness. Nothing can be truly existent if it is indeterminate or indefinite. Indeterminateness not only makes identity impossible, but by definition, *it also nullifies the very concept of being.* If we can show that all things are indeterminate or indefinite, we will have accomplished the task of confirming that they are *not-beings.* In Buddhist terminology this is Svabhāva-Śūnyatā—Emptiness of Self-being or Selfhood.

To discern the indeterminateness of all things, a brief examination will do. An object observed from different positions will show different shapes and forms. A man can be simultaneously hated by his enemies, loved by his mate, respected by his children, and ignored by birds and animals. A symphony by Beethoven can be appreciated as a great piece of musical entertainment, or be scorned by one who is tone-deaf as sheer senseless and nerve-wracking noise. In the subatomic field we have witnessed the phenomenon of indeterminateness; that is, matter can be like both a particle and a wave, or more accurately: the particle-like properties and the wave-like properties of matter cannot both be measured exactly (or with completely arbitrary accuracy) at the same time. A box weighs nine pounds only when it is measured on the ground; it would become almost weightless if it were weighed in an orbiting satellite. What we see in these examples all points to one fact: nothing has a definitive nature. Everything is indeterminate; things are such and such only in relation to so and so in a particular frame of reference. Their determinateness is found only in terms of certain conditions and within certain arbitrary realms. This fact of indeterminateness is also called relativity—x is x only in relation to y under certain conditions.

An important point to remember here is that when we say nothing has a definitive nature, we are speaking from the viewpoint of a higher truth. We have no argument with the fact that Henry Ford was definitely a rich man, that water is definitely H_2O, and that the sun definitely rises every morning in the east. These are all practical truths from a conventional point of view. But when the frame of reference is changed, different conclusions will result; Henry Ford may not be regarded as a rich man, and the sun may not rise in the east every morning. Because things observed from different realms become dif-

ferent and may even appear to contradict one another, as in the case
of the particle- and wave-like natures of matter in quantum phenomena, we conclude that from the viewpoint of higher truth all things
are indeterminate, indefinite and devoid of a Self-being or Selfhood.

Here the reader may ask what we mean by "higher truth," and
to what does this so-called higher truth refer. By higher truth, we mean
an observation that is not bound by any particular realm or frame of
reference; it rises above all frames of reference and all positions. It is
an organic and Śūnyatālistic approach, free from the bonds of particularity and partialities. This organic approach is also the totalistic approach of Hwa Yen philosophy. More about this will be discussed in
the next section, but it is proper to point out here that this totalistic
approach has its foundation in Svabhāva-Śūnyatā, for if there were a
Svabhāva of any sort, no totalistic observation would be possible.

Another aspect of the Emptiness of Selfhood is discovered when we
try to understand it through a reversed approach by asking the question, "If all things did possess a Selfhood what would happen then?"
The answer is that in that case, it would be impossible for any kind of
change to take place.

Svabhāva is by definition in diametrical opposition to impermanence and change. Hence, there would be no production of any
sort; progress would be rendered impossible, and all efforts would be
in vain. The acceptance of Selfhood or Self-being is tantamount to
the denial of phenomenal reality which manifests all sorts of changes:
progress and regression, arising and ceasing, ups and downs. Hence the
famous dictum of Nāgārjuna:

> It is because of Emptiness
> That all things and events can be established.
> Without Emptiness nothing can be established.[15]

What we have said indeed sounds very curious: "Because all things
are empty in their own-being, they can all exist. Should they possess
an own-being, none of them could exist." At the first glance this
sounds absurd, but some reflection will convince us of its truth and
significance. Parmenides could not accept non-being; therefore, he
could not accept change. A reverse argument is given in the case of
anātman (No-Self) doctrine. People entertain the fond belief that
rejection of ātman, the permanent self or soul, would shatter the basic
doctrine of Buddhism. If there is no permanent soul how can the

efficacy of karma be established? What is the use of making any spiritual effort if there is no self to receive the fruit? The truth is, the No-Self doctrine (anātman) is no more at variance with facts than the Eternal-Self (ātman) doctrine. Self, considered as the permanent entity of one uniform immutable nature, is impervious to any form of change; it will automatically render karma, progress and change impossible. It is exactly because of this difficulty that Buddha refused to accept the permanent self and propounded the doctrine of No-Self. It is precisely because of this truth of No-Self that karma, change and spiritual achievement are made possible.

This reminds us of the metaphor of zero discussed before. Because zero contains nothing, it can denote anything. For example, when we say a man is worth six figures—$000,000—we are not committing ourselves to an exact figuring of the person's bank account. The sum of six figures, represented by six zeros, is very flexible, extremely "non-Svabhāva," so that any exact number can be substituted afterwards—such as, $863,245. Because zero is non-being, it has great possibilities; it can become or function as any being. In the same way, because all things are devoid of Selfhood, they are dynamic and full of possibilities. Buddhist Emptiness, therefore, does not destroy or demolish things; on the contrary, it establishes all things. All that it destroys are men's clinging and attachments.

The Svabhāva Way of Man's Thinking

To understand Svabhāva and its implications it would be helpful to study the Svabhāva way of thinking that characterizes man's mind. The Svabhāva way of thinking is typified in the treating of an action or event as a fixed entity or substance. For instance, a question such as: "What will happen to my fist when I stretch my fingers?" will immediately make us aware that the "substantive fist" does not represent an entity but a hidden action, an event. Our Svabhāva way of thinking has preconditioned us to treat the fist as an independent and unitary substance, which, in reality, is a structural action co-originated by the interdependent relationship of fingers, palm, muscle-tensions and so forth. The Svabhāva way of thinking is to regard things as being independent, unitary, static, and fixed; whereas, the "non-Svabhāva" way of thinking would regard them as being interdependent, structural, dynamic and fluid. The former is bound, clinging and definitively restricted; the latter is free and open to infinite possibilities. Table I co-ordinates these points of contrast between the two.

TABLE I   Two Ways of Thinking

The Svabhāva Way	The Niḥsvabhāva Way
independent	interdependent
unitary	structural
entity-substance	events and actions
static	dynamic
fixed	fluid
bound	free
definitively restricted	infinite possibilities
clinging and attachment	release and detachment
being	non-being
thatness	whatness

A parallel to the niḥsvabhāva way of thinking is found in the late Korzybski's general semantics. His "non-Aristotelian" approach, I think, is very close to the doctrine of Asvabhāva or Niḥsvabhāva. To avoid what he called the "internalized" Aristotelian way of thinking, Hayakawa, Korzybski's follower, proposed some rules to follow.[16] The first is *indexing*. Because of our innate Svabhāva way of thinking, certain names tend to bring up definitive and fixed opinions toward the named object—for example, hippies, Jews, Communists, automation, and so forth. To avoid the fixed and partisan opinions that these words tend to bear, we ought to index them: $hippies_1$, $hippies_2$, $hippies_3$; $Communist_1$, and $Communist_2$. This will remind us that not all hippies and Communists are alike. The similarity which causes them to be classed under one name should not overshadow their individual diversity. The second rule is to use *dates*. Everything is constantly changing, but since man's ideas and beliefs do not change at the same pace, words and names may not accurately represent the reality in question. We should, therefore, date the words: $Mao\ Tse\text{-}tung_{1936}$; $Mao\ Tse\text{-}tung_{1958}$; $Mao\ Tse\text{-}tung_{1968}$; $U.S.A._{1868}$; $U.S.A._{1968}$; annual $income_{before\ April\ 15}$; annual $income_{after\ April\ 15}$; and so on. Another rule is to use *hyphens*. Because the Svabhāva way of thinking tends to isolate the inseparable, interdependent events into separate entities, we ought to use hyphens: time-space, psycho-somatic, bio-chemistry, geo-physics, social-economic, yin-yang, compassion-wisdom (karuṇā-prajñā), noumenon-phenomenon, and so forth. By connecting two or more different concepts with hyphens, we can see at once the structural elements of reality in an organic and totalistic manner, thus avoiding the inherent misrepresentation of Svabhāva concepts. There are more rules proposed by Korzybski, but these three should be sufficient to make the parallel clear.

The Svabhāva way of thinking is pervasive. There seems to be no possibility of avoiding it before one attains the Prajñā insight of Enlightenment, for each and every concept man holds is inherently Svabhāva-bound. It is our belief that a concept, especially a good concept, should not be equivocal or vague; it should be clear and definitive as exemplified by the precise language of science and law. A trivial example: the word *bicycle* denotes a vehicle with two wheels, not three or four wheels; it is clear and definitive. But for this very reason, it is also fixed, exclusive and Svabhāva-bound. At the very first moment when the word *bicycle* looms up in one's mind, it conveys only a fixed image of the object. It does not reveal its *non-svabhāva* nature at all! If one is eccentric enough, he can of course at the second, third and consecutive moments add explanatory notes as an amendment: "Beware! Bicycle is not something unitary or fixed, it is a structural compound momentarily changing. . . ."

Needless to say, these explanatory notes themselves are also Svabhāva-bound, and to water down their inherent Svabhāva flavor, further explanatory ideas are required. This can go on ad infinitum. This sounds unnecessary and even ridiculous, but it also reflects the fact that Svabhāva clinging is intrinsic in all our thoughts. In my first few months in the U.S., I learned how the Svabhāva way of thinking works. When I wanted to buy some food and drink for a snack, I always went six long blocks away from home to a grocery store to get them. It never occurred to me that these items were readily available in a nearby drugstore. When the word "drugstore" first emerged in my mind, it suggested nothing but a place to buy drugs, and now only as an afterthought can I amend this restricted Svabhāva tendency through corrective concepts, by reminding myself that the drugstore is almost equivalent to a department store in the U.S. So, the Svabhāva tendency is most distinctly exposed in the *initial moment* when the idea first looms up. In the consecutive moments, however, it tends to become more fluid and flexible, moving towards an orientation that is more organic and operational.

Comments on the Third Argument (for "form is Emptiness") *

Since the external world is a sum-total result of collective karma and the projection of one's own mind, subject to change and extinction, we can conclude that all things are empty.

This argument is used mainly by the Yogācāra school to verify the Emptiness of the external world which is regarded as merely a projection of man's consciousnesses.[17] If we go to Colorado we can see the Rocky Mountains, but not everywhere else. This, according to common sense, verifies the true existence of the Rocky Mountains in the external world. But Yogācāra, the Buddhist Idealism, claims that from a higher viewpoint, these mountains which appear to be existing in an external world, are a delusion projected by men's Ālaya Consciousness and their common karmas. The fact that everyone sees the existence of a definite thing in a definite space, does not mean that this thing is truly existent; *it only means that everyone has the same common karma to project the same picture on the same spot.* When a man sees, smells and tastes water, his experience differs radically from that of a fish. To a man water is something tangible and definitely existent, but a fish living in the water may never feel its existence at all, just as men do not feel the existence of still air. The Buddhist tradition asserts that when a deva or god sees the water contained in a lake, he sees it as nectar not water; the same will become pus and blood when a hungry ghost sees it, and it becomes a poisonous liquid or fire when a denizen of hell sees it. This again testifies to the fact that water has no Selfhood. Conditioned by different common karmas, it appears as different things to different sentient beings. If there were a substantive, true entity called "water," this variation and indeterminateness would not be possible. Again, it is because of the very fact that no water ever existed as such in the first place that the phenomenon of non-svabhāva is made possible.

* See p. 69.

THE DOCTRINE OF
THE ABSOLUTE EMPTINESS

In discussing "form is Emptiness," we have reviewed the essential aspects of Svabhāva Śūnyatā, the Emptiness of Selfhood. To explore the deeper aspect of Śūnyatā doctrine, we now proceed to examine the Thorough or Absolute Emptiness (Chinese: Pi Chin K'ung; Sanskrit: Atyanta-Śūnyatā; Tibetan: mThah. Las. hDas. Pahi. sToṅ. Pa. Nyid.) which is an outstanding feature and the essence of Prajñāpāramitā teaching. The Absolute Emptiness is a thorough negation of everything, including itself, for Śūnyatā itself must also be negated if it is a genuine Emptiness. This is why among the twenty Emptinesses,[18] there is one called the Emptiness of Emptiness (Śūnyatā Śūnyatā). If we assert Emptiness, and regard it in any way as existent, we then repudiate our own stand and admit the absurdity of all we have said previously. Absolute Emptiness denotes a sphere of ultimate transcendency—that which goes beyond all dharmas and notions (pāramitā). This is what the Zen Buddhists mean by: "You should empty all beings, but never substantiate the Emptiness . . . Not even a single hair is to be attached . . . When you come to a place where Buddhas are present, you should hurriedly pass through it; when you come to a place where there is no Buddha you should never linger even for a moment!" Thorough Emptiness (Pi Chin K'ung) is synonymous with Absolute Emptiness, but the word *absolute* here does *not* suggest positivity, certainty, authoritativeness, unquestionable finality or the like, as denoted by general usages. Absolute here means *"free from,"* derived from the original meaning of the Latin word *absolvere,* "to set free," "to release"; for instance, absolute alcohol means alcohol that is free from mixtures. So Absolute Emptiness suggests an Emptiness that is free from or rising above all forms of existence and concepts. The stress here is unmistakably on the transcending prospect.

The essence of Absolute Śūnyatā is given in the third paragraph of the *Heart Sūtra.*

> O Śāriputra, the characteristic of the Emptiness of all dharmas is not arising, not ceasing, not defiled, not pure, not increasing, not decreasing.

Men are involved in a world wherein they see the phenomena of arising and ceasing, purity and defilement, increasing and decreasing. To counter this discrimination and illustrate the other side of reality—the empty side—the *Heart Sūtra* points out that the "characteristic" of the Emptiness of all dharmas is that it is not arising, not ceasing, not defiled, not pure, not increasing, and not decreasing. All conditioned things (samskṛta) have the characteristics of arising and ceasing, but Śūnyatā transcends both; it neither arises nor ceases. The traditions of Buddhism hold that men and saṁsāra are defiled, that Nirvāṇa and Buddhas are pure, but Śūnyatā, as the absolute, rises above both purity and defilement. When one reaches the state of advanced Bodhisattva-hood, his merits and Wisdom will increase to the infinite dimension and his passion-desires and bad karma will decrease in equal measure, but Śūnyatā, as the absolute, transcends both; it neither increases when one attains Enlightenment, nor decreases when one wallows in the mud of saṁsāra.

Absolute Śūnyatā and the Doctrine of Being

Some Buddhist thinkers believe that these six negations in three pairs— i.e., not arising, not ceasing, not pure, not defiled, not increasing, not decreasing—denote the *eternal nature* of Śūnyatā: Śūnyatā remains so all the time, without arising or ceasing, increasing or decreasing. . . . They also denote Śūnyatā's *pervasiveness:* it is always so everywhere. Above all they denote Śūnyatā as being the *equalness* or *identity* of all dharmas. Thus, in Śūnyatā everything is equal and non-differenti- ated. From the Buddhist viewpoint, the danger of this trend of thought, as some critics have indicated, is that it tends to fall into the "heretical" view of eternalism (śāśvata-vāda) or realism (satkāya-dṛṣṭi) of one kind or another. Typical examples of this bent are seen in the Upaniṣads and in Thomas Aquinas' theory of Essence and Being. At first glance, the teaching of the Upanishads and that of Mahāyāna Buddhism seem to be very much alike. But when one compares them further, some unmistakable differences emerge. To pinpoint the exact differences between various mystical traditions is extremely difficult; the similarities always seem to overshadow the divergence. An unbiased and valid comparison between these schools requires first-hand mystical experiences of both traditions plus exhaustive studies in their docu- mentary sources. A competency of such caliber is extremely rare if it exists at all. In the pages to follow I shall present my personal observations on the problem, but they should not be treated as conclusive evaluations of the subject.

The distinctive feature of Absolute Emptiness lies in its self-negating or thorough-transcending aspect. Even Emptiness itself is empty and without a selfhood. This is called the Emptiness of Emptiness (Śūnyatā Śūnyatā). In contrast to this the doctrine of the Upanishads asserts a divine or universal ground of all things, variously called the ultimate, the pure existence, the Being of all beings, and the like. The pioneers of the Upanishads asked, "What is this world rooted in?. . . . What was the wood and what the tree from which they fashioned forth the earth and heaven?" The answer they gave was "The world is rooted in Brahman. Brahman was the tree out of which they carved heaven and earth." Brahman is like the basic element gold, out of which the golden bowl, the golden ring and necklace were made. Although the bowl, ring, and necklace are different in form, they remain gold without change. The *Chandogya Upanishad* says, "Just so, my dear, by one nugget of gold, all that is made of gold becomes known. The modification is only a name arising from speech, while the truth is that it is just gold, " (*Chan. Upa.* 6. 1. 5.). In this sense, Brahman is the substratum of all things; it is the unitary source, the "cosmic scotch tape" that sticks all things together. In Brahman all things find their root and unity. Now, what is this one element or substratum that all things share in common and in which they find their unity? The answer is that all things, regardless of their divergent forms and natures, share in Being (Sat) as their root without exception. The *Bṛhadāranyaka Upanishad* (2. 5. 15.) says, "As all the spokes are held together in the hub and felley of a wheel, just so in this Brahman, all beings, all gods, all worlds, all breathing creatures, all these selves are held together. . . ." "With food as an offshoot, seek for water as the root; with water . . . as an offshoot, seek for Being as its root. All these creatures . . . have their root in Being. They have Being as their abode, Being as their support," (*Chan. Upa.* 6. 8. 6.).

In direct opposition to the Buddhist emphasis on Emptiness or non-being, the Upanishads stress the primary importance of Being: "In the beginning, my dear, this was Being alone, one only without a second. Some people say, 'In the beginning this was non-being alone; one only without a second. From that non-being, being was produced.' But how indeed, my dear, could it be thus? . . . How could being be produced from non-being? On the contrary, my dear, in the beginning this was Being alone, one only without a second," (*Chan. Upa.* 6. 2. 2.). The stress on the substrative Being is very clear here. When we compare this to the Buddhist teaching of Thorough Emptiness (Śūnyatā Śūnyata) a sharp contrast becomes evident.

Among the various forms of śāśvata-vāda (eternalism) the most succinct one, I think, is Thomas Aquinas' thesis on the *Act of Existing,* or the *Act of Being* (ipsum esse). The easiest way to introduce this doctrine, I think, is first to distinguish the difference between *whatness* and *thatness* or essence and existence. Whatness, or essence, denotes the attributes, forms, nature or quiddity of a thing; whereas thatness, or existence, denotes the actuality, the "is-ness" the immediate presence, or the act of existing of a thing. In a sentence such as: "Ice cream is cold and sweet," the words *cold* and *sweet* denote the whatness or essence of ice cream, but not the ice cream per se or its pure existence. Two different usages of the verb *to be* should be observed here. In a sentence such as: "John is a man," or "John is short," the verb *is* plays no more than the role of copula. It signifies simply that it is of the essence (or whatness) of John to be a man, or that the *accident,* "short," is in the *substance,* "John." The copula *is* points always to the predicate, not to the subject. But in a sentence like: *John is,* or *God is,* the verb refers only to the subject: no attribute, or whatness, of the subject is mentioned. It signifies only one fact: John exists. Nothing except the actuality of the subject is suggested here. According to Étienne Gilson, this is a sentence with the strongest existential sense possible, for it refers only to the act of existing of the subject. If I understand it correctly, the thatness of a thing is exactly its "is-ness" or "beingness." Tables and trees are all different in their forms and attributes, but they all share one thing in common; they all participate in the act of existing or "is-ness," "beingness." In "is-ness," therefore, all things find their roots and unity.

In the treatise, *On Being and Essence,* Thomas Aquinas produces a great many discussions on essence, but very few on existence. It is extremely interesting to note that all the titles of the six chapters in his book, except the first one, deal with the subject of essence, not existence. Not even the word "existence" is mentioned in them. Why? Was it not existence, rather than essence, that the author wanted to discuss as the primary subject? Could it be that he found there was not much that could be said about existence after all? Did he find that in discussing existence, he must eventually use the awkward medium *essence?* The fact is that at the very moment you say something about thatness it will immediately become some form of whatness. So, thatness can be grasped intuitively, but cannot with ease be described verbally. At first sight, thatness seems to be something mysterious and inconceivable, for how can we conceive anything without the application of whatness, explicitly or implicitly? Actually, thatness or the act of existing is very simple and concrete; there is nothing mysterious or profound about it at all. "What is first presented to the thought when we say *is,* is the very act of existing, that is, that absolute actuality which actual existence is," observed Étienne Gilson.[19] Jacques Maritain wrote:

> Thus, the primordial intuition of being is the intuition of solidity and inexorability of existence. . . . It is a reasoning without words, which cannot be expressed in articulate fashion without sacrificing its vital concentration. . . .[20]
> Here everything depends on the natural intuition of being—on the intuition of that act of existing which is the act of every act and the perfection of every perfection, in which all the intelligible structures of reality have their definitive actuation, and which overflows in activity in every being and in the intercommunication of all beings.[21]

To quote further explanations of these philosophers would only cloud the issue and make this discussion more confusing. The following case is a simple example to illustrate the point. When an Australian aborigine was brought to New York City, he was bombarded with all sorts of sights and sounds which he had never experienced before. There was no vocabulary in his memory that could designate the kaleidoscopic phenomena properly. He was led to see a Boeing 747, an IBM machine, and an atomic power plant. He could not understand what they were and didn't even know how to name these monsters, but when he encountered these objects face to face, he could see and feel their concrete existence. He could not say the words "atom-smasher" or "IBM" properly. There was not a single word emerging from his mind at this moment of initial encounter. Nevertheless he had an intuitive feeling of grasping some actuality of the object—a comprehension of their "beingness." When he was brought before an IBM machine, he stared at it, and with his mouth wide open he uttered the sound, "Ah!" Next, when he was shown the 747, he again stared at it and uttered the sound, "Ah!" What does this *Ah* convey? *It conveys the simple fact of experiencing a certain intrinsic actuality or concrete existence.* This most direct and vivid experience is presumably what Aquinas called "the act of existing." The intuitive feeling of beingness requires no words or symbols to sustain or express it. It is intrinsically beyond whatness and all nameable attributes. This pristine feeling of "beingness" also *precedes* the split of subject/object dichotomy and affiliations.

We have used different words and terms to describe the same idea. To simplify the matter further, readers should refer to the following formula:

Thatness = beingness = "is-ness" =pure existence = the actuality of a thing ="it-is-thereness" = the act of existing = divine ground = universal substratum = Brahman = Being of beings.

Now, the Buddhist stand on the intuitive feeling of Being or thatness is diametrically opposed to that of the Upanishads and Aquinas. Instead of glorifying this "beingness" and augmenting its significance to theological or soteriological levels, Buddhism believes that this intuitive *grasping of being,* or actuality, is *an expression of men's deep clinging and attachment.* It is the very root of all sufferings and delusions in saṁsāra! Liberation or Enlightenment is the result of a *total annihilation* of this deep-rooted, innate *clinging to "beingness."* This is why Thorough Emptiness, the negation of all beings, plays such an important role in Buddhist thought and practice. The transcending aspect of Brahman found in the Upanishad literature can easily be confused with that of the Prajñāpāramitā teachings. The Thorough Emptiness of Buddhism and the "Beingness" (Sat) of the Upanishads are both inaccessible through words and ratiocinations. They both transcend all symbols, thoughts, and antithetical relationships, but this does not mean that they are the same. The Upanishads affirm the *ultimate substratum, the Great One;* whereas, Buddhism stresses the *Thorough Emptiness* without attachment to any Self-being or Svabhāva.

The negative statement concerning the nirguna Brahman (Brahman without attributes), seems only to suggest that Brahman *is not this, not that* (neti, neti). However, it does *not* suggest that Brahman itself is devoid of its own-being or Selfhood. In contrast, Buddhist Śūnyatā affirms both the *it-is-not* and the *there-is-not* aspects;

that is, on the one hand, Absolute Śūnyatā *is* not this and not that, and on the other, it *has not selfhood* either. It is thoroughly empty itself; there is not an iota of being of any sort. But the Brahman of the Upanishads is a different story; although Brahman here is inconceivable, formless and beyond all attributes, it does have a substantial own-being or Selfhood. The famous "neti, neti" statement in the Upanishads (*Bṛhad. Upa.* 3. 9. 26.) suggests only the *it-is-not* aspect of Ātman; it does not include a *there-is-not* aspect of Thorough Emptiness. "The Self *is not* this, *not* that. It *is* ungraspable, for it *is not* grasped. It *is* indestructible, for it *is not* destroyed. It *is* unattached, for it *cannot be* attached to. It *is* unbound; it *does not* suffer. . . ." [22]

Nowhere in Vedic literature can we find the clear evidence of an idea similar to Buddhist Thorough Emptiness. Thus we can understand why many Buddhist thinkers regard the Pure Being of Ātman as merely a form of subtle innate clinging to the fundamental consciousness (the Ālaya Consciousness), which is the basic cause of saṁsāra; attachment to it will impede true liberation. In all fairness, this accusation is hardly justifiable unless it can spell out the differences with precision and in detail. Now, let us read a passage from the *Concise Prajñāpāramitā Sūtra*,[23] in explanation of Absolute Emptiness and in contrast to the Upanishad doctrines of eternal Being.

> Subhūti said, "O Kausika, a Bodhisattva who aspires to the glorious vehicle should abide in the Prajñāpāramitā with the teaching of Emptiness. He should not abide in form, in feeling, conception, impulses or consciousness; he should not abide in form that is transient *or eternal*. . . . He should not abide in the fruit of arhatship . . . not even in Buddha's Dharmas. In this manner he should benefit and deliver infinite sentient beings."
>
> Whereupon Śāriputra thought, "Where then should a Bodhisattva abide?"
>
> Subhūti, knowing his thought said to him, "What do you think, Śāriputra? Where does Tathāgata abide?"
>
> Śāriputra said, "Tathāgata abides nowhere. This no-abiding mind itself is the Tathāgata. Tathāgata does not abide in conditioned things, nor in the unconditioned. The Tathāgata who abides in all dharmas is neither abiding nor non-abiding. Just so, a Bodhisattva should also rest [his mind] in this manner."
>
> At that time in the assembly many gods thought, "Even the languages and letters of the Yaksha demons are intelligible, but what Subhūti has just said is unintelligible."

Knowing their thoughts, Subhūti addressed the gods, "In that, there is no speech no demonstration and no hearing."

The gods thought, "What Subhūti intended to do was to make the doctrine easier for us to understand, but what he has done is to make the doctrine more subtle, profound, and obscure."

Reading their thoughts, Subhūti said to the gods, "If a devotee wants to attain the state of Stream-Winner, Once-Returner, No-Returner or Arhat,[24]. . . he should not depart from this deep insight. . . ."

The gods thought, "Who can understand and agree with what Subhūti has just said?"

Subhūti knew their thought and said, "I say sentient beings are like dreams and magical delusion. Stream-Winners . . . Arhats are also like dreams and magical delusions."

The gods said, "Subhūti, are you saying that the Buddha's Dharmas are also like dreams and magical delusions?"

Subhūti said, "Yes, I say Buddha's Dharmas are like dreams and magical delusions. I say Nirvāṇa is also like a dream and a magical delusion."

The gods said, "O Subhūti, are you really saying that even Nirvāṇa is like a dream and a magical delusion?"

Subhūti said, "O dear gods, if there were something that was more superior even than Nirvāṇa, I would still say that it is like a dream and a magical delusion. O dear gods, there is not the slightest difference between Nirvāṇa and dreams and magical delusions."

The doctrine of Thorough Emptiness is clearly expressed here. It is difficult to find parallel statements of this kind in the Vedic literature or in other sources of religious scriptures.

Absolute Śūnyatā and Absolute Transcendence

Living in a world that is full of polarities, a man sees light and darkness, truth and falsehood, pleasure and pain, abstract and concrete, positive and negative, right and wrong. Absolute Śūnyatā, however, goes beyond all these polarizing dualities, just as it transcends the "irreducible" substratum of Being. This is called the not-two Dharma-gate, or the Dharma-gate of non-duality in the *Vimalakīrti Sūtra*. Let us now read a few passages from this Sūtra in which a discussion of this topic occurs in a great assembly of Bodhisattvas.[25]

At this time Vimalakīrti said to all the Bodhisattvas, "Good sirs, how can a Bodhisattva enter the Dharma-gate of non-duality? Each of you with your eloquence please tell it as you like. . . ."

Virtue-Top Bodhisattva said, "Defilement and purity make two. If you see the real nature of defilement, you [will realize that] purity has no form, then you conform to the character of cessation. This is entering the Dharma-gate of non-duality. . . ."

Good-Eye Bodhisattva said, "One mark and no mark are two. If one knows that one mark is no mark, and yet does not cling to no mark, he penetrates into the state of equality, and is said to have entered the Dharma-gate of non-duality. . . ."

Puṣya Bodhisattva said, "Good and evil make two. If you do not arouse good or evil, but penetrate to the limit of no-form, thus attaining the full realization, you enter the Dharma-gate of non-duality. . . ."

Pure-Conviction Bodhisattva said, "The conditioned and the unconditioned dharmas make two. If one can depart from all numbers, his mind will be like empty space; with pure Wisdom he encounters no obstruction whatsoever. This is entering the Dharma-gate of non-duality. . . ."

Narayana Bodhisattva said, "Mundane and supra-mundane are two. The very nature of mundane is empty, which is the same as the supra-mundane. In them there is no entering, no coming out, no overflowing and no dispersing. This is entering the Dharma-gate of non-duality. . . ."

Good-Wit Bodhisattva said, "Saṃsāra and Nirvāṇa make two. When one sees the nature of saṃsāra, then there is no saṃsāra, no bondage, no liberation, no burning and no relieving. He who understands this enters the Dharma-gate of non-duality. . . ."

Lightening-God Bodhisattva said, "Insight and ignorance make two. The true nature of ignorance is insight itself. Insight cannot be grasped; it is beyond all numbers. To be equal in them without duality is to enter the Dharma-gate of non-duality. . . ."

Delight-Vision Bodhisattva said, "Form and Emptiness of form are two. However, form itself is empty, not when it ceases to be, but by its very nature. In the same way, feeling, conception, impulses and consciousness are empty. . . . He who realizes this is entering the Dharma-gate of non-duality. . . ."

Jewel-Seal-in-Hand Bodhisattva said, "To like Nirvāṇa and to dislike the world make two. If one does not like Nirvāṇa nor loath the world, then there is no duality. Why is this so? Because if there is bondage, then there is liberation. If from the beginning there is no such thing as bondage, who would ever seek for liberation? He who realizes that there is no bondage and no liberation will have no likes or dislikes. This is entering the Dharma-gate of non-duality. . . ."

Truth-Lover Bodhisattva said, "Real and unreal make two. He who truly sees, does not even see the real, how much less the unreal? Why? Because this is not something that can be seen by the eye of the flesh. Only the Wisdom-eye can see it, and yet for this wisdom-eye there is nothing seen or unseen. This is entering the Dharma-gate of non-duality. . . ."

Thus, each and every Bodhisattva spoke in turn; then they all asked Mañjuśrī, "Please tell us, what is the Bodhisattva's entering the Dharma-gate of non-duality?"

Mañjuśrī replied, "According to my understanding, to have no word, no speech, no indication and no cognition, departing away from all questions and answers is to enter the Dharma-gate of non-duality." Thereupon Mañjuśrī asked Vimalakīrti, "We have spoken, each for himself. Now, good sir, you must tell us what is the Bodhisattva's entering the Dharma-gate of non-duality."

Then Vimalakīrti kept silent, without a word. Whereupon Mañjuśrī praised him in earnestness, "Oh great, oh marvelous! Not to have even words or letters, this is truly entering the Dharma-gate of non-duality!"

While this chapter on entering the Dharma-gate of non-duality was preached, five thousand Bodhisattvas in the assembly all entered the Dharma-gate of non-duality and reached the state of no-arising-Dharma-maturity.[26]

Absolute Emptiness in the Heart Sūtra

In the third paragraph of the text of the *Heart Sūtra*, we read: "Therefore in the Emptiness there are no forms, no feelings, conceptions, impulses, or consciousness; no eye, ear, nose . . . no ignorance and also no ending of ignorance; no old age and death . . . no Truth of Suffering, no Truth of the Causes of Suffering, of the Cessation of Suffering, or of the Path. There is no Wisdom, and there is no attainment whatsoever."

In this paragraph we see that all the important and fundamental teachings of Buddhism are rejected: the five skandhas, the eighteen dhatus, the Four Noble Truths, including Nirvāṇa and the holy Path;

are all abolished. Is this what the long-sought-after transcendental Wisdom has actually seen? Immediately the text says, "There is no Wisdom, and there is no attainment whatsoever." So even Enlightenment and Buddhahood are finally scuttled. Now, is this Absolute Emptiness simply a synonym for nihilism? The answer is an emphatic No! Nihilism, in all its various forms, affirms the non-existence of some thing or some principle. But this affirmation itself is true and must be adhered to. In other words, it does not negate its own propositions as Absolute Śūnyatā or Śūnyatā Śūnyatā does. Śūnyatā Śūnyatā is not nihilism; it is absolute transcendentalism. The absolute is neither existence nor nothingness; it is simply inconceivable and indescribable through the conventional means of words and thought. To talk about it is to speak play-words! When one reaches this realm, there is simply nothing that can be said. This is why Vimalakīrti kept silent when he was asked to describe the absolute (the Dharma-gate of non-duality). This is the reason for the Buddha's silence, and for his answer to Upasīva's inquiry about Nirvāna:

> He who has gone to rest, cannot be measured;
> For there [in Nirvāna] nothing can be named.
> When all dharmas are abolished,
> So are all passages of speech.

Here one is likely to raise the objection that the Absolute Śūnyatā is *meaningless* since it does not even assert its own stand. If one wants to say something meaningful at all, one must affirm whatever one tries to say; otherwise it would be much better to keep one's mouth shut! The astonishing Buddhist answer is that to say something meaningful, one does not have to affirm what he says. The speaker's remark was not made to assert a philosophical proposition but to bring his audience to the yonder realm to confront the Absolute face to face. Śūnyatā is not a doctrine of philosophy; if it is anything at all, it is a *therapeutic device* for the cleansing of men's innate clingings. Nāgārjuna, the leading exponent of Śūnyatā, has made this point very clear. He says, "Because I have no acceptance whatsoever, I am free from all faults." Just as a man by throwing one stone kills two birds, so Nāgārjuna's thoroughgoing rejection of all philosophical positions serves two purposes. The first is to make him immune to committing any philosophical fault, and the second is to expose the futility and foolishness of all philosophical reasonings by reducing the philosophical positions of his opponents to absurdity. He demonstrates the necessity of transcending these philosophical jungles by direct realization of the Thorough Emptiness. In his epoch-making treatise, *Mādhyamika-Kārikās* (13. 7), Nāgārjuna says:

> If there is a thing that is *not* empty,
> Then there must be some thing that *is* empty.
> Since nothing is non-empty,
> How can there be an empty thing?
> The Victorious One proclaims Emptiness
> In order to refute all viewpoints;
> He who holds that there is an Emptiness
> All Buddhas will call incurable.

Śūnyatā, therefore, should not be considered to be a something which somehow exists somewhere. One has to rise above his intellectual habitude to perceive it. On the other hand, if one does not cling to Emptiness, he cannot be accused of being nihilistic. A famous koan of Zen master Chao Chou is a good illustration of this point:

A monk asked Chao Chou, "What should one do when there is not a thing to carry?" Chao Chou looked at him and said, "Lay it down!" The monk said, "Since there is nothing at all to carry, what should I lay down?" Chao Chou said, "In that case, then take it up!" The monk was immediately enlightened.

At the outset the monk had already attained some kind of shallow realization of Emptiness, but he clung to it and could not free himself to play in the dynamic flow of events. He still had the perplexity of what to do next. Chao Chou, the truly enlightened master, saw this right away; so he said to him, "Lay it down," meaning lay down your so-called Emptiness. But the monk, who was deeply involved in the dead-emptiness, fought back by saying, "Since there is not a thing to carry, what should I lay down?" Chao Chou replied, "In that case, then take it up!" This totally unexpected remark awakened the monk from his dead-emptiness and brought him to true Enlightenment. The critical point to notice in this dialogue is the last remark, "Take it up," because by freeing oneself from clinging to the dead-emptiness, one can participate in every activity in the world without losing the Śūnyatā insight. After all, form is Emptiness, and Emptiness is form, and there is not the slightest difference between them. Thorough Emptiness should not, therefore, be treated as nihilistic or dead-emptiness;

it is the dynamic Svabhāva Śūnyatā in its tranquil and transcending aspects.

In summary, there are two basic reasons why Absolute Śūnyatā cannot be equated with nihilism: first, it is self-negating or self-transcending as we have just seen; second, it plays an indispensable role in "supporting" all dharmas. Because of Śūnyatā, all things can exist; without Śūnyatā, nothing could possibly exist. Śūnyatā is therefore extremely dynamic and positive; in the words of the *Heart Sūtra* this is called "Emptiness is form." It should also be noted that Absolute Śūnyatā is not different from Svabhāva Śūnyatā; we distinguish two Śūnyatās here merely for the sake of describing the various facets; Śūnyatā represents only the totality of one truth.

The Ten Similes of Emptiness

If the Absolute or Thorough Emptiness implies not a nihilistic void, but absolute transcendency—that which abides neither in being nor in non-being, why then should the word "empty" (śūnya) be adopted at all? Chinese Buddhist thinkers have summarized ten reasons for this.[27]

1. *Emptiness implies non-obstruction* . . . like space or the Void, it exists within many things but never hinders or obstructs anything.

2. *Emptiness implies omnipresence* . . . like the Void, it is ubiquitous; it embraces everything everywhere.

3. *Emptiness implies equality* . . . like the Void, it is equal to all; it makes no discrimination anywhere.

4. *Emptiness implies vastness* . . . like the Void, it is vast, broad and infinite.

5. *Emptiness implies formlessness or shapelessness* . . . like the Void, it is without form or mark.

6. *Emptiness implies purity* . . . like the Void, it is always pure without defilement.

7. *Emptiness implies motionlessness* . . . like the Void, it is always at rest, rising above the processes of construction and destruction.

8. *Emptiness implies the positive negation* . . . it negates all that which has limits or ends.

9. *Emptiness implies the negation of negation* . . . it negates all Selfhood and destroys the clinging of Emptiness (pointing to the thorough transcendency that is free from all abiding) .

10. *Emptiness implies unobtainability or ungraspability* . . . like space or the Void, it is not obtainable or graspable.

Although these ten similes, expressed in a poetical language, cannot describe all aspects of Thorough Emptiness, they do illustrate certain of Śūnyatā's most important characteristics. The word Emptiness may not convey the meaning of absolute transcendency exactly, but it comes closer to the idea than any other word available to man.

ŚŪNYATĀ AND LOGIC

The Prajñāpāramitā literature is full of paradoxical statements. At first sight, they appear to be illogical and to contradict sound reasoning. For instance, in the third paragraph of the *Heart Sūtra* everything is negated including the Path, Nirvāṇa, and Enlightenment, but in the fifth paragraph, the former stand seems to have been reversed, for it says that all Buddhas, by relying on Prajñāpāramitā, have attained Enlightenment. The *Diamond Sūtra* is even more explicit in the paradoxical nature of the Prajñā truth. "The so-called good dharmas are not good dharmas. . . . Buddha says that all minds are not minds; therefore, they are minds." If we use M to represent the subjects of these statements, the form would be:

$$M = \sim M, \therefore M$$

which appears to be illogical, because it is in direct opposition to the basic Law of Identity in Aristotelian logic. But the fact is that this argument is perfectly logical, and the reason is a very simple one which we shall discuss later.[28]

It should be noted that the very concept of the Emptiness of Emptiness (*Śūnyatā Śūnyatā*) is against the basic premise of logic. Let us use B to represent being and $\sim$B to represent non-being or Śūnyatā. Śūnyatā Śūnyatā can thus be represented as $\sim B \neq \sim B$, or $B = \sim B$, or $X \neq X$,[29] which is in direct opposition to the basic Law of Identity in logic. In testing the validity of an argument, if the result is in contradiction to the basic form of $P = P$—which may also be expressed as $P \lor \sim P$ is true (the Law of the Excluded Middle), or $P \cdot \sim P$ is false (the Law of Contradiction)—then the argument is considered to be invalid or logically untrue. Now the question is: *How can we verify this basic Law of Identity, the archtypal mode upon which all logical thinkings must rely?* Many logicians seem to believe that this is unnecessary. They think that this is an inquiry the philosophers should undertake; it is not exactly the business of logicians. A logician's task is to see how the logical principles or *forms* work in computations. He should never bother with the verifiability of the basic premises of logical principles such as $P \lor \sim P$, $A = A$, and so forth.

In his book *Symbolic Logic,* Irving Copi observed:

> . . . in an ideal science *all* propositions should be proved, by deducing them from others, and all terms should be defined. But this would be 'ideal' only in the sense of being impossible to realize. Terms can be defined only by means of other terms whose meanings are presupposed and must be antecedently understood if the definitions are to explain the meanings of the terms being defined (p. 168).
>
> Every deductive system, on pain of falling into circularity or a vicious regression, must contain some axioms or postulates which *are assumed* but *not proved* within the system . . . *they are not proven within the system itself.* . . . Any argument intended to establish the truth of axioms is definitely outside the system, or extra-systematic (p. 172).

Logicians today do not claim that axioms in deductive systems are *self-evidently* true, as traditionally claimed in Euclidean Geometry. "No claim is made that the axioms of any system are self-evidently true. Any proposition of a deductive system is an axiom of that system *if it is assumed rather than proven in that system*" (p. 172). According to this view, the basic premise of logic expressed in the form of $A = A$ is therefore *a presumption, not a proven truth.* Some readers will contend here that the Law of Identity can always be verified by empirical evidence. No one in his right mind would deny that a man is a man or a dog is a dog. Besides, the efficacy of the computer is the best verification of logical thinking whose "primordial" premise is still based on the Law of Identity and its extensions. To this argument I would only add that the fond belief that the Law of Identity is incontrovertibly and universally true in terms of empirical evidence has been denied by the phenomenon of indeterminacy and relativity as mentioned before in our discussion of Svabhāva Śūnyatā. Besides, this argument, based on empirical evidence, would certainly not be accepted by logicians, because it has deviated from the cherished belief that logical thinking is entirely deductive and analytical and that empirical verifiability is entirely irrelevant.

Now, if we go beyond the bounds of logic and look at this problem from different angles and ask: *What does "A is A" mean? How can we verify it?* Immediately we will find an existential impasse. Everyone uses the expression "A is A" in various situations, but few would seriously ask its intrinsic meaning. When we say "A is A" what do we really mean? The question is extremely difficult to answer. Some people say that it simply means *"A exists as itself."* But we must push it further and ask, "What do you mean by 'A exists as itself'?" The respondent would indeed be hard pressed to answer this. A pseudo answer such as: "It means that A has a self-entity which is identical with itself but not something else," may be employed, but this question, because of its "primordial" nature, is almost impossible to answer. "A exists as itself" is not a *conceptual proposition* but an *existential feeling of is-ness,* the feeling of perceiving a substantial entity (Svabhāva).[30] It is an intuitional, but not a ratiocinative statement. To the next question: How can we prove or verify "A is A"?, the plain answer is: it cannot be proven. If, for example, we want to prove or disprove that A, B, or C is a dime, we can simply try to fit A, B, or C into the definition of dime—a metal coin with such and such weight, size, thickness, and design. If they correspond with this description, they are considered to be dimes. The process of verification is therefore a process of *correspondency-testing;* that is, seeing whether this fits into that. Now, a process of *fitting this into that* (fitting A into B) cannot be applied in the case of *fitting this into this* (fitting A into A). The former holds a contrast of at least two different entities (A and B); whereas the latter holds only one entity (A). The verification process through correspondency-testing, which requires at least two different entities to make the idea of *correspondence* meaningful, is not applicable to the case of A = A (or the Law of Identity), since it has no more than one entity. If you say that "A is A" can also be verified through the correspondency-testing process, by fitting the entity A into the definition of the same, my answer is that you are doing something quite meaningless, for two reasons. First, each and every time you perform this "testing" process, the result will invariably be positive; therefore, it is unnecessary and useless. One of the essential elements of verification is that an element of doubt or uncertainty must always be present; in the situation "A is A" there is no doubt or uncertainty involved. And second, this so-called "testing" process is a contrived operation, artificial and meaningless. It is in fact a *reaffirmation,* not a *verification.*

Since the Law of Identity cannot be verified within a system that uses its own contents as a criterion for verification, to prove or disprove the Law of Identity we must go beyond or outside it. The Law of

Identity is unverifiable so long as we remain in its fold, for it will always appear to be an existential "reality" to us requiring no other proof to sustain itself.

Now, the fact that "A is A" is an intuition or existential reality should not exclude the existence of other forms of intuitions such as: *A is not A, therefore A*—the existential reality of Prajñāpāramitā. These two different intuitions actually belong to two different realms without impeding each other. But if we insist that they contradict each other and that we must choose one and exclude the other, which one then should we choose? Which one is considered to be more important or "truer" than the other? Mahāyāna Buddhism obviously thinks that the orientation of śūnyatā is "truer" and more important. Why? Because it is broader and deeper in its dimensions. We know that the principles of higher truths always embrace or supersede those of lower ones but not the reverse. With the apparatus of algebra, difficult problems in arithmetic can be solved easily, but this is not true the other way round. When higher principles of morality are evoked, the lower ones are abnegated if necessary. This testifies to the fact that the principles of higher realms are always more inclusive and of greater depth and thus more important. The Law of Identity is perfectly true in the realm of mundane truth (saṁvṛti-satya), but it becomes insufficient and even erroneous when it is applied to the subject matter of higher dimensions. The Law of Conservation and the Law of Parity are perfectly true in classical physics, but they no longer hold true when applied to the realm of sub-atomic physics. In the same way "A is *not* A, therefore A" in Prajñāpāramitā, is a more inclusive viewpoint than "A is A because it exists as itself" from common sense. The Prajñāpāramitā says that *A is A* not because it exists as such, but because it has no Selfhood, or it is non-A. Prajñāpāramitā affirms the identity of A just as the common sense does when it deals with matters on the mundane level; but in addition, it also points out the nonsvabhāva and illusive nature of A. Backed by this rationale, the Mahāyānists believe that the śūnyatā orientation is more inclusive and of a higher dimension.

Another difference between Absolute Śūnyatā and logical thinking is worth mentioning here. In logic, the Principle of the Excluded Middle asserts that any statement is either true or false. The Law of Contradiction asserts that nothing can be both true and false. Two negatives always make a positive: $\sim (\sim X) = X$. But Śūnyatā Śūnyatā, the negation of the negation of beings, does not necessarily imply a positive being. In the system of Prajñāpāramitā, two negatives do not automatically become positive as the principle of the Excluded Middle dictates. Following the same reasoning, the Principle of Contradiction (no statement can be both true and false) is also transcended. Something can indeed be both true and false at the same time, at least *in different dimensions*. For instance, the Law of Conservation holds true in classical physics, but is untrue in atomic physics. The logician's argument on this point is that if all the words used in a proposition were strictly defined in a finite area and complete in their denotations, then the Principles of Identity, of Contradiction and of the Excluded Middle would be perfectly true. The sentence "USA is USA" may not be true if the former means USA 1880 and the latter means USA 1968, but a statement such as: "USA 1880 is USA 1880" is perfectly true and unobjectionable.[31] Prajñāpāramitā replies that USA 1880—or any entity in the phenomenal world—*cannot be strictly determined,* since they are all relative and without a Selfhood. "A is A" is completely meaningless if A cannot be strictly defined in its most rigorous and universal sense, and this is exactly the situation—no strict determinacy of anything is obtainable in our world. Hence, "A is white" (w_a) and "A is not white" ($\sim w_a$) can be both true and false (the abnegation of the Principle of the Excluded Middle), not only because A can become different things in different realms, thus altering its truth value as we have mentioned before, but most important of all because "A is not A," since it does not have an own-being or self-identity in the strictest universal sense. It has an identity *only in the conventional and restricted sense*. Prajñāpāramitā has no argument with and no objection to the common sense belief that a dog is a dog, or that limestone is heavier than water, so long as they are confined to the conventional and pragmatic sense. Only when we extend the conventional orientation to a universal dimension of absolute truth does Prajñāpāramitā proclaim its dissent. "A is A" is perfectly real in the realm of conventional truth (saṁvṛti-satya), but unreal from the viewpoint of the totalistic Ultimate Truth (Paramārtha-Satya). The paradoxical statements in Prajñāpāramitā literature can thus be easily explained by allocating the different truth values to different dimensions in the Two Truths system of the Middle Way Doctrine (Mādhyamika) which will be explained below.

The Two Truths System

Nāgārjuna says in his *Mādhyamika-Kārikās*:[32]

> Based on [the system] of Two Truths
> Buddhas have preached the Dharma to men.
> Mundane truth is the first, and Ultimate
> Truth the second. He who knows not
> These Two Truths can never understand
> The profound meaning of Buddha's teachings.

All religions face the same problem of how to relate man to God, and to reconcile the finite with the infinite. The perennial tension between the mundane and the transcendental is also easily detectable in Buddhist doctrines. To solve this problem, many theories have evolved; the system of Two Truths is a typical example. In order to accommodate men and their conventions, the existence and efficacy of all dharma-events in the phenomenal world are affirmed. This is called the mundane truth or the conventional truth (saṁvṛti-satya). To point out the delusory and empty nature of all beings and the reality of absolute transcendency, the Ultimate Truth (Paramārtha-satya) of a higher level was also given. With this Two Truths system, the problems of being and non-being, men versus Buddha, finite and infinite, and so forth can all be solved with consistency and ease. When Buddha says that men and gods exist, that karma and saṁsāra exist, that the Four Noble Truths and Three Bodies (Trikāya) of Buddha exist, that a river is a river and a tree a tree, he is talking from the standpoint of saṁvṛti-satya. When he says that heaven and earth do not exist, that saṁsāra and Nirvāṇa do not exist, that Buddhahood and Enlightenment do not exist, He is talking from the viewpoint of Paramārtha-satya. The paradoxical statement of the *Diamond Sūtra*—"Man's mind (M) is not man's mind (∼M); therefore, it is called man's mind (M): $M = \sim M, \therefore M$"—can now be easily explained. The first M is the assertion of man's mind in the mundane truth; its negation, ∼M, is the denial of man's mind in the Ultimate Truth. The third M represents Māyā, the nature of man's mind, in which the merging or identification of mundane and transcendental is expressed. Here we see the vital point that the Two Truths should never be treated as two separate entities in two distinct and divided categories. From the viewpoint of the Round Doctrine of Hwa Yen Buddhism, they are completely identical or non-dual. Any trace of dichotomy would indicate a sign of Svabhāva clinging. The concept of the Two Truths itself is only valid when we, standing firmly on this side, try to describe the other side and its paradoxical relationship with this side. It is only an expedient device to explain away the delusory tension between the mundane and the transcendental for people who are deeply rooted in this side. The purpose of preaching the Two Truths system is to go beyond the system itself and see the non-distinctive nature of the two. When all relativities are transcended, all pairs and duals are demolished. A wondrous state of great freedom (Ta Tse Tsai) in which all polarities merge into one vast totality will be revealed. In this state of non-dual totality, one then fully realizes the meaning of the "Emptiness is form and form is Emptiness" of the *Heart Sūtra*. This non-distinctive aspect of mundane and transcendental should perhaps be given a special name for clearer understanding, such as the Non-Dual Śūnyatā in contrast to the Absolute Śūnyatā.[33]

But let us return to our discussion of the Two Truths system. This system not only attempts to solve the problem of being and non-being by putting them in the spheres where they properly belong, thus dissolving the apparent illogicality of paradoxical statements, but it also functions as a pointer to the transcendental absolute. This is illustrated in Chi Tsang's Two Truths on the Three Levels.[34]

The Two Truths on Three Levels

On the first level, mundane truth affirms the reality of all things in the phenomenal world. A small problem arises here, however, when one raises the question of whether the sun is truly no larger than a disc running tirelessly in the sky, or whether the earth is flat, since they are perceived in such an experiential manner. Civilized people would reject these naïve views at once despite the fact that they are empirically true. So, even in our empirical world, truths have many different levels. Truths of the lower levels are mercilessly discarded when the higher ones are adduced. Thus it is shown here that in the Ultimate Truth of the first level, the existence of all beings according to mundane truth are denied.

The second level claims that the belief in being or in non-being alike is mundane truth, while the denial of both is the Ultimate Truth. This is to say that both the mundane and Ultimate Truths of the en-

TABLE II A simplification of Chi Tsang's Two Truths on Three Levels

Mundane Truth	Ultimate Truth
1. Affirmation of being: Δ	1. Denial of being: $\sim\Delta$
2. Affirmation of either being or non-being: $\Delta \vee \sim\Delta$	2. Denial of either being or non-being: $\sim(\Delta \vee \sim\Delta)$
3. Either affirmation of either being or non-being or denial of either being or non-being: $(\Delta \vee \sim\Delta) \vee \sim(\Delta \vee \sim\Delta)$	3. Neither affirmation nor denial of either being or non-being: $\sim[(\Delta \vee \sim\Delta) \vee \sim(\Delta \vee \sim\Delta)]$

tire first level, when viewed from a higher standpoint, can be ascribed only to the sphere of mundane truth on the second level. This is because the affirmation of either being or non-being is still a form of clinging to "extremes." The Śūnyatā of the Middle Way means the transcending of all extremes: saṁsāra and Nirvāṇa, finite and infinite, pure and defiled, existence and non-existence . . . all these can be regarded as extremes in that they are Svabhāvically construed. The Ultimate Truth rises above them, and this transcendency is expressed here on the second level as the denial of both being and non-being. Following the same reasoning, the combination of the mundane and Ultimate of the second level is to be construed as mundane of the third level, and the denial of them combined is the Ultimate. Through this dialectic contemplation, *one is progressively led to the absolute transcendence.* For the sake of clarity, a diagram of symbols is given in Table III to substitute for the previous table of the Two Truths on Three Levels.

TABLE III

Mundane	Ultimate
1. Δ	1. $\sim\Delta$
2. $\Delta \vee \sim\Delta$	2. $\sim(\Delta \vee \sim\Delta)$
3. $(\Delta \vee \sim\Delta) \vee \sim(\Delta \vee \sim\Delta)$	3. $\sim[(\Delta \vee \sim\Delta) \vee \sim(\Delta \vee \sim\Delta)]$

The arrow marks indicate the dialectical process of approaching absolute transcendence by progressively relinquishing being, non-being, and all dualities. This progression makes evident the fact that Absolute Emptiness is essentially non-abiding.

Two points of criticism have been raised here to rebut this process of dialectics. The first is, why should this dialectical process be limited to three levels. Following the same reasoning, we can extend the dialectical progression to the fourth, the fifth—up to infinite levels. Chi Tsang seems to have given no sufficient reason why the dialectics should be limited to only three levels. Another criticism was raised by the Reverend Yin Shun, the famous Mādhyamikin in contemporary China, that despite the complicated language and compound sentences used in the second and third levels—such as, "either affirmation of either being or non-being, or denial of both being and non-being" and so forth—what it actually amounts to is still the basic idea of being or non-being, and the attitude of affirmation or negation. Now, if we pay attention to the table, we will discover the following facts: all the mundane truths of the three levels are positive statements or assertions, and the Ultimate Truths are negative statements or negations regardless of whether they are expressed in simple or complicated forms. Looking at the table, indeed, we immediately see that the three levels in the right column all bear the marks of negations; whereas, in the left column, they all bear tacit positive marks. The truth is that the simple words *being* (*Yu*) and *non-being* (*Wu*) have much greater depth and implication than the mixture of being and non-being expressed in compound sentences.[35]

The Non-Abiding Nature of Śūnyatā

In spite of all these objections, Chi Tsang's system of Two Truths on Three Levels does serve an important function: to point out the *non-abiding* nature of Śūnyatā. There are different ways of illustrating the non-abiding nature of Śūnyatā in the various traditions of Buddhism; Chi Tsang's was the scholarly way, that is, through dialectics and philosophical reasoning. In contrast, we also find the down-to-earth approach of Zen Buddhism. A man asked a Zen master to explain the First Truth—the Ultimate Truth—to him. The Zen master kept silent for a while and said, "Well, if I tell you the First Truth, it will become the Second Truth!" The deep insight and ingenuity of these Zen masters in demonstrating the non-abiding nature of the Ultimate is truly remarkable.

Monk Shao, the outstanding disciple of Kumārajīva, of China illustrates the non-abiding nature of Tao [36] in the following way.

All things have their companions.
But Tao stands alone.
Outside of Tao there is nothing;
In It there is no duality.
Without outside or inside, It includes
The Primordial One and embraces
The eight realms and ten thousand things. . . .

It is not one, not many, not dark not bright,
Not arising, not ceasing, not empty, not existent,
Not up, not down, not construction, not destruction,
Not moving, not rest, not going, not coming,
Not profound, not shallow, not wise, not ignorant,
Not contradicting, not harmonious. . . .
Not new, not old, not good, not bad. . . .
Not alone and not a pair. . . .

But why is this so?

Because, if you say It has an inside,
It embraces the entire universe.
If you say It has an outside,
It accommodates and establishes all things.

If you say that It is small,
It covers wide and far.
If you say that It is large,
It penetrates the realm of atoms.

Call It one; It bears all qualities.
Call It many; Its body is all void.

Call It light; It is obscure and dark.
Call It dark; It is illuminatingly bright.

Say It arises; It has no body and no form.
Say It becomes extinct; It glows for all eternity.
Call It empty; It has thousands of functions.
Say It exists; It is silent without shape . . .
Call It high; It is level without form.
Call It low; nothing is equal to It.

Say It constructs; It scatters all the stars.
Say It destroys; things last from the days of old.

Say It moves; It remains in silence.
Say It stands still; It runs with all things.

Say It returns; It leaves without saying farewell.
Say It leaves, when the time comes, It returns.

Call It deep; It mingles with all beings.
Call It shallow; Its root cannot be seen.

Call It poor; It has a thousand treasures and merits.
Call It rich; nothing exists in the vast Ultimate . . .

Say It is alone; It consorts with ten myriad things.
Say It pairs; It is empty and alone. . . .

Therefore, Tao cannot be expressed by one name, and the Truth cannot be illustrated through one doctrine. Here I have only explained it very briefly, for how is it possible to plumb the depth of Tao?

Further Discussions of True Emptiness

With the foregoing introduction to the various aspects of the Śūnyatā doctrine, we can now return to the discussion of True Emptiness as stated in the second paragraph of the *Heart Sūtra:* "O Śāriputra, form is not different from Emptiness, and Emptiness is not different from form. Form is Emptiness and Emptiness is form. . . ."

In what sense does this statement mean that form is Emptiness and Emptiness is form? Does it mean form and Emptiness are only partially identical with each other? If so, there must be some part of form which differs from Emptiness and vice versa. If this is the case then the so-called True Emptiness here is no better than a partial or nominal Emptiness. Obviously, the text does not mean that form and Emptiness are only partially identical, for it says explicitly in the previous sentence that form is not different from Emptiness and Emptiness is not different from form. Prajñāpāramitā does not allow any being—or a portion of any being—to be excluded from Śūnyatā. Partial Emptiness is, therefore, definitely not the meaning we seek. Now, if form is *completely* identical with Emptiness and vice versa, we will then run into the bizarre corollaries that a pencil is a chicken, a typewriter is an eyeball, and that when Miss Harrison of Unionville, New York, drinks whiskey, John Clifford in Lafayette, Indiana, becomes drunk without touching a drop of alcohol. Why should this be so? Some explanations are needed here. The following form of argument immediately strikes us as illogical: A is Chinese, B is Chinese, therefore A is B. The error in this argument lies in the fact that although A and B both share the Chinese nationality, they do not share other things in common. In other words, they are partially identical but *not completely* identical. This can be seen in the following diagram in which A and B share a participation in X (Chinese nationality), but remain otherwise separate and independent.

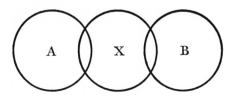

This diagram demonstrates that A and B are only partially identical, not completely or thoroughly identical as they are in the next diagram.

Now, if "A is Emptiness and B is Emptiness" is to mean that A or B is *completely identical* with Emptiness and with no differences whatsoever, the natural corollary would be that A is B and B is also A. Everything is identical with everything else—all in one and one in all; all *is* one and one *is* all. This is exactly what the mystics have said about their visions of reality. The Zen master Fu Ta Shih said, "A cow ate grass in Chin-Chou, but the horse in I-Chou became satiated." Isn't this fantastic if not outrageously absurd? Here, we are indeed touching upon the core problem of Prajñāpāramitā.

Regardless of the difficulties, it is entirely possible for us to understand why forms are Emptiness. This can be reasoned out and comprehended with a certain degree of clarity. But in explaining or comprehending "Emptiness is form," we will immediately run into a curtain of fog. The starting point, Emptiness, is itself vague and remote from us. It is common knowledge that few Buddhist teachers can avoid the difficulties of explaining "Emptiness is form" to their audiences. The easy way out of this dilemma is to say that since form is Emptiness, then Emptiness must also be form. We can rest right here. Or, if we are not content with this argument, we can demand a more positive explanation of "Emptiness is form," but we will then have to face statements as fantastic as: a pencil is a man; I drink beer, but you get drunk; when a man walks on a bridge, the bridge flows but not the water, and the like. In fact, the whole task of Hwa Yen doctrine is to try to explain the tenet of "Emptiness is form," in a positive manner. The Hwa Yen Realm of Totality, discussed in the first chapter, is none other than an existential description of the principle of the identical-ness of form and Emptiness. The numerous fantastic statements of Hwa Yen—such as, "throw the past into the future, bring the future into the past; put the entire universe in an atom," and so forth—are also natural corollaries of the basic teaching of "form is Emptiness and Emptiness is form."

We are now facing at least three kinds of problems: the logical, the empirical, and the spiritual. *First,* what is the logical justification of these contradictory statements, if any? *Second,* how is it possible to have such fantastic experiences as claimed? What are their justifica-tions? *Third,* the bizarre statements just mentioned seem to violate the ordering of the world; how then can the principles of Totality establish any order, especially the spiritual order which is the primary concern of Buddhism? Certain aspects of these questions were answered before, and some will be dealt with in the next section when we discuss the Hwa Yen Philosophy of Totality.

THE SIGNIFICANCE OF ŚŪNYATĀ

The last part of the fourth paragraph of the *Heart Sūtra* reads: "Because there is nothing to be attained, a Bodhisattva relying on Prajñā-pāramitā has no obstructions in his mind. Because there is no obstruction he has no fear, and he passes far beyond all confusions and imaginations and [finally] reaches the ultimate Nirvāṇa." The message here is that if a Mahāyāna practitioner, a Bodhisattva, can rely on the teaching of Absolute Emptiness, all obstructions in his mind, such as greediness, enmity, passion-desires and, above all, the innate clinging of Selfhood, will all be dissolved into naught. With the realization of Emptiness, he conquers the root of ego; with the eradication of ego, he in turn conquers all fears and confusions and reaches the ultimate liberation of Nirvāṇa. Here we see that śūnyatā should never be treated as merely a philosophical idea, for it also has great religious significance and implications. Because there is no almighty God, salvation (or liberation in Buddhism) is only attainable by one's own efforts through the realization of Emptiness. Śūnyatā is, therefore, not only an ontological reality but in a certain sense also a "soteriological" instrument. This is why Prajñāpāramitā is also called "The Mother of All Buddhas," symbolized in the form of Mother Tārā in Tantric Buddhism:

> Beyond thinking and all words,
> The Perfection of Wisdom
> Arises not nor ceases,
> Like the void space.
> Those with direct insight
> Alone can behold Her.
> To the Mother of all Buddhas,
> In the past, present, and future,
> I make sincerest obeisance.

Śūnyatā's other significance is its total negation of Svabhāva and the Svabhāva way of thinking. This becomes instrumental not only in philosophical inquiries but also in man's spiritual growth. A mind imbued with Śūnyatā is vast, dynamic and compassionate, because the veil of self and Selfhood has been removed and the radiance of Dharma-dhātu in the all-embracing Buddha-Mind has shone forth.

The Śūnyatā doctrine of Prajñāpāramitā is exalted by Mahāyāna as *the* most important teaching of Buddhism. A Bodhisattva without Prajñāpāramitā is like a fish without water. He may undertake all the spiritual endeavors—charity, patience, observing precepts, practicing meditation and so forth—but all these good conducts, meritorious as they are, cannot lead him to liberation nor to the transcendental plane of infinity to fulfill the Bodhisattva's illimitable vows and acts. Without Śūnyatā, his goodness is limited in the narrow confines of finitude. The six basic Bodhisattva's spiritual practices, or the six Pāramitās— the Perfection of Alms-giving, the Perfection of Discipline, of Vigor, of Patience, of Meditation, and of Intuitive Wisdom—all depend on the practice of Śūnyatā. Without Śūnyatā or the Prajñā insight, one may practice alms-giving or observe the rules of discipline, but this cannot be construed to be the *Perfection* of Alms-giving or the *Perfection* of Discipline. These are good deeds but not Pāramitās (Perfections). The Mahāyāna Doctrine of the *Six Pāramitās Sūtra* [37] says:

> Again O Maitreya, that is only the observation of pure discipline, and it cannot be considered to be a Pāramitā, because the practicer observes the disciplines by taking forms. He cannot reach the supreme [infinity]. Why is this so? Because [if one observes discipline by taking forms,] all that he can receive are the mundane fruits in saṁsāra. In time they will all be exhausted. But, if one observes disciplines [not for himself but] for the sake of all sentient beings, and in doing so also observes the Emptiness of the First Principle, without taking the form of self and others, then he is said to truly practice the Perfection of Discipline [Sīla Pāramitā. . . ."

The significance of Śūnyatā can be seen from another angle by examining the long-striven-for goal of Buddhism. The final objective of every religion is to achieve a unification of polarities: the mortal becomes immortal; the created joins the creator; the finite and the transient unite with the infinite and the everlasting; the wanderer eventually returns to his heavenly home; and so forth. In the historical religions, this unification is achieved mainly through the grace of God, but since this is considered implausible or secondary in Buddhism, an alternative is needed. This is the important role Śūnyatā plays. It is because of Śūnyatā that the merging or dissolving of all dualities is made possible. This we have seen in the discussion of the Not-Two Dharma Principle (or the Dharma-gate of non-duality) mentioned before in the *Vimalakīrti Sūtra*. Without Śūnyatā, the unification of samsāra and Nirvāṇa, the merging of the finite and infinity, and the interpenetration and mutual containment of all beings on all levels would not be possible. There is no other way to enter the mansion of infinity except to go through the door of Emptiness. It is repeatedly emphasized in the bulk of Prajñāpāramitā literature that without the realization of Emptiness, the infinite compassion and altruistic deeds of a Bodhisattva are not possible. The unique quality of a mature Bodhisattva lies in the thorough integration of the insight of Emptiness and the spontaneity of compassion in his personality. The way to Buddhahood is to do all good deeds with a spirit imbued with Thorough Emptiness, free from all attachment.

In concluding our discussion of Śūnyatā, one more point should be stressed. The most troublesome topic, and the one which always recevies the most tenacious resistance in the discussion of Prajñāpāramitā, is its paradoxical or "illogical" aspect. To solve, or at least mitigate this problem we must bear in mind that the conception of Śūnyatā is not Śūnyatā per se. The former is an abstraction projected and created by men's minds; whereas, the latter is a direct experience encountered in Enlightenment. What this means is that conceptual Śūnyatā is vastly different from existential Śūnyatā. We can create or construct a concept of Śūnyatā, but we cannot directly perceive Śūnyatā itself through conceptualizations. It is true that the concept of śūnyā (empty) can be in contradiction to the concept of bhāva (being), but Śūnyatā itself is not opposed to beings. If Śūnyatā is *something,* then it can be in opposition to something else, but since Śūnyatā is not a something at all, how can it be opposed or contradictory to anything? "Form is Emptiness and Emptiness is form" is a description of existential reality, not a theorization of an abstract philosophical concept. When Bodhisattva Avalokiteśvara says "Form is Emptiness," he does not intend to give his audience an idea or concept; he merely tries to relate a hard-to-describe first-hand experience. Furthermore, the self-negating and "fluid" nature of Śūnyatā is inherently against the construction of any concept that is Svabhāva-bound. Since all concepts are naturally Svabhāva-bound, any concept of Śūnyatā necessarily falls short of its goal, hence the formation of a concept of Śūnyatā usually defeats its own purpose. That is why, eventually, the enlightened sages must remain silent.

The next question is, how can we help but treat Śūnyatā as a concept or a "something"? The answer is that this difficulty is unavoidable and can be overcome only through direct realizations. The point to note here is that although Śūnyatā is not a concept itself, a concept of Śūnyatā can serve as a pointer to the otherwise inaccessible target. But the pointer is to be discarded when the target is hit. When one reaches the other shore, the ferry boat is left behind.

NOTES [Part II, Section I]

1. Edward Conze, *Buddhism, Its Essence and Development* (New York, 1951), pp. 130–31.
2. See chapter ten of the *Vimalakīrti Sūtra*.
3. See note 12 of Part I.
4. Form (rūpa): although rūpa usually implies only the form, color or shape of a thing, here, in the sense of rūpaskandha (the aggregation-of-forms), it implies a very wide range of things. Any matter, or thing so long as it holds any form or extension is considered to be rūpa. This is the first of the five skandhas; the other four skandhas—feeling, notion, impulse, and consciousness—are all mental functions. Rūpa is used here to denote matter or material in contrast to the mind. The common expression is "sê hsin erh fa—form and Mind, the two dharmas." Because of its special usage here, the word *Form* is capitalized at certain places.
5. See Śankara's comment on chapter III, 19 of *Māndūkyopanishad* (Mysore: Sri Ramakrishna asrama), pp. 180 and 188. See Chandradhar Sharma's *Indian Philosophy, A Critical Survey*, pp. 261–67, for Śankara's philosophy of Māyā and Brahman.
6. See Theodore Stcherbatsky's *Buddhist Logic* (Gravenhage, 1958), pp. 79–81.
7. *Ibid.*, p. 95.
8. See *Vimalakīrti Sūtra*, chapter 3. Taisho 474, p. 541.
9. *Taisho* 1776, pp. 353–54.
10. Parmenides' philosophy on change and Being—see Arthur Fairbanks' *The First Philosophers of Greece* (London, 1898), pp. 86–97.
11. The outstanding difference in the interpretation of Svabhāva is seen between the Gelupa School and the three Old Schools of Tibetan Buddhism, i.e., Ningmapa, Khagyupa and Sakyapa. The founder of Gelupa, Master Tsungkhapa, invented a very peculiar definition of Svabhāva; as a result, he created a new Mādhyamika Philosophy which, in the author's opinion, seems to be a kind of Other-Emptiness (gShan.sToṅ.Pa), or Emptiness of Absence. To put it simply, this philosophy claims that the Svabhāva of a dharma is empty, but not the dharma itself, "When we say the vase is empty, we do not mean the vase itself is empty . . . what is empty is the Svabhāva of that vase."
12. Smṛti-upasthāna (Pali: sati-patthāna) is a meditational device concentrated on

maintaining an awareness or mindfulness of the functions of body, feelings, mind and mind-objects. Contemplation is taken to the minutest detail. The constant awareness of these "transient" and "conditioned" objects will gradually bring one to the realization of the truth of No-Self (anātman), hence Enlightenment. It is the core of Hīnayāna meditation practice. See Nyanaponika's *The Heart of Buddhist Meditation*.

13. This definition is based on Hsüan Chuang's interpretation in the first chapter of *Ch'êng Wei Shih Lun*. See *Taisho* 1585, pp. 1–5.

14. The hundred dharmas of the Yogācāra School can be said to be another device to break down the notion of "Self." Except for the six asaṁskṛta dharmas (the unconditioned dharmas) the other ninety-four dharmas can be either directly ascribed to the "Self," or to its associated elements. See *The Essentials of Buddhist Philosophy* by Takakusu, p. 94a.

15. See *Mādhyamika-Kārikās*, Chapter 24, stanza 14.

16. See *Language, Meaning and Maturity* by Hayakawa, pp. 28–29.

17. See Vasubandhu's *Trimśikā* and Fung Yu-Lan's *A History of Chinese Philosophy*, pp. 299–338.

18. The twenty Emptinesses:
    1. The Emptiness of the Internal Elements.
    2. The Emptiness of the External Objects.
    3. The Emptiness of both the Internal Elements and External Objects.
    4. The Emptiness of Emptiness (śūnyatā-śūnyatā).
    5. The Emptiness of the Great.
    6. The Emptiness of Ultimate Reality.
    7. The Emptiness of the Conditioned.
    8. The Emptiness of the Unconditioned.
    9. The Emptiness of Going Beyond all Extremes; the Absolute Emptiness, or the Thorough Emptiness (Sanskrit: Atyanta-śūnyatā).
    10. The Emptiness of No Beginning and No Ending.
    11. The Emptiness of the Undeniable.
    12. The Emptiness of the Ultimate Essence.
    13. The Emptiness of all dharmas.
    14. The Emptiness of all Marks.
    15. The Emptiness of the Past, the Present, and the Future.
    16. The Emptiness of the Non-Existence of Selfhood.
    17. The Emptiness of Being.
    18. The Emptiness of Non-Being.
    19. The Emptiness of Self-Being (or Selfhood).
    20. The Emptiness of Other-Being.

19. See Étienne Gilson, *The Christian Philosophy of St. Thomas Aquinas*, p. 41.

20. Jacques Maritain, *Approaches to God* (New York, Harper, 1954), pp. 4–5.

21. *Ibid.*, p. 3.

22. ". . . sa eṣa, na iti, na ity ātmā, agṛyaḥ, na hi gṛhyate, aśīryaḥ na hi śīryate, asaṅgaḥ na hi sajyate . . . ."

23. *Taisho* 227, p. 540.

24. These are the four stages of Enlightenment of the Hīnayāna School.

25. *Taisho* 475, pp. 550–51.

26. No-arising-Dharma-maturity (Sanskrit: annutpattika-dharma-kṣānti): although there are various translations for this term, I believe that the word kṣānti here does not mean "patience" or "endurance" but denotes a state of maturity or advancement in which the śūnyatā realization is so strong that it enables one to endure all adverse conditions. Traditionally, it is said only those Bodhisattvas who have reached the Eighth Stage (the Eighth Bhūmi) of Enlightenment can attain this realization. But some say those of the First Stage or the First Bhūmi are able to do so.

27. *Taisho* 1668, p. 615. It is doubtful that this Śāstra was Nāgārjuna's original

composition, it was probably written by some Chinese Buddhist scholar.

28. See "The 'Round View' and Logical Consistency," in Section Two of this Part.

29. To avoid the regular, logical thinking that two negatives imply a positive, Śūnyatā-Śūnyatā is not symbolized here as $\sim (\sim B)$, but instead as $\sim B \neq \sim B$, or $x \neq x$ to illustrate the point.

30. See the discussion on the clinging of being in this section, on page 93, 94.

31. See Irving Copi's *Introduction to Logic* (New York, 1953), pp. 252–55.

32. See *Mādhyamika-Kārikās*, chapter 24, stanzas 8 and 9.

33. Although the phrase *Non-Dual Śūnyatā* (pu êrh k'ung hsin) appears occasionally in the Prajñāpāramitā literature, it is used in a general and descriptive sense, and not as a 'proper noun' to denote a special name.

34. *Taisho* 1854, pp. 90–91.

35. See Yin Shun's *Commentary on The Middle Way Essay (Chung Kuan Lun Chiang Chi)* (Taipei, 1963), pp. 41–42.

36. *Pao Tsang Lun, Taisho* 1857, pp. 144–45. The word *Tao* should be treated as an equivalent of Śūnyatā or Tathatā here.

37. *Taisho* 261, p. 890.

Section Two
The Philosophy of Totality

MUTUAL PENETRATION AND MUTUAL IDENTITY—THE TWO BASIC PRINCIPLES OF HWA YEN PHILOSOPHY

With the foregoing explanation of the Philosophy of Emptiness as a foothold, we may now proceed to discuss the Philosophy of Totality as construed by the four Hwa Yen masters, Tu Shun, Chih Yen, Fa Tsang, and Ch'eng Kuan. The gist of Hwa Yen philosophy can be summarized in two phrases: *mutual penetration* (or mutual entering), and *mutual identity*. Mutual identity is almost an equivalent of the *Heart Sūtra's* dictum that form is Emptiness and Emptiness is form, whereas mutual penetration corresponds to the principle of dependent-arising of the Śūnyatā doctrine which states that no thing, whether concrete or abstract, mundane or transcendental, has an independent or isolated existence, but all things depend upon one another for their existence and functions. The mutual penetration principle of Hwa Yen, however, seems to have gone one step further; it makes the concept of dependent-arising more explicit by proposing the following three graphic phrases: simultaneous-mutual-arising, simultaneous-mutual-entering, and simultaneous-mutual-containment, which are indicated in the diagram below.

$$\text{mutual penetration} = \begin{cases} \text{simultaneous-mutual-arising} \\ \text{simultaneous-mutual-entering} \\ \text{simultaneous-mutual-containment} \end{cases}$$

To explain these three ideas, let us return to our familiar example of a cup of water, which can be viewed as merely a form of liquid to quench one's thirst, as the compound H_2O, as aggregates of molecules, as the fleeting particles in the sub-atomic field, as a manifestation of causality, or as the expression of the two-in-one form-Emptiness of the

Śūnyatā doctrine. Looking at this cup of water, we see that all these different "entities" of different realms arise simultaneously. The liquid, the H_2O, the aggregates of molecules, the fleeting particles, and so on all arise simultaneously in a harmonious manner without impeding one another. They do not arise intermittently or discontinuously; they co-arise at the same time. This is the so-called principle of *simultaneous-mutual-arising*.

Since men tend to see things from one particular viewpoint, thus becoming partial and arbitrary, they are liable to forget the totalistic integrity of reality. The observation of this principle can, therefore, remedy partiality and narrowness on the one hand, and augment men's perspective of the totalistic reality on the other.

Now, these different "entities" of different realms not only arise simultaneously, but they *penetrate into* and *contain* one another without the slightest hindrance or impediment. The H_2O, the molecules, and the particles are not in a different cup, but in the same time they mutually-arise, enter-into, and contain one another smoothly in this same cup of water. We may envision this as the rays of light from many lamps overlapping and penetrating into one another without impediment. The totalistic reality is expressed here in terms of simultaneous-mutual-penetration of things in various realms of the phenomenal world. Here no transcendental reality is involved. Up to this point, Hwa Yen philosophy corresponds almost exactly to Alfred North Whitehead's Philosophy of Organism. Here both Hwa Yen and Whitehead stress the mutual-penetrating and mutual-containing aspects of existence in order to disclose an organic and totalistic view of reality. Parallel to the example of water given before, Whitehead, in making his point, made a rough division of six types of occurrences in nature. The first type is human existence, including body and mind; the second includes all sorts of animal life, insects, the vertebrates and other genera, all varieties of animal life other than human; the third type includes all vegetable life; the fourth consists of the single living cells; the fifth consists of all large-scale, inorganic aggregates; the sixth type is composed of the happenings on an infinitesimal scale, disclosed by the minute analysis of modern physics.[1] Now, all these functionings of nature influence each other, require each other, and lead on to each other; any change or mutation of any particular type of existence will effect the others. Whitehead explains, "The list has purposely been made roughly, without any scientific pretension. Sharp-cut scientific classifications are essential for scientific method, but they are dangerous for philosophy, because such classification *hides* the truth that the different modes of natural existence *shade off into* each other." [2] In other words, what science tries to do is to artificially separate the inseparable, organic whole, by its own selection for a particular and restricted purpose. As far as philosophy is concerned, this approach is not only dangerous but at times misleading, for it reveals one aspect at the cost of concealing the other. The organic totailty is therefore short-changed. Whitehead elaborates this. "There is the animal life with its central direction of a society of cells. There is the vegetable life with its organized republic of cells. There is the cell life with its organized republic of molecules. There is a large-scale, inorganic society of molecules with its passive acceptance of necessities derived from spatial relations; there is the infra-molecular activity which has lost all trace of the passivity of inorganic nature on a larger scale. . . ." These different genera (or realms) are mutually dependent, mutually subsisting; they cannot be understood in isolation—they are an organic whole. "Therefore, there is a dual aspect to the relationship of an occasion of experiences as one relatum, and the experienced world as another relatum. The world is included within the occasion in one sense, and the occasion is included in the world in another sense. For example, I am in the room, and the room is an item in my present experience, but my present experience is what I now am." [3] What Whitehead was trying to say here is exactly what Hwa Yen calls simultaneous-mutual-containment. Nothing in this universe is an isolated event. The existence of event A depends on events B, C, and D, and vice versa. Not only do they depend on each other, but they subsist and "contain" one another in the sense that there is an inter-immanence between all things. Everything is at once an image and also a reflector of all other things.

> We have to construe the world in terms of the general functionings of the world. Thus as disclosed in the fundamental essence of our experience, the togetherness of things involves some doctrine of mutual immanence. In some sense or other, this community of the actualities of the world means each happening is a factor in the nature of every other happening. . . . The whole antecedent world conspires to produce a new occasion. . . . The only intelligible doctrine of causation is founded on the doctrine of immanence. . . . We are in the world and the world in us. . . .

> The body is ours, and we are an activity within our body. . . .
> This fact of observation, vague but imperative, is the foundation
> of the connexity of the world, and of the transmission of its types
> of order. . . . [4]

In the Hwa Yen terminology, what Whitehead has stressed is exactly
the simultaneous-mutual-containment aspect of reality. The difference
is that the style and the approach with which the Hwa Yen philosophers express themselves are more poetic and devotional than philosophical.

The Metaphor of the Ocean-Mirror Samādhi

In the first part of this book, The Realm of Totality, we mentioned
Ch'êng Kuan's ten reasons for the causes of the infinite Dharmadhātu
of Non-Obstruction. The sixth reason is useful here to elucidate the
principles of simultaneous-mutual-arising and simultaneous-mutual-
containment: *Because all dharmas are like reflections or images, the
principle of Non-Obstruction is seen.* Using the reflections in a mirror
as an illustration, the Dharmadhātu of Non-Obstruction is presented
through three arguments.

1. Since all things are images, they are not real entities. Their existence
   is not self-subsistent but depends on other things. Thus the truth of
   Māyā-Śūnyatā (Illusion-Emptiness) is seen.

2. Because the innumerable images reflected from a mirror all arise
   abruptly at the same time, the simultaneous arising (t'ung-shih
   tun-c'hi) of infinite things is seen.

3. Because each and every thing in the universe is simultaneously a
   reflector (mirror) and a reflection (image), the Non-Obstruction of
   mutual containment (t'ung-shih hu-shê) is seen.

The first argument is very obvious, and we have discussed it in the
previous section on Śūnyatā, so no elaboration is needed here. The
second and third arguments may, perhaps, best be illustrated by means
of an interesting metaphor known as the "Ocean-Mirror Samādhi"
(Hai Chin San Mei, or Hai Yin San Mei) —a quite famous and frequently used term in the Hwa Yen vocabulary.

According to the totalistic Hwa Yen viewpoint, each and every
thing in the universe is at once a "mirror" and an "image." It is a mirror, because it reflects all things; it is an image, because it is simultane-

ously reflected by all other things. This is to say that inasmuch as one thing is—at least in *some* manner—related to all other things, it reflects them all; and inasmuch as the existence of any particular thing must depend on other things, it can be said to be an image, or reflection, of objects other than itself. In addition to this metaphorical sense of reflection between subjects and objects, there is a mystic conviction that the True Mind, the transformed Ālaya Consciousness, like a great mirror, is limpid, serene, and illuminating, literally capable of reflecting or perceiving all things in a spontaneous manner. We notice here that the term "reflection," as used in the former case, is primarily a figurative expression denoting a certain abstract concept; whereas, in the latter case it is a graphic description of a certain mystic experience. Although both usages are implied here, the latter seems to be the more important, and therefore, predominant usage.

Now, what does the fanciful term "Ocean-Mirror Samādhi" mean? It denotes something like this. If the entire ocean in all its colossal size and power is taken as a huge mirror, it could easily reflect all the manifold phenomena of the vast firmament. This mirror, the greatest one conceivable in the world of men, would not only reflect the numerous formations of clouds, rains, and storms from many continents, but also the innumerable stars, galaxies, and sentient beings' activities therein —including such wondrous scenes as the kingdom of gods and the kingdom of devils. Not only the magnificent garments and exquisite adornments that beautify the lustrous bodies of the angels, but also the malignant glares and grimaces that make the devils' faces dreadful, would all be simultaneously reflected in this great "ocean-mirror," without one minute detail being omitted. Fa Tsang comments on this: "The so-called Ocean Mirror [is a metaphor that] symbolizes the innate Buddha Mind. When [the manifold] illusions are exhausted within, the mind will become serene, limpid, [and unruffled,] and the infinite reflections of all phenomena will appear at one time. This may be compared to the stirring up of ocean waves when the wind blows; and their subsidence when it stops, leaving a calm and pellucid surface where all reflections may clearly be seen."

This illuminating ocean-mirror-like Buddha Mind is not, in essence, different or isolated from any man's mind; the two, in fact, reflect each other in a most wonderful manner. To explain this mystery of simultaneous containment and reflection, a parable—which we paraphrase—is set forth by Ch'êng Kuan in his *A Prologue to Hwa Yen*.

A monk is preaching the Dharma to his disciple in a room where hangs a mirror. The mirror, the monk, and the disciple symbolize the True Mind, the Buddha, and man, respectively. The mirror reflects a picture of two individuals facing each other; one is preaching, and the other is listening. To describe the interrelationship of the participants of this phenomenon, we can either say that *the monk within the mirror of the disciple* is preaching the Dharma to *the disciple within the mirror of the monk,* or we can say that *the disciple within the mirror of the monk* is listening to the Dharma preached by *the monk within the mirror of the disciple.* When Buddha preaches the Dharma to man, it is not a two-way relationship—one preaches and the other listens, but a *four-way* relationship—the Buddha who is within man's mind preaches the Dharma to man who is within Buddha's mind, and the man who is within Buddha's Mind listens to the preaching of *the* Buddha who is within man's mind.

The mutual containment aspect is clearly seen in this parable. More on this True Mind doctrine in relation to Hwa Yen will be discussed in the next section.

The Obstructions of Disclosure and Concealment

Totality is usually hidden from man, because he tends to see one thing at a time from one particular frame of reference. His inherent Svabhāva way of thinking conditions him not to do otherwise. This can be seen in the way we talk and think. When we say, "Water is something for drinking," we automatically exclude or *conceal* its other multiplex aspects, such as H_2O, aggregates of molecules, and so forth. Usually when we make an assertion of something, we reveal that aspect but conceal the others. But reality is a totalistic whole—the non-svabhāva version of simultaneous arising and containment of infinite realms. So, the realm of Hwa Yen Buddhahood is essentially a complete and total revelation of all. It conceals nothing whatsoever. This, however, posits an extremely difficult problem for the Hwa Yen philosophers. Because man's very basic pattern of thinking is Svabhāva and realm-bound, it is hard for him to think or talk of the multiplex positions and their interrelationships and mutual subsistence simultaneously. In the vocabulary of Hwa Yen this is called *the obstruction of the concealment and disclosure.* In contrast to this, Hwa Yen stresses the co-existence, or simultaneity of the hidden and the displayed, which is also called the

Non-Obstruction of concealment and disclosure. Ch'êng Kuan comments on this in his commentary on the "Principle of Simultaneous Establishment of Concealment and Disclosure in Secrecy" in *A Prologue to Hwa Yen.*

> On the eighth date of a [lunar] month, half of the moon is bright and the other half dark; the very appearance of the bright part [the disclosed] affirms but does not negate the existence of the hidden part. Likewise, the manifestation of something always implies the existence of the unmanifested or concealed part of the same thing. At the moment when the bright part of the moon is disclosed, the dark part also "secretly" establishes itself. This is the reason for the so-called simultaneous establishment of concealment and disclosure in secrecy. . . . To use another parable, the size of the moon, as seen by men on earth, is no larger than a big ball, but a moon-dweller [supposing there were one] would see it as a colossal world. The perception of the moon as a ball, or as a world, does not increase or decrease the size of the [total] moon itself. When the large aspect is seen, only the aspect-of-large is disclosed, and the aspect-of-small is thereby hidden; and vice versa. . . . [The point to note here is that *infinite forms* of a given object will show forth when the frame of reference is not set on one specific stand or dimension, but on Totality].

Ch'êng Kuan's exposition on this principle is quite explicit, but to elaborate it further let us look at another plain example. Many Europeans and Americans regard Mr. Winston Churchill as a great man, a hero to be admired and envied; to many Russians, Germans, Asians and Africans, he may be regarded as a person to be despised. To his intimate friends and relatives, Mr. Churchill may be an entirely different person, unknown to the general public. To his physician Mr. Churchill is no more than an ordinary Homo sapien with some sort of malfunction or disturbance in some organ. He is infinitely small when measured against the solar system, or the Milky Way, but he becomes enormously big when compared with an atom or a molecule. In the Hwa Yen dialogue, this is equal to saying that when this version of Churchill is displayed, the other versions are concealed or hidden, and yet the display of *this* by no means annihilates *that*. On the contrary, at the very moment when *this* is displayed, all the infinite *thats* are simultaneously and secretly established without the slightest hindrance or obstruction. It is a great pity that the human mind can only function in a one-at-a-time, from-one-level pattern, thus deprived of the opportunity of seeing the infinite versions of a given thing at once. Even from the pragmatic viewpoint, the attachment to one particular aspect or standpoint often proves to be disastrous. If military men plan their strategy only upon those data which are disclosed or apparent, but fail to take into account the hidden data, they are obviously courting catastrophe. Were not the majority of cases of military defeat in history due to a lack of seeing the hidden facets of the enemy's side? Also bearing witness to this point is the familiar story of the Buddhist fable that five blind men touched a different spot of an elephant; each of them then gave a different description of what an elephant really is, and the discrepancies among the descriptions eventually led to a foolish quarrel—to the amazement of the spectators. The problem, of course, is that we can hardly be a true spectator of ourselves. Bound by our inherent Svabhāva limitations, we do not often see the picture of Totality unless we make a strenuous effort to grasp it. Take another example, the question: "What is a man?" is impossible to answer without giving a specific frame of reference. The respondent is entitled to rebut the questioner, "What do you mean? To what specific area does your question refer?" To delimit, and to specify is therefore a constant necessity in human language and communications. But to define an object from any specific frame of reference is to elicit a portion from the totality of that being. That which is elicited or stressed is called by Hwa Yen the disclosed (hsien), or the host (chu), and that which is ignored or minimized, is called the hidden (yin), or the guest (pin). Man sees the disclosed and clings to it, but he is usually blind to the hidden. Total revelation of all the aspects of any given being is evidently inaccessible to every man; it is actually a realm of infinity beyond man's reach.

The "Round View" and the "Round Doctrine"

The so-called simultaneous-mutual-arising, mutual-penetration, and mutual-containment are but descriptions of *infinity* in a totalistic orientation. To make these concepts clearer and to see their resultant corollary it would be helpful to grasp first the core of Hwa Yen philosophy which, in my opinion, is best reflected in Tu Shun's "Cessation and Contemplation in the Practice of the Five Doctrines" (Wu Chiao Chih Kuan).[5]

To demonstrate that this teaching is beyond intellect and apart from words, two approaches are taken: [1.] the elimination of men's views, and [2.] the revelation of the Dharma. Now, the first—the *elimination of men's views:*

QUESTION: Do the dharma of dependent-arising exist or do they not?

ANSWER: No, they do not exist. They are of themselves void. Because all things in dependent-arising are devoid of Selfhood, so they are all void.

QUESTION: Then, they are void [indeed]?

ANSWER: No, they are existent, because things in dependent-arising have been existing from beginningless time. [Otherwise] this very question could not arise.

QUESTION: Then are they both existent *and* void?

ANSWER: No, because the void and the existent are completely merged into one. In the realm where the void and the existent merge, all the dharmas of dependent-arising become non-differentiated; thus there is not the slightest trace of any form of dichotomy. This truth can be illustrated by the metaphor of the golden ornaments and the gold of which they are made.

QUESTION: Then they are neither void nor existent?

ANSWER: No, because both [the void and the existent] can co-exist without one impeding the other. This is because [in the light of] the mutual-supporting aspect of the void and the existent, the dharmas of dependent-arising can simultaneously establish themselves.

QUESTION: In that case, in the final analysis are they all definitely void?

ANSWER: No, because [in the light of] the mutual-merging aspect of the void and the existent, they lose the meaning of existence as such. Things are void and not existent when viewed in the light of the void negating the existent; they are existent and not void when viewed in the light of the existent negating the void. When viewed [in the light of] simultaneous-negating, they both vanish. [When viewed in the light of mutual-establishment, they are both existent.]

We notice that regardless of how the questioner changes his stand and proposition, the answerer (representing Hwa Yen) invariably gives him a reply of "No!" This is not because the answerer has a malicious intention to frustrate the questioner, *the whole purpose is to eliminate men's views,* as pointed out at the beginning. The intention is that whatever view man holds be rejected as fallacious or one-sided, *because it discloses one aspect but conceals the other.* Now, if we continue to read the next paragraph, the revelation of the Dharma, we see that the answerer reverses his position completely. All the same questions, which he formerly rejected, he now accepts without the slightest qualm! He switches all the "noes" to "yeses"!

> Now, the second—*the revelation of the Dharma:*
>
> QUESTION: Do the dharmas of dependent-arising exist?
> ANSWER: Yes, because the phantom-existences are there.
>
> QUESTION: Are they void then?
> ANSWER: Yes, since they are devoid of Selfhood, they are void.
>
> QUESTION: Are they not only void, but also existent?
> ANSWER: Yes, because they do not impede the existence of one another.
>
> QUESTION: Are they neither void nor existent?
> ANSWER: Yes, because in the light of mutual-negation they both are annulled. In short, it is because of dependent-arising that things do exist; it is because of dependent-arising that things do not exist; it is because of dependent-arising that things not only exist but also do not exist; and it is because of dependent-arising that things neither exist nor do not exist. By the same token, one is one and one is not one; one is both one and not one, and one is neither one nor not one; many are many and are not many, and both many and not many, and are neither many nor not many. . . . Following the same reasoning, many are many and one is one, they are many, but also one; and are neither one nor many. . . . In brief, *all these reasonings are possible because of the Non-Obstruction and complete merging of the positive and the negative way of observation.* This is made possible because the nature of dependent-arising is intrinsically free from all bindings.

From these statements we can clearly see that the Hwa Yen way of viewing things is quite different from the customary way. The same questions are answered by yes and no, by both and neither. This appears to be against all reason, but the core and spirit of the Hwa Yen teaching lies right here. We notice that the answerer shifts his position each time the questioner tries to pin him down. He changes the frame of reference in every round when the same question, or a question in the same category, is put before him. In other words, when a question referring to category A is asked, the answer is given with reference to category B. Is this fair and sound? The reply is, that if the answerer is bound by a specific realm, his answer will be unfair and wrong; but if he is not so bound, his conflicting answer will not be incorrect. His is the totalistic or the "Round" view not tinged by the slightest Svabhāva tendency, for after all, right or wrong are meaningful only when a certain standpoint of a realm is preconceived and pre-fixed as we have seen before. If one can appreciate this "all-righteous" way of viewing things, which is also called the Round View or Round Reasoning (Yüan Chiao Chien) by the Chinese Buddhists, the principle of mutual entering and mutual identity will at once become self-evident. Mutual entering is but an expression denoting the interconnection and influence of things as seen in the light of "Round Totality," and mutual identity is their non-differentiation and mergence. Some Zen stories will be helpful here to illustrate the point, because both Zen and Hwa Yen are trying to say the same thing through different approaches.

A Zen master said, "If you have a staff, I shall give you one; if you do not have a staff, I will take one away from you."

Monk Fa Ch'ang visited Ma Tsu and asked him what was the Buddha? Ma Tsu said, "Your mind is Buddha." He immediately gained Enlightenment. Then he stayed in a remote mountain for many years. To test him out, Ma Tsu sent a monk to visit him. The monk asked Fa Ch'ang, "What did you gain from Ma Tsu which has enabled you to stay for so many years in this place?" Fa Ch'ang said, "He told me that the mind itself was Buddha." The monk said, "But Ma Tsu has changed his teaching now, he is now saying that it is neither mind nor Buddha." Fa Ch'ang said contemptuously, "This old fellow always tries to confuse people. Let him have his neither mind nor Buddha, I still hold my 'mind *is* Buddha.'" Being informed of this remark, Ma Tsu was very pleased and said, "Now the plum is really ripened."

The point is that he who has reached the realm of Non-Obstruction or Totality cannot say something incorrect *no matter what he says*, for he is no more Svabhāva-bound but is in a dimension of the "Round-Doctrine" (Yüan Chiao).

There is another familiar Zen story prevalent in the West which in my opinion expresses the Hwa Yen "Round View" exactly. Two monks, A and B, were arguing about a doctrinal problem; each insisted on his own opinion and rejected the other's as fallacious. Monk A said, "I am going to see our master and let him arbitrate," so he entered the chamber of the master who was at that time accompanied by an attendant monk who stood behind him.

"O Master!" cried monk A. "I just had an argument with B. My interpretation of such-and-such passage in a Sūtra is this . . . but B had a different interpretation and insists that I am wrong. Please tell me who is right and who is wrong?"

The Master said, "You are right!"

Monk B heard about this and rushed to the Master. "Master! How can you say that A is right? According to the authoritative commentary of so-and-so, my interpretation should be right, and his wrong."

The Master said, "Yes, you are right!"

The attending monk who stood behind the master and saw the whole event could no longer maintain his patience. He proceeded forward and whispered to the master, "O Master, you can either say A is right or B is right, but how can you say both of them are right?"

The Master turned his head and looked at the protester with a smile, saying, "Yes, you are also right!" [6]

The reader can clearly see that the Zen Master could have answered "No!" to these three monks as well, without violating his own principles. He was a man in the dimension of Non-Obstruction.

The "Round View" and Logical Consistency

Now, what would be the right word to describe and evaluate this "Round-View" of Hwa Yen? Fantastic, extraordinary, monstrous, illogical, or just pure nonsensical? Whatever the impression one may get from this brief introduction to the thought of Hwa Yen, two questions must be answered before one can make any sense out of this strange philosophy. First, how can anyone justify this kind of monstrous thinking which brazenly violates all principles of logic? And second, how can Hwa Yen establish any order—social, moral, spiritual, or otherwise—at all?

THE FIRST PROBLEM: The Hwa Yen "Round Doctrine" is a violation of all logical principles. The question has already been discussed in a previous chapter, but to make the point more explicit, we now claim that *all Hwa Yen and Śūnyatā arguments are perfectly logical.*

Let's see a typical example of argument-form from the Prajñāpāramitā literature. In the *Diamond Sūtra* we read: *"The so-called world is not a world; therefore, it is called a world."* This argument form can be translated and symbolized as follows:

1. A is X

2. A is not X

3. ∴ One is many; or the son of a barren woman is amphibious; (or any bizarre statement one can think of).

In symbols, we have the above statements as the following:

1. P

2. ~P / Q

The logical validity of this argument form can be swiftly established thus:

3. P v Q   (1 addition)

4. Q   (2,3 disjunctive syllogism)

No logician can deny the logical validity of such deductions of elementary logic. So, in this predicament, logician Irving Copi asks: "What is wrong here? How can such meager and even inconsistent premises make any argument in which they occur valid? It should be noted first that if an argument is valid because of inconsistency in its premises, it cannot possibly be a sound argument. If they are inconsistent with each other, the premises cannot possibly all be true. . . ."[7] *The reasoning Irving Copi offers here is not the reason of a logician, but of a metaphysician.* His swift claim that "if an argument is valid because of inconsistency in its premises, it cannot possibly be a sound argument," is arbitrary and partial. He does not specify here the criteria that constitute a so-called "sound argument." Again, "if they are inconsistent with each other, the premises cannot possibly all be true." This statement clearly indicates the rigid, Svabhāva-bound belief that inconsistency necessarily implies falsehood, and that the Law of Identity and Non-Contradiction enjoys the exclusive right to be the only sine qua non of all truths. This narrow orientation was examined and refuted in our discussion of the Śūnyatā doctrine. In the calculus game of proving the validity of any given argument, the student of logic who engages in the game will invariably be thrilled and relieved when all of a sudden the negative form of a premise appears in his calculations. Now he knows that the game is over, and the problem solved. Is it not ironic, that in seeking logical validity, the despised inconsistency can become a staunch ally? Whatever the philosophical implications of this irony, it is irrefutably evident that the paradoxical arguments in the Hwa Yen and Prajñāpāramitā literature are all one hundred percent logically valid. What should be stressed here is the fact that if a proposition and its negation can both be simultaneously established, whatever the derived conclusion is, it must be logically valid. The all-righteous "Round View" of Hwa Yen is the natural corollary of the mutual identity of being and non-being. This "Round View" is the inescapable consummation of the dialectics of mysticism. The whole question, therefore, is not whether these statements are *logically valid,* but whether they can be *empirically true,* and whether inconsistency in a particular dimension can become consistency and harmony in another. The answer is a definite *yes* as we have seen in our previous discussions.

THE SECOND PROBLEM: If a claim can be accepted and denied at the same time by the so-called "Round Doctrine" of Hwa Yen, how can it establish any order at all?

The answer is that a principle or order is valid and effective only in a specific realm, beyond which it no longer applies. The orders of lower realms are renounced when they become insufficient, and then the orders of higher realms are evoked or sought. This is evident in physics, social science, ethics, and elsewhere. What should be emphatically stressed here is the fact that neither Prajñāpāramitā nor Hwa Yen has the slightest intention of sabotaging any order in any realm. In fact, they uphold all orders by allocating their validity to respective dimensions in an interpenetrating and non-obstructive manner. The inviolable truth of the Law of Identity on the conventional level is firmly held by all Buddhist schools. An enlightened master of Hwa Yen Dharmadhātu, if invited to design a computer machine *for men,* would still follow the two-value system of logic as a basic guideline, as any computer designer would do. When a particular realm is specified and defined, no conflicting or contradictory principles are allowed therein. Water is definitely something to drink, but not something to burn, so far as everyday common sense is concerned. One may extract hydrogen from water and make it burn, but that does not belong to this specific dimension in question and therefore no equivocal or conflicting claims are admitted here. Hwa Yen never rejects logic or order; it merely transcends them in its Dharmadhātu embrace. On the other hand, one should always remember that Hwa Yen is based upon an orientation towards Totality. It views things not from one particular dimension, but from all dimensions. It includes all and establishes all. This is made possible because of the aforementioned two principles; namely, the Non-Obstruction of mutual penetration and of mutual identity. Liberation from the binding of the order of one particular realm does not mean the destruction or vitiation of that order but its relocation and enlargement. The higher orders often *appear to be* in conflict with the lower ones, but this is only so because of men's Svabhāva orientation. Totality is a great harmony of the co-existence of all realms. In Totality nothing is rejected or obstructive; here inconsistency becomes Non-Obstruction.

We are now living in an age in which the absolute has surrendered to the relative. Our vision, flexibility, and to some measure, our tolerance are immeasurably greater than those of our forefathers. Men have indeed freed themselves from many senseless bonds and barriers which once enslaved their ancestors. But this new freedom and perspective have also created a Svabhāva relativism that brings confusion and despair. A Svabhāva-bound relativism is destined to cause all sorts of self-defeating situations. For instance, with relativistic pretensions man can easily make excuses for himself and for his wrongdoings. In such a case, the true cause of his wrongdoing is not the relativity of moral values which he claims to be true but his *preference for a particular course of conduct*. Being Svabhāva-bound, he is not a true believer of relativism. Man's inherent partiality and preference for a particular course or idea (Svabhāva-graha) inextricably condemns him to be anti-relativistic. *His relativism, at best, is partially but not totalistically oriented*. The Hwa Yen relativism, if such a term is applicable at all, is a thorough-going totalistic relativism. That is to say, because it is totalistic and Śūnyātalistic, it absolutely transcends all bindings of all particularities as well as all relativities. The Thorough Emptiness of Śūnyatā, hinted at in the thundering silence of Buddha and Vimala-kīrti, points to the absolute, transcendent aspect of reality; whereas Hwa Yen Dharmadhātu points to the positive and all-embracing aspect of reality. Buddhism is neither relativism nor absolutism, it can be said to be neither or both *depending on the pedagogical need of a specific situation*. It is a widely held belief that Tathāgata is free from all views.[8] This slipperiness, repulsive to many but attractive to a few, is the outstanding characteristic of Mahāyāna Buddhism.

A DISCUSSION OF MUTUAL IDENTITY

As mentioned before, the Non-Obstruction of Dharmadhātu is made possible by the principles of mutual penetration and mutual identity. By approximation, we can picture mutual penetration as the co-arising of multiplex events in various dimensions within a given object, or we can imagine it as many rays of light from different lamps overlapping and interpenetrating simultaneously. But no amount of groping, fumbling, or approximation can bring us closer to a complete understanding of mutual identity. The impossibility of drawing even a fictive picture of mutual identity is clear enough to reflect the insurmountable difficulty of this whole problem. The main reason for this difficulty is that the great majority of men have never had such a firsthand experience. Man lives in a world of distinctions, not of mutual identity. His mind is predominantly—if not entirely—directed towards distinct objects and their relationships. There is therefore no way for him even to think about mutual identity, a principle of which he has no direct experience.

Direct experience and perceptions provide the elemental data for the creation of symbols and words. The linking of words in a structural arrangement constitutes what we call thinking. But the dimension of mutual identity is intrinsically beyond all Svabhāva symbols; the thinking process itself is therefore unable to apprehend it. The powerful capacity to manipulate symbols which characterizes man and distinguishes his mind from that of animals is simply inadequate to handle the problem of non-distinction and mutual identity—a realm that is accessible only by going beyond all symbols.

Mutual identity simply means that all different things are one; therefore, to approach it, it is necessary to pass through a ground that all things share in common in order to eliminate the apparent differences and thus reveal the true universal identity. This common ground is designated in Buddhism as the Buddha Mind, Suchness, Emptiness, or the universal principle (Li). It is through the merging of the distinct matter (Shih) into the non-differentiated principle (Li) that the truth of mutual identity is revealed. This reduction of phenomenon into noumenon is called in the Hwa Yen vocabulary the Non-Obstruction of Li (principle) against Shih (events) and is best explained in Tu Shun's "Cessation and Contemplation Practice in the Five Doctrines." [9]

OBSERVATION ON THE COMPLETE MERGING (NON-OBSTRUCTION) OF LI AGAINST SHIH

The complete merging of Li and Shih into one unity can be observed through the fusing of two principles—those of *Mind as Suchness,* and of *Mind as Changing.* The former is Li, and the latter in Shih. This is to say that both the view of existence and the view of non-existence become completely merged in a perfectly harmonious manner; thus, although [from a certain standpoint] either one may be hidden or revealed, there is no obstruction whatsoever between the two. The [truth of the] non-dual implies that all dharmas of dependent-arising are truly void or seemingly existent. Since the Void is the non-void, it again becomes existent. Since the Void and the existing are not two, they completely merge into one unity. When the idea of duality dies out, there is no obstruction between the Void and the existing. Why? Because the true and the illusory mutually reflect, penetrate, and embrace each other. What does this mean? This means that the Void is a void which obstructs not the existing, for the Void itself is the eternal existing; and the existing is one which impedes not the Void, for existence itself is the eternal Void. The existing is the non-existing, or an existing that is apart from the extreme of existing. The Void is the non-void, [or that which is] apart from the extreme of the void. Since the Void and the existing are completely merged, they become non-dual; therefore, no obstruction whatsoever exists between them. Since they both annul each other, they are both free from the two extremes. Thus the Sūtras say:

When one penetrates deeply into dependent-arising, he cuts off all erroneous views; no more then will he be bound by habitual thoughts of being or non-being.

> Because of dependent-arising,
> All dharmas arise and vanish.
> If one understands this truth,
> He will soon reach Buddhahood.

> The profound Buddha-matrix is ever
> Escorted by the Ego-Consciousness,
> The split of this duality condemns

Men to wander in saṁsāra. But the wise
Divorce themselves from this duality.

The defiled and yet not-defiled—
This is most hard to understand;
The non-defiled and yet defiled—
This too is hard to understand.

For these reasons Buddhism teaches the combined exercise of
cessation and contemplation [śamatha and vipaśyanā], and exhort
the united, or the mutual-nourishing of compassion and Wisdom.
. . . The so called mutual-nourishing of compassion and Wisdom
means that while the existing is the self-same Void, it does not
lose [the position of] being the existing. Thus, compassion can
nourish Wisdom without abiding in the Void. [By the same token,]
while the Void is the self-same existing, it does not lose [the position of] being the Void. Thus, Wisdom can nourish compassion
without abiding in the existing. [From another viewpoint] since
the great compassion abides not in the Void, it must follow the
existing and embrace all beings; and since the great Wisdom
neither adheres to, nor includes the existing, it always abides in
the void but does not vanish. [The so-called] vanishing is the
vanishing of the non-vanishing, or the vanishing-and-yet-not-
vanishing; [and the so-called being is the being of the non-being,
or the being-and-yet-not-being]. Since the being is the non-being,
although numerous phenomena appear, they are not existing;
since the vanishing is the non-vanishing, the Void remains as
such and is not annulled. Since the nature of the Void remains as
such and is not annulled, saṁsāra and Nirvāṇa are not one; and
since the numerous phenomena are not existing, saṁsāra and
Nirvāṇa do not differ. Why? Because the perfect merging of the
Void and the existing is one and yet not one. This can also be
stated in four different principles.

1. Because the existing is the self-same Void, [Buddha] abides not
   in saṁsāra.

2. Because the Void is the self-same existing, [Buddha] abides
   not in Nirvāṇa.

3. Because [of No-Selfhood,] the Void and the existing [are merged
   into] one piece and yet both remain: [Buddha] not only abides
   in saṁsāra, but also in Nirvāṇa.

4. Because the Void and the existing negate each other, and thus
   are both annulled, [Buddha] neither abides in saṁsāra nor in
   Nirvāṇa.

[All these four principles are made possible because of the truth of Svabhāva Śūnyatā].

Using the waves of water as a metaphor, the undulating forms [of the water] are the waves, the uniform wetness is the water. There is no wave that differs from the water—the wave itself is the self-same revelation of the water; there is no water that differs from the waves—it is water itself that makes the waves. The very fact that water and waves are one does not impede their being different; [the very fact of their being different does not hinder their being one.] Not impeding the difference, to abide in the waves is to abide in the water. Why? Because water and waves are different and yet not different. The Sūtras say:

Sentient beings are themselves the manifestations of Nirvāṇa; they need no further extirpation. Nirvāṇa is the nature of sentient beings; it needs no further growing.

Tathāgatas do not see any saṁsāra; nor do they see Nirvāṇa; Nirvāṇa and saṁsāra contain no difference whatsoever.

In the realm of the unconditioned [asamskṛta], the conditioned [samskṛta] appears, yet the nature of the unconditioned is by no means impaired; this is also true in the realm of the conditioned. . . .

From Fa Tsang's commentary we can clearly see that the principle of mutual identity is essentially a state of non-differentiation and all-inclusiveness realized by the merging of all antithetical entities, such as being and non-being, saṁsāra and Nivāṇa, the conditioned and unconditioned dharmas, and so forth. This dimension of total merging of antithetical entities is brought into the open by the removal of "obstructions"—namely, those Svabhāva barriers that stand in the way of Dharmadhātu in that they regard any given entity as deterministically self-so but not otherwise. For example, one is determinately one, but not many; being is definitely not non-being; phenomenon is never noumenon; the past is never the present or the future, and so forth. Obstruction, in short, is the Svabhāva determinateness and inflexibility delusively envisioned by men. Non-Obstruction, on the other hand, is the removal of these Svabhāva barriers. In the Gist of Hwa Yen Sūtra (Hwa Yen Chin Chih Kuei) [10] Fa Tsang expands the basic principle of Non-Obstruction into ten divisions.

1. The Non-Obstruction of nature and form.

2. The Non-Obstruction of immensity and smallness.

3. The Non-Obstruction of one and many.

4. The Non-Obstruction of mutual penetration.

5. The Non-Obstruction of mutual identity.

6. The Non-Obstruction of the hidden and the displayed.

7. The Non-Obstruction of the subtle ones.

8. The Non-Obstruction of Indra's net.

9. The Non-Obstruction of the ten times.

10. The Non-Obstruction of host and guest.

In a slightly different manner, these ten Non-Obstructions are also called the ten mysteries in other Hwa Yen literature.

1. The mystery of simultaneous completion and mutual correspondence.

2. The mystery of Non-Obstruction of immensity and smallness.

3. The mystery of the mutual compatability of one and many in dissimilarities.

4. The mystery of mutual identity of all dharmas in freedom.

5. The mystery of the establishment of concealment and disclosure in secrecy.

6. The mystery of mutual containment of the subtle ones.

7. The mystery of the realm of Indra's net.

8. The mystery of illustrating the truth through phenomena.

9. The mystery of the various formations of the ten times.

10. The mystery of the perfect illuminating host and the guests.

These ten mysteries or Non-Obstructions are synonyms of the so-called shih-shih wu-ai fa-chieh, the Non-Obstruction-Dharmadhātu of Events against Events. To explain the idea of shih-shih wu-ai, the crown of Hwa Yen philosophy, it is appropriate to review first the so-called four Dharmadhātus, propounded by the first patriarch of the Hwa Yen School, Master Tu Shun.

THE PHILOSOPHY OF THE FOUR DHARMADHĀTUS

The four Dharmadhātus as set forth by Tu Shun in his remarkable essay *On the Meditation of Dharmadhātu* are as follows.

1. The Dharmadhātu of Shih—the realm of phenomena, or events.
2. The Dharmadhātu of Li—the realm of noumena, or principles.
3. The Dharmadhātu of Non-Obstruction of Li against Shih—the realm of principle against events in total freedom and merging.
4. The Dharmadhātu of the Non-Obstruction of Shih against Shih—the realm of events against events in total freedom and merging.

Li and Shih are two important words in the vocabulary of Hwa Yen, but before we further define their meanings, it would be helpful to mention first a significant fact concerning the Chinese way of thinking. In Chinese, a train is called a "fire car" (huo chê); a bicycle, a "foot-stepping car" (chiao ta ch'ê); an automobile, a "gas car" (ch'i ch'ê); a truck, a "cargo car" (huo ch'ê); a sled, a "snow car" (hsüeh ch'ê); and so forth. From this example one can see clearly that the Chinese way of thinking is to picture a universal idea first, in this case the word *ch'ê* or car, and then to use an adjective to modify it in order to single out the specific object from the family-group which the universal idea represents. But in the English language, almost every object has a specific name ascribed to it for its identification. No direct relationship is detectable from English words like *train, bicycle, carriage, sled,* and *automobile.* Each of these words has an independent and solid character denoting a particular thing in an unmistakable manner. Although in English we have the words *vehicle* and *car* to denote the whole family of carriers equipped with wheels, we do not, as a rule, combine these terms with an adjective to identify the particular type as the Chinese do. Every object usually has a specific, pointed, and exclusive name. The word *vehicle* is used exclusively to denote a certain group of instruments that move and transport persons or things —it represents an abstract or universal idea that can seldom be used for denoting a particular and concrete thing or event. It would be ridiculous to say "foot-vehicle," "snow-vehicle," or "gas-vehicle" in English, but to the Chinese mind, it seems equally ridiculous to create so many unrelated names to denote objects in the same family. These names are not only difficult to remember, but also inefficient indications of membership in the "one great, harmonious family." By comparison, the Chinese way of thinking tends to be synthetic rather than analytic—and is thus particularly congenial to the enterprise of philosophizing.

If the main concern of philosophy is to search for an ever more universal truth, the application of "synthetic" words will be unavoidable in any philosophic enterprise. Since Hwa Yen is a philosophy dealing with the problem of Totality, it cannot help but use all sorts of "synthetic" and overlapping words. The wider and more vague the connotations of a word are, the more useful that word might be for Hwa Yen. To Hwa Yen a word is quite useless if it is not flexible and yet inclusive. These two Chinese words, Li and Shih, are therefore chosen by Hwa Yen philosophers to wrestle with the problem of Dharmadhātu, since they possess these qualities.

Looking at the multiple meanings of Li and Shih, the evidence for the above statements becomes apparent at once. Li, in different contexts, can mean "principle," "universal truth," "reason," "the abstract," the "law," "noumenon," "judgment," "knowledge," and so forth. Shih can mean a "thing," an "event," the "particular," the "concrete," "phenomenon," "matter," and so on. With Li and Shih so construed, the four Dharmadhātus can now be explained in the following manner.

The Dharmadhātu of Shih (Events)

This is the realm of phenomena, in which all things are seen as distinct and different objects or events. A river flows, a tree grows, birds fly and fish swim, the fire is hot, and the ice cold—all the multitudinous phenomena which occur in the empirical world are of this realm. Things and events are looked upon here as distinct and independent objects.

The Dharmadhātu of Li (Principle)

This is the realm in which only the abstract principles which underlie phenomena, and the immanent reality (tathatā) that upholds all dharmas, are seen. It is a realm beyond sense perceptions, a realm grasped only by intellect or intuition. All the principles and laws that dictate the events in the phenomenal world belong to this category. For instance, if one is thrown from a horse, he will fall at a particular spot. That particular spot is entirely predictable when all the factors involved are considered, and it is thus said to be dictated by a combination of various physical laws, such as gravity, inertia, and so forth. The reliable recurrence of the four seasons and of day and night are not accidental events; they are as they are and not otherwise because they are dictated or governed by a combination of various Lis or laws. Li is, therefore, the invisible controller of all events. Of all the different Lis, the Hwa Yen philosophers seem to have in mind primarily the ultimate Li—namely, tathatā (suchness or thatness) either interpreted as the universal One Mind (I Hsin) or as Emptiness (K'ung). There is no evidence however that different criteria to distinguish the *various kinds* of Lis and their interrelationships have ever been proposed by Hwa Yen philosophers. For example, the Lis that dictate the movement of physical objects have not been clearly distinguished from the ultimate Li of tathatā. The interrelationships between Li and Shih are well elaborated, but those between Lis in different categories have never been clearly defined. In short, Li is conceived of here as the all-inclusive and many-sided principle, fundamental for all existence, yet indeterminable in its contents. The Dharmadhātu of Shih and the Dharmadhātu of Li cannot be regarded as two separated realms. They are inseparable and interdependent, forming a unified whole. They are listed here as two separate realms only for the sake of illustration. In his essay *On the Golden Lion,* Fa Tsang uses the golden lion as a metaphor to explain the Dharmadhātu of Li and of Shih. The metal, gold, can be construed as symbolizing the non-differentiated noumenon of Li, and the artifact, lion, as the differentiated phenomenon, or Shih. Thus the interdependence and mutual identity of Li and Shih is made clear. The manifold relationships and observations made between Li and Shih, however, are far more complex than what is presented in this simple metaphor. So let us now turn our attention to the study of the third Dharmadhātu, the Non-Obstruction of Li against Shih, which is the key principle of Hwa Yen philosophy.

The Dharmadhātu of Non-Obstruction of Li against Shih (Li-shih Wu-ai)

This is the realm where Li and Shih are seen as the inseparable unity. A concrete event (Shih) is seen here as an expression of a certain abstract principle (Li), and the principle (Li) as the testimony of the manifesting event (Shih). Without one, the other would become meaningless; thus, in this realm, Li and Shih taken together become a more meaningful concept. Suppose, in the Great Depression of 1929, I saw a man jump from a window on the top floor of a tall building in New York City. I could see it as merely a physical object crashing towards the ground, drawn by the force of gravity and following a certain definite trajectory; or I could see it as a repercussion of the devastating failure of the economy at the time. Whether I treat it as an example stemming from physical or economic principles, it clearly demonstrates that an event (Shih) is always an expression of some underlying principle (Li), and vice versa. Li and Shih are not only inseparable and mutually interpenetrating, but they are also completely identical or non-dual (advaya). This is the so-called Non-Obstruction of Li against Shih, parallel to the dictum of "form (Shih) is Emptiness (Li), and Emptiness is form" in the śūnyatā doctrine.

Tu Shun, the founder of the Hwa Yen School, gave a rather detailed exposition of the Non-Obstruction of Li against Shih in his essay *Meditation on the Dharmadhātu*.[11]

The Meditation observes:

Ten principles are set forth here to elucidate both the fusion and dissolving of Li and Shih, their co-existence and extinction, co-operation and conflict [as reflected in the principle of the Non-Obstruction of Li and Shih]:

1. The principle that Li [must] embrace Shih.
2. The principle that Shih [must] embrace Li.
3. The production of Shih must rely on Li.
4. Through Shih the Li is illustrated.
5. Through Li the Shih is annulled.
6. Shih can hide the Li.
7. The true Li is Shih itself.
8. Things and events [Shih-fa] themselves are Li.
9. The true Li is not Shih.
10. Things and events [Shih-fa] are not Li.

The Meditation observes:

1. *The principle that Li [must] embrace Shih.*

Li, the law that extends everywhere, has no boundaries or limitations, but Shih, the objects that are embraced [by Li], has limitations and boundaries. In each and every Shih, the Li spreads all over without omission or deficiency. Why? *Because the truth of Li is indivisible.* Thus, each and every minute atom absorbs and embraces the infinite truth of Li in a perfect and complete manner.

COMMENT: This principle is quite obvious, and needs no elaborate explanations. The law of gravity, for instance, extends itself everywhere. It is efficacious at all times in all places on earth. In this sense, Li is considered to be indivisible and without boundaries or limitation. In contrast, Shih, the particular thing or event has limitations and boundaries. Because Li is indivisible, the total body of Li, but not its fragments, must embrace Shih. For we cannot even imagine how a fragment of the law of gravity can be effective at all. Another point that should be mentioned here is that in the Chinese language, there are no different forms for singular and plural nouns. The distinction between singular and plural is made by adding adjectives which modify the noun. Therefore, the words *Li* and *Shih,* given in the essay, can be construed to be either singular or plural. Hence, we can never be sure of whether Li or "Lis" is meant in a specific context, or what the exact philosophical implications are. But the presumption is that the word *Li* used in the Hwa Yen literature usually indicates the totality of all Lis—physical, ethical, ontological and spiritual alike.

The Meditation observes:

2. *The principle that Shih [must] embrace Li.*

Shih, the matter that embraces, has boundaries and limitations, and Li, the truth that is embraced [by things], has no boundaries or limitations. Yet, this limited Shih is completely identical, not partially identical, with Li. Why? Because the Shih has no substance—it is the selfsame Li. Therefore, without causing the slightest damage to itself, an atom can embrace the whole universe. If one atom is so, all other dharmas should also be so. Contemplate on this.

COMMENT: The key sentence in this argument is, "Yet this limited Shih is completely identical, not partially identical, with Li." This point has been discussed in the previous section on Śūnyatā doctrine, that Emptiness (Li) and form (Shih) are completely identical—and not partially identical—with each other. An atom can, therefore, embrace the whole universe without damaging itself. Here we see that by reducing Shih into Li, the fourth Dharmadhātu of Non-Obstruction of Shih against Shih (an atom embracing the universe) is deduced.

The Meditation observes:

This all-embracing principle is beyond [the comprehension of the] ordinary mind and is difficult to understand. It cannot be depicted [properly] by means of any metaphor of this world. [But being compelled now to illustrate the subject, the following metaphor is used.]

The entire ocean is [embodied] in one wave, yet the ocean does not shrink. A small wave includes the great ocean, and yet the wave does not expand. Though the ocean simultaneously extends itself to all waves, it does not by this fact diversify itself; and though all waves simultaneously include the great ocean, they are not one. When the great ocean embraces one wave, nothing hinders it from embracing all other waves with its whole body. When one wave includes the great ocean, all other waves also include the ocean in its entirety. There is no obstruction whatsoever between them. Contemplate on this.

Ch'êng Kuan commented on this paragraph as follows.

Ocean is used here to symbolize the Li, and waves the Shih. . . . How can the great ocean be [contained] in one wave? It can, because the ocean is indivisible. How can the one great Li be [contained] in one Shih? It can, because Li cannot be divided. One wave can embrace the great ocean, because it is identical with the ocean. An atom can embrace all Li's, because it is the selfsame Li. . . .

COMMENT: The third sentence of the text reads: "The entire ocean is [embodied] in one wave, yet the ocean does not shrink." It can be reasoned that if there were an extremely intelligent and well-informed person, given time, he would be able to deduce the contents of the ocean from the information contained in one wave. In this case, the ocean need not be shrunk to the size of a wave to be "contained" in that wave. This is quite understandable, but the next sentence says, "A small wave includes the great ocean, and yet the wave does not expand." From the empirical viewpoint of men, a small wave certainly cannot include the entire ocean without itself expanding. This impossibility, according to Hwa Yen, is derived from the fact that man is confined within a certain realm, and so long as he cannot transcend it, he must obey the dictates of the restrictive time-space order within such a

dimension. But the totalistic Dharmadhātu is not restricted or confined by any particular time-space order in any realm. On the other
hand, if a wave must expand to a size larger than the ocean in order
to include it, then it must be a Svabhāva wave and ocean precluded
from the Hwa Yen sphere of Non-Obstruction, which flatly claims that
without altering the size of a small atom, the entire universe is contained within it.

> The Meditation observes:
> Though the ocean simultaneously extends itself to all waves, it
> does not by this fact diversify itself; and though all waves simul-
> taneously include the great ocean, they are not one. When the
> great ocean embraces one wave, nothing hinders it from embracing
> all other waves within its *whole* body. When one wave includes
> the great ocean, all other waves also include the ocean *in its en-
> tirety*. There is no obstruction whatsoever between them. Con-
> template on this.

COMMENT: This paragraph is better understood when it is contem-
plated in silence than when it is explained in words.

> [At this juncture] one may raise [the following] question. "If the
> Li embraces an atom with its *total* body, why then is it not small?
> If the Li does not reduce itself to the same size as the atom, how
> can you say that its *total* body embraces the atom? Furthermore,
> when an atom includes the nature of Li, why is it not large? If the
> atom does not equal Li and thus become great and vast, how can
> it embrace the nature of Li? This reasoning is self-contradictory
> and unreasonable."

COMMENT: The simplest answer to these challenges is that all these
problems are produced by the Svabhāva way of thinking and Hwa Yen
Totality is entirely free from it. But Tu Shun, with great patience and
thoroughness, gave his answer from many different angles to demonstrate the non-Svabhāva way of reasoning.

> The Meditation observes:
> ANSWER: Setting Li and Shih face to face, they are neither
> identical nor different; thus they can [each] totally include [the
> other], yet not impair their respective positions or order.
>   First, to see Shih from the position of Li, four principles are
> found.

    a. Because the reality of Li does not differ from Shih, its totality dwells in each Shih.

    b. Because the reality of Li and Shih are not identical, the principle of Li always stretches to infinity.

    c. Because the non-identity is the non-difference itself, boundless Li is completely included in an atom.

    d. Because the non-difference is the non-identity itself, the one atom's Li is boundless and without division.

COMMENT: There is no better example of the non-Svabhāva way of thinking than is indicated in the above statement. The first principle, "Because the reality of Li does not differ from Shih, its totality dwells in each Shih," is a stress on synthesis or unification (ho). Conversely, the second principle puts its stress on separation or division. This shows that *the totalistic approach is not invariably synthetic* in its attempt to reduce all differentiation into the non-differentiated whole. Division and distinction are also embraced in the fold of Totality. It is only through the absolute freedom from any Svabhāva bondage (chi wu tzŭ hsin), be it a form of unification or of division, that Hwa Yen Totality can be approached. Using the vocabulary of Mādhyamika, the first principle indicates the Transcendental or Ultimate Truth (Paramārtha-satya) and the second, the conventional truth (saṁvṛti-satya).

    The statement of the third and fourth principles seem to be difficult to understand. How do we explain a sentence such as "Because the non-identity is the non-difference itself, boundless Li is completely included in an atom"? The expedient answer to this problem is that the so-called "non-identity" here denotes the distinct objects or Shih, and the non-difference denotes Li or tathatā. So, this statement merely rephrases the fact that the distinct things in the world of convention are exactly the non-differentiated Emptiness. Non-identicalness can be easily symbolized as $\sim (A = A)$, and non-differentiation as $\sim[\sim (A = A)]$. The so-called "non-identicalness equals non-differentiation" is tantamount to the symbolization of $\sim (A = A) \equiv \sim[\sim (A = A)]$ or simply $P = \sim P$ which is the familiar fundamental doctrine of all mysticism.

    The opponent then raises another question.

When boundless Li embraces an atom, do we find, or not find, the reality of Li in other atoms [at the same time]? If we do, then it means that Li exists outside the atom, hence Li is not totally [engaged in] embracing an atom. On the other hand, if the reality of Li is not found outside the atom, then you cannot say that Li embraces *all* things [Shih]. Hence your argument is self-contradictory.

ANSWER: Because the nature of Li is omnipresent, harmonious, and fusing,[12] and because the innumerable things [Shih] are [mutually] non-obstructive, therefore the [truth of Totality] exists both inside and outside [of Li and Shih] without obstruction or impediment. [To elaborate on this,] four reasons are given [from the viewpoint of both inside and outside of Li and Shih].

COMMENT: The gist of the argument in this paragraph is that since both Li and Shih are totally merged into a unified whole, they are both inside and outside; therefore, there is no inconsistency whatsoever involved. The statement, "Because the innumerable things [Shih] are [mutually] non-obstructive; therefore, [the truth of Totality] exists both inside and outside of Li and Shih without obstruction or impediment," is the pledge of the fourth Dharmadhātu of shih-shih wu-ai, The Non-Obstruction of Shih against Shih. Here we see it is difficult to treat the Non-Obstruction of Li against Shih and of Shih against Shih as separate topics; they are intimately interconnected. An elaboration of one will necessarily involve the other.

The Meditation observes:
From the standpoint of Li:
a. While Li embraces *all things* with its *total* body, it by no means impedes the existence of this total body in one atom. Therefore, to be outside is to be inside.
b. While the total body [of Li] exists in one atom, it does not impede the existence of this total body in other things. Therefore, to be inside is to be outside.
c. The nature of non-duality is omnipresent; therefore it is outside and it is also inside.
d. The nature of non-duality is "beyond all"; therefore it is neither outside nor inside.

The first three reasons are given to illustrate the non-difference of Li from all Shih, the last to illustrate Li's non-identity with Shih. It is because Li is neither identical nor different from Shih, that outside and inside are seen without obstruction.

COMMENT: It has often been noted that the Buddhist way of thinking does not usually follow the pattern of "either . . . or"; its common
pattern is close to that of "both . . . and." This inclusive way of
thinking, when pushed to its extreme, will inevitably bear the fruit of
the elusive Round Doctrine of Hwa Yen. The text in the last paragraph clearly indicates this point. The all-inclusive and slippery Li is
everywhere and nowhere; therefore it is both inside and outside of a
thing. It is identical and also different from Shih not because this is so
in terms of so and so, with a view towards relativity, *but because the
principle of Non-Obstruction and of the all-merging Totality necessarily demands such a corollary.* Again, the principle of Non-Obstruction implied in the text can also be explained in another manner.
When we speak of the *whole* population of a town, county, or state,
this so-called "whole" is really only relative. From the viewpoint of
higher dimensions, say the nation or the globe, these "wholes" are but
a part or fragment. These "wholes" are, therefore, relative and realm-
bound—being restricted within a delimited sphere. In contrast, the
totalistic whole or Li (Ch'uan Li) of Hwa Yen is not in the slightest
sense realm-bound. How then can this kind of Li be restricted within
the limit of any realm? This thought, "to be inside is to be outside,"
merely re-emphasizes the non-obstructive nature of Li.

The Meditation observes:

From the standpoint of Shih:

a. When one thing [Shih] includes Li with its total body, it does
   not impede all other things from including Li in its entirety.

b. When all things embrace Li, they do not impede one atom
   from embracing [Li] in full. Therefore to exist outside is to
   exist inside.

c. Because all things embrace [Li] simultaneously in each and
   every manner, therefore all things are completely inside [Li]
   and at the same time outside [Li] without any obstruction.

d. Because all different things do not impair one another, by setting one against the other, it is neither within nor without.

Contemplate on this.

COMMENT: In principle *c,* the so-called *inside* Li means that each
and every individual Shih embraces the universal Li; and outside Li
means that this pair of Shih/Li is not exactly that pair of Shih/Li. The
"neither within nor without" statement of principle *d* seems to be a

restatement of the Two Truths system: in the realm of the truth of convention, entity A cannot be said to be contained within entity B; otherwise, orders in the phenomenal world would be disrupted or impaired. On the other hand, in the realm of Ultimate Truth, entity A is not outside B because of their mutual identity in Li.

The Meditation observes:

3. *The production of Shih must rely on Li.*

This means that Shih has no other essence [than Li]; it is because of Li that Shih can be established, for all causations are devoid of self-nature. It is also because of this No-Selfhood that all things come into being. The waves push the water and make it move, and owing to the contrast of water and wave, motion is produced. By the same token, it is because of the Buddha-matrix [Tathāgata-garbha] that all dharmas can come into being. Contemplate on this.

4. *Through Shih the Li is illustrated.*

When Shih grasps Li, Shih is emptied and Li is substantiated; and because Shih is emptied, the Li that "dwells" in the total Shih vividly manifests itself [i.e., Li is disclosed and Shih is hidden], as when the form of a wave is annulled, the body of the water appears naked. Contemplate on this.

5. *Through Li the Shih is annulled.*

When Shih grasps Li and makes Li emerge, the form of Shih is annulled, and the only thing that clearly and equally appears is the sole and true Li. Beyond the true Li, not a single piece of Shih can be found. When the water annuls the waves, not one wave remains. [In other words, the reason here is] to keep the water in order to exhaust the waves.

6. *Shih can hide the Li.*

The true Li follows and establishes causal events. However since these causal events are against Li [in so far as the world of convention is concerned], the result is that only the events appear, but Li does not appear, [as ordinary men only see the tangible Shih in their daily experience but not the abstract Li]. Similarly, when water becomes waves, the aspect of motion appears while the aspect of stillness does not appear at all. The Sūtra says, "The Dharmakāya that circles and wanders in the five lokas [in saṃsāra] is called a sentient being." Hence, whenever a sentient being appears, the Dharmakāya always [follows] but does not [necessarily] manifest itself.

7. *The true Li is Shih itself.*

If a Li is true, it should not be outside of Shih. There are two reasons for this. First, because of the principle of dharmanairātmya [the emptiness-of-Selfhood-of-dharmas]. Second, because Shih must depend on Li, [Shih] itself is but hollow without any substance. Therefore, only if Li is identical with Shih through and through can it be considered to be the true Li. [Taking again the parable of water and waves:] since the water is waves themselves, no motion can be excluded from wetness. This is why we say that the water itself is the waves. Contemplate on this.

8. *Things and events [Shih fa] themselves are Li.*

All things and events of dependent-arising are devoid of Selfhood, hence they are identical with reality [Li] through and through. A sentient being is therefore Suchness per se without [going through] annihilation. Similarly, when the waves are in motion they are exactly identical with water at the same time, and there is no difference between them whatsoever.

9. *The true Li is not Shih.*

The Li that is identical with Shih is not Shih as such. This is because the true Li is different from the illusory, and the real is different from the unreal; also that which is depended upon is different from that which depends. Likewise, the water that is identical with waves is not waves as such, for motion and wetness are different.

10. *Things and events [Shih fa] are not Li.*

The Shih—that which is embodied in the total Li—is not always Li as such, because its form and nature are different, and because that which depends is not that which is depended upon. Although the total body of [Shih] is in the Li, things and events can also vividly appear. Likewise the waves—that which is totally embodied in water—are not always the water, for the meaning of motion is different from that of wetness.

The above ten principles all consist in dependent-arising. To see Shih from the standpoint of Li, we find forming [chen] and annulling [huai], unification [ho] as well as separation [li]. To see Li from the standpoint of Shih, we find revealing as well as concealing, one as well as many. [In the great Totality, therefore,]

contradiction and agreement all become harmonious with no im-
pediment and no obstruction, and all in all arise simultaneously.
One should meditate on this deeply to let the *view* clearly appear.
This is called the "Meditation of the Harmony and Non-Obstruction of Li and Shih."

COMMENT: The last paragraph reminds us that the principle of
Non-Obstruction of Li and Shih discussed in Tu Shun's essay was
written primarily for a spiritual purpose; that is *to let the view of*
Dharmadhātu emerge clearly before one's mind. It is, after all, not a
philosophical inquiry but an instruction in spiritual meditation. The
conclusion observes that in the great Totality even contradictions and
agreements have all become harmonious. Absolute harmony in terms
of the totalistic consistency is the mark of Hwa Yen Dharmadhātu.

The Dharmadhātu of Non-Obstruction of Shih against Shih (Shih-shih Wu-ai)

In the third Dharmadhātu of Li against Shih, we have seen how the
realm of Non-Obstruction is reached by reducing all Shih into Li not
merely as a non-differentiated whole but as a totalistic harmony of all
antitheses that is at once dynamic and unimpeded. So far as facilitating
men's comprehension of the principle of Non-Obstruction is concerned, this reasoning process of reducing the distinct phenomena
(Shih) into noumenon (Li) is perhaps necessary, but the realm of
Non-Obstruction itself, if it is a true fact, needs no such rationalization
for its existence. *It is simply so and profoundly so.* That is to say, no
reduction of Shih into Li is at all necessary to validate the Non-Obstruction of Shih against Shih, *which is the ultimate and the only*
Dharmadhātu that truly exists. The other three Dharmadhātus—the
Dharmadhātu of Shih, of Li, and of the Non-Obstruction of Li against
Shih—are merely explanatory expediencies to approach the fourth
Dharmadhātu of Shih-shih Wu-ai. They have no independent entity or
existence. The only Dharmadhātu that actually exists is Shih-shih Wu-
ai, and in its dimension each and every individual Shih enters into and
merges with all other Shih in perfect freedom, without the aid of Li.
This Non-Obstruction of Shih against Shih is elaborated through
either the so-called ten Non-Obstructions, or through the ten mysteries
by Fa Tsang and Chih Yen. To facilitate our discussion of Shih-shih

Wu-ai, let us first read Ch'êng Kuan's explanations on the meaning of Non-Obstruction in his essay *A Prologue to Hwa Yen*.[13]

> The Non-Obstruction of Totality in complete freedom [yüan-t'ung wu-ai] is to say that this very body of Buddha is Li and also Shih; It is one and also many; It is the dweller and also the world that is dwelt upon. It is the man who teaches and also the Dharma that is taught. It is identical with this and also with that; the same as sentient and as insentient beings. It is deep and also vast. It is the cause as well as the effect. . . . This is to say that the true Body of Buddha Vairocana is the great Dharmadhātu itself. Nothing is different from It. No divine revelation is required here to validate Its simultaneous identity with all beings since nothing is outside of the embrace of the Body of Dharmadhātu. . . .
>
> "It is one and also many" can be interpreted in two ways: either in the sense of the one Body-of-Reality [Dharmakāya] being completely identical with the numerous Bodies-of-Transformation [Nirmāṇakāya], or in the sense of the revelation of one Buddha's Body, in one location, [necessarily implying] the revelation of other Buddha's Bodies in other locations, since the one is identical with the many Bodies. . . . Because It is all-embracing, stretching out in every direction like space, we say that It is vast, and because It transcends all forms and shapes and even goes beyond the mark of Emptiness, we say It is deep. . . . "It is cause and It is also effect" means that there is no cause [in the light of Shih-shih Wu-ai] which can be regarded as truly different from effect and vice versa . . .

It is obvious that this completely free Non-Obstruction of Totality or Shih-shih Wu-ai is simply an annotation of the basic principle of mutual identity. In an elaborate style, it is now presented in the so-called ten Non-Obstructions. (See pp. 136–137.)

1. The Non-Obstruction of nature and Form.
2. The Non-Obstruction of immensity and smallness.
3. The Non-Obstruction of one and many.
4. The Non-Obstruction of mutual penetration.
5. The Non-Obstruction of mutual identity.
6. The Non-Obstruction of the hidden and the displayed.
7. The Non-Obstruction of the subtle ones.
8. The Non-Obstruction of Indra's net.
9. The Non-Obstruction of the ten times.

10. The Non-Obstruction of host and guest.

When given in a slightly different manner, these ten Non-Obstructions are also called the ten mysteries.

1. The mystery of simultaneous completion and mutual correspondence.
2. The mystery of Non-Obstruction of immensity and smallness.
3. The mystery of the mutual compatability of one and many in dissimilarities.
4. The mystery of the mutual identity of all dharmas in freedom.
5. The mystery of the establishment of concealment and disclosure in secrecy.
6. The mystery of mutual containment of the subtle ones.
7. The mystery of the realm of Indra's net.
8. The mystery of illustrating the truth through phenomena.
9. The mystery of the various formations of the ten times.
10. The mystery of the perfect illuminating host and guests.[14]

Without going into details, the reader can see promptly that the ten Non-Obstructions and the ten mysteries are synonymous—if not exactly identical—concepts. Therefore, an explanation of one will cover both. We will examine the latter, since they are more popular and better known.

It should be noted here that the so-called ten mysteries can actually be reduced to five or six principles. There is no compelling reason to make them *ten* except the Hwa Yen philosopher's obsession with this "auspicious and perfect number" which was considered to be indispensible in compositions. This procrustean approach, which orginated in the *Hwa Yen Sūtra* itself, has created an artificial style, thereby sometimes stifling the flowing spirit of its literature to the point of boredom. In the author's opinion, these ten mysteries can be comfortably reduced to five or six without sabotaging the general content. In sequence of importance, we shall now comment on them.

An Elaboration of the Ten Mysteries

FIRST: *The principle of simultaneous completeness in correspondence.* In Fa Tsang's essay *On the Golden Lion* we read, "The gold and the lion are simultaneously established. They are perfectly complete [in all aspects]. This is called the principle of simultaneous completion of mutual correspondence."

This is the chief principle among the ten mysteries; the other nine are merely elaborations of this basic principle. It can either be interpretated as representing the principle of Non-Obstruction of Li against Shih, or as the Non-Obstruction of Shih against Shih. In the former case, the gold is looked upon as Li or noumenon and the lion as Shih or the phenomenon; the two are mutually penetrating into and identical with one another. But since all these ten mysteries are supposedly elaborations of Shih-shih Wu-ai, an even better interpretation would be as follows. In the infinite Dharmadhātu, each and every thing (Shih) simultaneously includes all the rest of Shih and Li in perfect completion, without the slightest deficiency or omission, at all times. To see one object is, therefore, to see all objects and vice versa. This is to say a tiny individual particle within the minute cosmos of an atom actually contains the infinite objects and principles in the infinite universes of the future and of the remote past (of both mundane and transcendental categories) in the perfect completeness without omission. This implies not only the Non-Obstruction of space and time but more significantly, it implies the simultaneous existence of all causes and effects. In the dimension of Shih-shih Wu-ai all causes and effects, regardless of kind or of realm, must be simultaneously established without hindrance or omission.[15] Should we consider this to be a form of absolute determinism? From men's viewpoint, this certainly appears to be the case. How can effects in the future be brought into the past without first being determined? Here again we encounter the familiar Svabhāva way of thinking: determinativeness precedes all entities and events. Indeed the Non-Obstruction of time is even more difficult to imagine than the Non-Obstruction of space.

Fa Tsang comments on this first principle.

The mystery of simultaneous completeness means that all the above mentioned ten principles [16] simultaneously establish themselves in correspondence, to form a [totalistic] dependent-arising, without the differentiation of past or future, beginning or end. In this dimension, all and all establish themselves in perfect consistency and freedom. This establishment of totalistic dependent-arising makes all things and principles mutually penetrate into one another, yet does not upset their orders in any individual realm. By the power of the Ocean-Mirror Samādhi, all and all [in the Dharmadhātu] now come into view simultaneously like reflections in a mirror.

SECOND: *The principle of the wondrous projection of Mind-Only.* The simplest and easiest way to establish the Dharmadhātu of Shih-shih Wu-ai is by reason of this principle, for all the ten mysteries can find their justification through this principle alone. Yung Ming, the great Zen Pure-Land master of the Sung Dynasty, compiled his one-hundred-volume masterwork *On The Zen Mirror* (*Tsung Chin Lu*) stressing almost nothing but the doctrine of Mind-Only. In commenting on the ten mysteries in the light of the doctrine of Mind-Only, Yung Ming observes the following.[17]

All the ten mysteries are established by this one principle of the wondrous projection of Mind. The ten mysteries are not something beyond the doctrine of the One Mind. For example, the mind-of-equality implies the element of One; whereas the mind-of-distinctions implies the element of many. Inasmuch as this One Mind is all minds, the principle of identity and the principle of simultaneous correspondence are seen. Inasmuch as all minds enter into this One Mind, the principle of mutual penetration is seen. When One Mind takes in all minds, it is the concealment, and when all minds support the One Mind it is the disclosure. Not violating the mind-of-distinction and yet revealing the mind-of-equality, is the meaning of one within many; not damaging the mind-of-equality and yet revealing the mind-of-distinction, is the meaning of many within one. The subtle mind does not obstruct the vast mind, nor the vast the subtle; this is the meaning of the establishment of distinction between one and many. The One-Mind is pure, and the mind-of-distinction is mixed; since this true One Mind is the selfsame mind-of-distinction; the pure is the mixed and vice versa. This is the meaning of the principle of the pure and the mixed attributes of various storehouses. The One Mind can take in all minds and return them to the One Mind, this is the meaning of Indra's net. The external world is a projection of Mind, and from this projected world, one can also realize the true Mind. This is the principle of relying on the phenomenal things to elucidate the truth. The fast and the slow, the long and short kalpas are all established by the accumulation of thoughts and are projected by this One Mind. This is the meaning of the ten times. Inconceivable Dharmas can be preached through the truth of this One Mind. Men are thus led eventually to the realm of the Absolute, which is beyond words and thoughts. . . .

Feng Yu-Lan, in explaining the ten mysteries also follows this easy way out by relying entirely on the Mind-Only doctrine in his comment on *On The Golden Lion.*

THIRD: *The mystery of the mutual compatability of one and many in dissimilarities.* Fa Tsang comments on this in his essay *On The Golden Lion.*[18] "The gold and the lion are mutually compatible in their establishment. There is no obstruction between one and many. However, within this [total and harmonious mergence] each Li and Shih still keeps its own individual position and existence, remaining as one or many, without disarray or confusion."

The absolute Li is one, but the phenomenal Shih are many, and yet each and every Shih is a manifestation of this Li. Therefore, one is many and many are one. Although one and many are mutually compatible or even identical, this does not mean the annihilation of either the "one" or the "many." On the contrary, because of the emptiness of Selfhood, both one and many can be established without obstruction. This is the meaning of the mutual compatibility of one and many in dissimilarities.

Chih Yen in his book *The Ten Mysteries of the One Vehicle Doctrine of Hwa Yen*[19] observes:

Now, using [the numbers one to ten as] a metaphor to illustrate the doctrine: if you [repeatedly] count from one to ten and then count back from ten to one, [you will soon realize that] the ten is within the one, and the one is also within the ten. Because of the very fact that one contains ten, the word "one" is meaningful. If there were no "ten," then there would be no "one." [That is to say, if there were only a singular "one" in the whole universe, this so-called "one" would be meaningless. The very meaning of "one" depends therefore on many]. . . . Thus, it is owing to their void nature that all causations can be established. . . . [On the other hand,] if one existed alone, in its selfhood, the establishment of ten [or many] would be impossible. If there is no ten [or many], the establishment of one will also become impossible.

And in the same essay we read: [20]

QUESTION: If one is ten itself, why then is there a need for ten at all? If so, would not the proposition itself become meaningless?

ANSWER: When we say "one is identical with ten" this "one" is not the same "one" that men ordinarily think of, but a "one" of dependent-arising [yuan chen I]. The Sūtra says:

The one is not the one [as men see it];
It is merely preached
To destroy the ideas of numbers.
With their shallow intelligence,
Men grasp all things tight . . .
Their clinging, ignorant minds
Regard "one as one for sure!"

This stanza, however does not tell us clearly what this "one of dependent-arising" is; it nevertheless explicitly states that men's erroneous "one" is a persistent and uncompromising grasping which manifests itself as an inveterate tendency to regard "one as definitely one." Fa Tsang then comments on this.[21]

The so-called "one" is not the one-with-Selfhood [Svabhava], [it is the one of] dependent-arising; therefore, when we say one contains ten [or one is identical with ten] we mean the "one" of dependent-arising. Because, if it were the "one" with Selfhood, it would be a one of self-sufficiency and of isolation, excluding all other considerations and alternatives; this sort of Svabhava-one, if it exists at all, would certainly contravene the truth of dependent-arising. Furthermore, a Svabhava-one would necessarily nullify the original meaning and function of the word "one." It is therefore, not the true "one," but an arbitrary "one," [delusively conjectured]. The "one" that is truly meaningful is the one of dependent-arising, the one that is embraced by, and identical with many. In brief, to elicit the aspect of singleness or multiplicity from the dependent-arising Whole, is what we call the one or the many of dependent-arising.

Question: If everything is void and without Self-being or Selfhood, how then is it possible to have the so-called "one" or "many" at all?

Answer: Contrary to what you have just said, it is because of the very fact that *all things are devoid of Self-being* that the causation of one and many can be established. [Or, to answer your question in another manner, it is owing to] the dynamic power of dependent-arising, which forever expresses itself in accordance with the merit of the Dharmadhātu as shown in Bodhisattva Samantabhadra's wondrous realm, that [things can manifest themselves and yet be void at the same time]. Thus one and many are always [mutually] reinforcing but not interfering with or damaging to one another.[22] The *Vimalakīrti Sūtra* says:

> From the basis of non-abiding
> All dharmas are established.

Also the *Mādhyamika-karikas* says:

> It is through the truth of Voidness
> That all dharmas are established.

FOURTH: *The mystery of the various formations of ten times.* Fa Tsang comments on this in his essay *On The Golden Lion.*[23]

> The lion is a dharma produced by causes and conditions. It comes into being and goes out of existence at every moment [kṣana]. Each of these instants can be divided into the three periods of past, present, and future; and in each of these periods, three more periods of past, present, and future can again be divided. In this way there exist nine ages, grouping them together we have one total Dharma-gate [to truth]. Although [from a certain viewpoint] these nine ages are separate from one another and individually keep their own formations, [in reality] they are all harmoniously and simultaneously merged in the one great moment without obstruction. This is the mystery of the various formations of ten times.

In his *Hwa Yen I Hai Pei Men* Fa Tsang made these observations.[24]

> Regarding the harmonizing mergence of one moment with the aeons . . . since a single moment has no substance of its own, it becomes interchangeable with the great aeons. Because the great aeons have no substance, they also embrace the single moment. Since both the single moment and the great aeons have no substance, all the marks of the long and the short are merged into [a great harmony], hence all the universes that are far away or near by, all the Buddhas and sentient beings, and all things and events in the past, present, and future come into view simultaneously. Why is this so? Because all things and events are projections of Mind. [Since time is inseparable from events,] if one moment becomes non-obstructive, all dharmas will [automatically] become harmoniously merged. This is why all things and events in the three times vividly appear within one moment as stated in the Sūtra:

> One moment is the hundreds of thousands of aeons
> and hundreds of thousands of aeons are one moment.

Fa Tsang in his essay *The Gist of Hwa Yen Sūtra* and Yung Ming in his *On the Zen Mirror* both use the lotus flower as a metaphor to illucidate the principle of the ten mysteries. The metaphor is quoted originally from the chapter of the Ten Dhyānas of the *Hwa Yen Sūtra*. "O Son of Buddha, this Bodhisattva has a lotus flower; its vast size extends to the limits of the ten directions. . . . Beholding it, all sentient beings pay their sincere homage by making obeisance before it." Ch'êng Kuan comments on this in *A Prologue to Hwa Yen*.[25]

> Since this flower is omnipresent, it also embraces all times. This is to say that the three times, and their triple divisions, when all converged into one moment, make the total of the ten times . . .
>
> Time is no entity of itself, and the [very concept] of time is established through the [observation] of the object, [in this case] the flower. Since the flower becomes non-obstructive, time also becomes non-obstructive.
>
> The Sūtra says:
>
> The infinite kalpas in the past
> Can all be placed in the present
> And the future; and the infinite
> Kalpas in the future can be placed
> In the past [and also in the present] . . .
>
> In the past there is the future,
> And in the future, the present . . .
> The infinite kalpas are but one moment,
> And that moment is the infinite kalpas . . .
>
> Realizing this, one knows
> The incalculable kalpas are but
> One moment, and that moment
> Is no moment, thus one sees
> The reality of the universe.

Here we notice that the doctrine of Non-Obstruction of the ten times again pivots on two principles—mutual entering and mutual identity. Because of mutual entering, the past can enter into the present and future, and vice versa. Because of mutual identity, all the three times can be "contained" or "dissolved" into the one moment of "eternal present," which is actually a moment without moment, or a moment of total freedom from all bondage and limitations.

FIFTH: *The mystery of the establishment of concealment and disclosure in secrecy.* Fa Tsang comments on this in *On The Golden Lion.* "When we look at the lion [as lion], there is only lion and no gold. That is to say the lion is disclosed but the gold is hidden. When we look at the gold, there is only gold and no lion; hence, the gold is disclosed, but the lion is hidden. If we look at them simultaneously, they are both disclosed and hidden. Being hidden, they are secret; being disclosed, they are evident. This is called the establishment of concealment and disclosure in secrecy." Because of its philosophical importance, we repeat the explanation on this critical point that Ch'êng Kuan gave in *A Prologue to Hwa Yen.* (See pp. 126–127.)

> On the eighth date of a [lunar] month, half of the moon is bright and the other half dark; the very appearance of the bright part, [the disclosed] *affirms but does not negate* the existence of the hidden part. Likewise, the manifestation of something always implies the existence of the unmanifested or concealed part of the same thing. At the moment when the bright part of the moon is disclosed, the dark part also "secretly" establishes itself. This is the reason behind the so-called simultaneous establishment of concealment and disclosure in secrecy. . . . To use another parable, the size of the moon, as seen by men on earth, is no larger than a big ball, but a moon-dweller [supposing there were one] would see it as a colossal world. The perception of the moon as a ball, or as a world, does not increase or decrease the size of the [total] moon itself. When the large aspect is seen, only the aspect-of-large is disclosed, and the aspect-of-small is thereby hidden; and vice versa. . . .[26]

A proposition usually stresses either a "this" or a "that" aspect of an organic totality, because this is the way men usually think. Four possibilities of the interrelationships between "this" and "that" should be considered, according to *A Prologue to Hwa Yen.*

> First, when we stress "this," or when "this" takes in "that," "this" is disclosed and "that" is hidden.
>
> Second, when "that" is stressed, or when "that" takes in "this," "that" is disclosed and "this" is hidden.
>
> Third, the fact that at the very moment when "this" takes in "that," it does not impede the process by which "that" takes in "this," testifies the truth of the simultaneity of both disclosure and concealment.

Fourth, at the very moment when "this" takes in "that" which is the disclosure of "this," "that" also takes in "this"; therefore the first cannot be considered to be [the absolute] disclosure. Therefore, in this observation we say disclosure has vanished. [Based upon the same reasoning,] when "that" is taken into "this," which is the hiding or concealment of "that," "that" is simultaneously taking in "this," which is not hidden; hence, the hidden has vanished. So, in this observation, we say it is neither disclosure nor concealment.[27]

This passage perhaps represents a typical example of the Hwa Yen totalistic way of thinking. Its significance for understanding Hwa Yen philosophy cannot be overstressed.

When this Non-Obstruction of disclosure and concealment is applied to the principles of Li and Shih, the formation of the ten viewpoints is made. Fa Tsang in his *Arousing the Thought-of-Enlightenment in the Hwa Yen Doctrine* commented on this.[28]

This again can be discussed from ten viewpoints:
1. When the abstract principle [Li] is viewed to subsist an event [Shih], the principle is hidden [because the event is displayed].
2. When an event is viewed to be identical with the abstract principle, the principle is displayed [because the event is hidden].
3. Because the principle and the event are inseparable, both the displayed and the hidden simultaneously establish themselves.
4. When the principle and the event are viewed as mutually negating, neither the displayed nor the hidden can be established.
5. Inasmuch as the principle "subsists" the event without losing itself, the very hidden is the displayed.
6. Inasmuch as the event is exhausted without nullifying other events, the displayed is the hidden.
7. Inasmuch as the preceding two principles are never separated from each other, both the displayed and the hidden are identical.
8. Inasmuch as the principle and the event mutually negate each other, they are both annulled, and neither the displayed nor the hidden is possible.
9. Inasmuch as the preceding eight principles all share the self-

same Li [truth] without obstructing one another, they are all displayed at the same time.

10. Inasmuch as these principles mutually negate one another, all assertions are nullified; thus, the at-onement of these principles is the selfsame non-at-onement.

SIXTH: *The mystery of Non-Obstruction of immensity and minuteness.* This principle was made by Fa Tsang to substitute Chih Yen's original second principle of the pure and mixed attributes of various storehouses. To explain this principle Ch'êng Kuan again used the metaphor of the lotus flower which was alluded to before.[29] The Sūtra says: "This Bodhisattva has a lotus flower; its vast size extends to the limits of the ten directions. . . . Beholding it, all sentient beings pay their sincerest homage by making obeisance before it."

This lotus flower extends to the edge of all Dharmadhātus, and yet it does not, by this fact, do violence to its own position. Because a portion is not a portion, and a non-portion is a portion, the immensity and minuteness can therefore both be free without obstruction or hindrances.

From this metaphor one can simultaneously draw four reflections.

1. It symbolizes the sole infinity: the lotus extends to the limits of all ten directions.

2. It symbolizes limitation and distinctions: there are sentient beings who, upon seeing it "from the outside," pay their homage to the flower.

3. It implies that infinity is the selfsame limitation: the infinite Li is the selfsame limited Shih.

4. It implies the annulment of both infinity and limitation: from the viewpoint of Śūnyatā, neither of them actually exists.

Ch'êng Kuan observes further in the same essay: "The so-called 'minuteness' is that which, having no space within itself, has no inside; the so-called 'immensity' is that which, having no boundary, has no outside. That which is without an outside, the vast Buddha-Body and Land, can enter that which is without an inside, the minute dust-mote. This is the Non-Obstruction of immensity and minuteness."

The Sūtra says:

All infinite Vajra Mountains
Can be poised on the tip of a hair. . . .

> A Bodhisattva who longs to know
> How the immense can be minute
> Arouses his first Bodhicitta
> And sets his mind on Enlightenment.

The large must include the small to be called the large, and the small must contain the large to be called the small. Because they have no Selfhood, the large and the small can mutually contain each other. Because they have no isolated existence, the wide and the narrow can each include the other. Thus we know that the so-called "large" is the large of the small, and the so-called "small" is the small of the large. There is no definite nature to the small, because it even stretches to cover all the ten directions, and there is no definite shape to the large, because all aeons are vividly revealed in one moment. Since the very small is the very large, Mount Sumeru is contained in a mustard seed; and since the very large is the very small, the ocean is included in a hair. If their Selfhood is not annulled, how can they enter and withdraw without handicap? On the other hand, because they all keep their original forms, they can stretch and roll up without impediments.

SEVENTH: *The mystery of the realm of Indra's net.* This is actually a repetition of the previous principle of the Non-Obstruction of immensity and minuteness. It is said in the *Hwa Yen Sūtra* that high above in heaven, on the roof of the palace of the God Indra, there hang innumerable ornaments in the form of small crystal marbles. They are interlaced in various patterns forming a great complex network. Because of the reflection of light, not only does each and every one of these marbles reflect the entire cosmos, including the continents and oceans of the human world down below, but at the same time they reflect one another, including all the reflected images in each and every marble, without omission. This parable is, in fact, a parallel to the demonstration of the interpenetration of realm-embracing-realm through the exhibition of inter-mirror reflections given by Fa Tsang to Empress Wu.[30] Ch'êng Kuan comments on this in *A Prologue to Hwa Yen.*

> Because a dust-mote is [identical with, or is] an expression of the ultimate Reality, it can therefore contain all things. . . . Since all the universes contained within a dust-mote are also expressions of Reality, they too contain all other universes . . . this observation goes on indefinitely, and thus realms-embracing-realms ad

infinitum are established. An illustration of this truth can be seen by either the demonstration of the interreflection of mirrors, or by the metaphor of the marbles of Indra's net. . . . The innumerable images reflected within a [crystal] marble is comparable to the infinite universes contained within a dust-mote. This, however, is only the first realm. When each marble [and its reflections are] seen in all the other marbles and vice versa, the realms-embracing-realms ad infinitum then come into view. . . .[31]

In the essay of *On The Golden Lion* Fa Tsang explains, "In each eye, ear, joint and hair of the lion, there is a golden lion. All the lions, in all hairs simultaneously enter into a single hair, and yet in each and every hair [of the lions], there again exist infinite lions. Each and every hair, in turn, brings these infinite lions back into the [original] single hair. In this manner there is an endless progression of realms-embracing-realms, just like the jewels of Indra's net. This is called the mystery of the realm of Indra's net." [32]

EIGHTH: *The mystery of the Non-Obstruction of the subtle ones.* This is a restatement of the principle that infinite universes do exist within a small atom or dust-mote, and within each and every dust-mote of these universes there again exist infinite universes. A view of realms-embracing-realms ad infinitum is thus established. The reason for the term *the subtle ones,* according to Ch'êng Kuan, is due to the infinitesimal smallness and "subtlety" of this sphere stretching far beyond the reach of man's comprehension. We read in the essay *On The Golden Lion:* "The gold and the lion may be [viewed] as the disclosed or the hidden, the one or the many, the pure or the mixed, the potent or the impotent. The one is the other, the host and guest interchange their radiance. Both Li and Shih equally reveal themselves. They are mutually compatible; neither is the least obstructive to the formation of the other. This is achieved even in the realm of the minute and the subtle, and is called the mystery of the Non-Obstruction of the subtle ones." [33]

NINTH: *The mystery of mutual identity among things in freedom.* This is a restatement of the basic principle of mutual identity. It reads thus in *On The Golden Lion:* "All the various organs of the lion down to each tip of hair all take in the lion in so far as they are all gold.

Each and every one of them completely penetrates the eyes of the lion in its embrace. The eyes are the ears, the ears are the nose, the nose is the tongue and the tongue is the body. In this manner they are all established in total freedom without any hindrance or obstruction.[34]

TENTH: *The mystery of the perfect illuminating ruler and retinues.* This principle stresses the fact that nothing can come into being alone by itself. Through the principle of dependent-arising things are brought into existence with a combination of factors. A main subject owes its existence to its associated factors and vice versa. However, in any particular event of a particular realm with a definite orientation no more than one subject is allowed, lest the phenomenal order be violated or nullified. Here, the orientation is not synthetic, it is analytical; it follows not the usual approach of "both . . . and," but the approach of "either . . . or."

Ch'êng Kuan comments on this in *A Prologue to Hwa Yen.*[35]

The Sūtra says that when Bodhisattva Fa Hui preaches the doctrines of the ten stages, innumerable Bodhisattvas of other universes all come to the assembly and claim that, in their own universes, their Bodhisattvas also preach the same doctrine; the meaning, principle and even the words are not different. [Although this implies the universal presence and validity of Dharma activities, what is significant here is that] when Fa Hui of this universe is treated as the ruler [or main subject] he cannot be treated also as the retinue [or the subordinate factors] at the same time. When all other Bodhisattvas in the ten directions are treated as retinue, they cannot be considered to be the ruler simultaneously. *This* ruler, when so designated, cannot see *that* ruler face to face at the same time. [So far as the inter-universe relationship of ruler and retinues is concerned] when a particular ruler in another universe is designated, the ruler here should be treated only as retinue. Therefore, we say that ruler and ruler do not see each other face to face, nor do retinues and retinues.

The implication of the above statement is that the all-merging Totality does not in any manner damage or impede the order of any *individual realm,* nor does it do any violence to a *broader order,* when two or more separate universes are treated as an integral unit.

This principle was proposed by Fa Tsang, and it was not included in Chih Yen's original list.

The Harmonious Mergence of the Six Forms

A discussion of the Hwa Yen philosophy of Non-Obstruction would be incomplete without mentioning the principle of the "harmonious mergence of the six forms" (lu-hsiang yüan-jung). Lu-hsiang yüan-jung seems to be merely a different way to explain the basic principles of mutual entering and mutual identity by observing the interdependency of three pairs of antitheses—wholeness and diversity (tsung hsiang and pieh hsiang), universality and particularity (t'ung hsiang and i hsiang), formation and distintegration (chen hsiang and huai hsiang) —which make up the so-called six forms. Fa Tsang explains this in his essay *On The Golden Lion*.[36]

> The lion [as an integrated entity] represents the wholeness [tsung hsiang]; whereas the five organs, inasmuch as they are different [from the whole], represent [the parts] or diversity [pieh hsiang]. Inasmuch as the lion as a whole and the various differentiated organs are both brought into being by the principle of dependent-arising, they share the quality of universality. At the same time, however, the eyes and ears do not overlap [in their functions] but keep their diversified particularities. Inasmuch as the combination of these various organs makes up the lion, there is the formation, and inasmuch as each of these organs occupies its own particular position, there is the disintegration.

Fa Tsang elaborates this further in his book *The Doctrines of Hwa Yen One Vehicle in Sections*.[37]

> Question: What is the so-called wholeness [tsung hsiang]?
> Answer: A house, for instance, is a good example for [wholeness].
>
> Question: [The so-called] house is but a combination of beams, [roof, walls, and so forth]. Which one among these elements is what you called the "house"?
> Answer: The beams [and so on] themselves are the house per se. Why? Because, all the beams, [roof, and walls] themselves can establish the house. Apart from beams [and so forth], there would be no house. As soon as the [concept] of beams is established, the [concept] of house is also simultaneously established.
>
> Question: If the beams can completely establish the house by itself without the [assistance] of tiles, [walls, floors, and so on], are you then implying that a house can be constructed by beams alone?

Answer: [No, this is not so], because if there were no tiles, [walls, or floors], the very name of beam would lose its meaning. The very concept of "beam" depends on tiles [and] walls. [The whole thing should be observed through a totalistic and organic approach.] Therefore, to say beams alone can form the house simply makes no sense here. . . .

On the other hand, the so-called diversity [pieh hsiang] means that the elements, the beams and so on, are different from the wholeness. Because, if there were no diversified distinctions among these elements, wholeness itself would not have been possible. No diversity means no wholeness. What does this mean? It means that because of the existence of diversities, wholeness is established; if there were no diversities, the establishment of wholeness would be impossible. Following the same reasoning, diversity is also established through wholeness.

Question: If wholeness *is* diversity itself [i.e. the principle of mutual identity], then the establishment of wholeness would be impossible [because your claim of mutual identity nullifies the separate existence of diversity and wholeness].

Answer: Contrary to what you have just said, it is just because wholeness is diversity itself that wholeness can be established [and not otherwise]. For instance, inasmuch as beams [and other parts] are the house itself, it is called the wholeness; [and inasmuch as the house] is beams themselves, it is called diversity. If beams are not the house itself, then they cannot be considered to be the [totalistically true] house. The mutual identity of wholeness and diversity is seen through this observation.

Question: But if the principle of mutual identity is true, how can you then assert the existence of diversities at all?

Answer: Contrary to what you have said, it is just because [the wholeness and diversities] are mutually identical that diversities can be established [and not otherwise]. Because, if the two are not identical, then wholeness must exist outside of the diversities and vice versa; hence, the impossibility of the wholeness of diversities. . . .

What is being stressed here is the fact that each component of any pair of antitheses, be it diversity or wholeness, formation or distintegration, the differentiated particulars or the non-differentiated universality, cannot be considered in isolation as if it had an independent existence (Svabhāva) . If there were no diversities, particularities, and disintegration, there would have been no wholeness, universality, and formation. Each component of the antithesis depends upon the others for its meaning and existence. They should be observed from an organic and totalistic orientation exemplified in the Hwa Yen concept of interpenetration and mutual identity. The parallel concept is found in the mutual identity of form and emptiness in the *Heart Sūtra*. Therefore, lu-hsiang yuan-jung is merely an extension of the same observation made in the Prajñāpāramitā literature.

NOTES [Part II, Section 2]

1. See lecture eight, "Nature Alive" in Whitehead's *Modes of Thought* (New York, 1938).
2. Ibid.
3. Ibid.
4. Ibid.
5. *Taisho* 1867, p. 512.
6. This story, though well-known in the West, may not be a story of Zen Buddhism. I have failed to locate its source in the Chinese Zen literature, but it is possible that it might be from certain Zen sources of a later period. Although its original source is unknown, it is an extremely important and pointed story.
7. Irving Copi, *Introduction to Logic* (New York, 1954), p. 273.
8. See T. R. V. Murti's *The Central Philosophy of Buddhism* (London: Allen and Unwin, 1955), pp. 45–50.
9. *Taisho* 1867, p. 511.
10. *Taisho* 1871, p. 594.
11. See the text in the third chapter of Part III.
12. Here the three words *omnipresent, harmonious and fusing* are just the translation of the one Chinese word *jung*, which in this context is extremely hard to render accurately. Taisho, 1884, p. 688.
13. Ch'êng Kuan, *A Prologue to Hwa Yen, Hwa Yen Su Ch'ao* (published by Hwa Yen Lien She, Taipei, 1966), Chap. II, p. 71.
14. See *On The Golden Lion* in chapter III. There are two different versions of the ten mysteries, the old and the new. The old ten mysteries were proposed by Chih Yen and the new by Fa Tsang. The list given here is the new version which changes the second mystery, the mystery of the pure and the mixed attributes of various storehouses, of the old version into the mystery of Non-Obstruction of immensity and smallness; it also changes the mystery of universal accomplishment through the projection of Mind-Only into the mystery of the perfect illuminating host and guest. See Ch'êng Kuan's *A Prologue to Hwa Yen*, Chap. V, pp. 29–33.
15. Ibid., pp. 29–37.
16. *Taisho* 1866, p. 505.
17. *Taisho* 2016, p. 644.
18. *Taisho* 1881, pp. 668–70.
19. *Taisho* 1868, p. 514. This is a selected and abridged translation.
20. *Taisho* 1868, p. 514.
21. *Taisho* 1866, p. 503.
22. *Taisho* 1866, p. 503.

23. *Taisho* 1881, p. 670.
24. *Taisho* 1875, p. 630.
25. Ch'êng Kuan, *A Prologue to Hwa Yen,* Chap. V, pp. 56–58.
26. Ibid., Chap. V, pp. 48–49.
27. Ibid., Chap. V, pp. 47–48.
28. *Taisho* 1878, p. 654.
29. Ch'êng Kuan, Chap. V, pp. 38–40.
30. See Fa Tsang's Hall of Mirrors in Part I of this book.
31. Ch'êng Kuan, Chap. V, pp. 51–53.
32. *Taisho* 1881, p. 669.
33. Ibid., p. 670.
34. Ibid., pp. 669–70. This is the sixth mystery in the text *On The Golden Lion;* whereas in Fa Tsang's new version it becomes the ninth mystery.
35. Ch'êng Kuan, Chap. V, p. 60.
36. *Taisho* 1881, p. 670.
37. *Taisho* 1866, pp. 507–508.

Section Three
The Doctrine of Mind-Only

THE MIND AND THE EXTERNAL WORLD

Ch'êng Kuan in his *A Prologue to Hwa Yen* gave ten reasons for the all-merging Dharmadhātu. The first reads,[1] "It is because all things are merely manifestations of the Mind, that all dharmas can all merge through and through, in the realm of Totality." He comments on this in the same volume. "This is to say that all things are projected by the True Mind. As the water in the great ocean manifests itself in waves with its total body, so the small and large forms of things are all transformed by the Mind; this is possible, because all dharmas are identical with the One Mind. Hence, if the mind enters the realm of Non-Obstruction, so will all the dharmas."

This first reason uses the Mind-Only Doctrine to validate the principle of Dharmadhātu, and it is held by many scholars to be the cardinal argument of Hwa Yen philosophy. On the surface, it seems that the doctrine of Mind-Only is repeatedly stressed in the Hwa Yen literature, giving us the impression that the entire Hwa Yen teaching is based on a philosophy of idealism. This is actually not the case. I, personally, believe that the three main philosophies—the philosophies of Emptiness, of Totality, and of Mind-Only—are equally important in the establishment of Hwa Yen doctrine. Among the three, however, the philosophy of Śūnyatā, rather than Mind-Only, seems to play a more vital role, for it is quite conceivable that the Hwa Yen Totality cen be established without the aid of the Doctrine of Mind-Only, *but not without the support of Śūnyatā.*

This is witnessed in the essay *On the Meditation of Dharmadhātu,* the most important philosophical essay of the Hwa Yen School. In the very beginning of the essay, the author, Master Tu Shun, tried to lay a sound foundation for the all-embracing Totality by first introducing the principles of the True Voidness. *Throughout the entire essay*

Mind-Only is never mentioned. Thus, we know that Hwa Yen Totality can be established by the principle of śūnyatā alone without resorting to the Mind-Only principles. This does not by any means imply that Mind-Only is unimportant. The convictions that the objective world is merely a projection of the Mind, that outside of the Universal Mind nothing whatsoever truly exists, that reality is discoverable within one's own Mind, that all value and meaning, however considered, consist in Mind itself, that liberation and Enlightenment are made possible by transforming one's own Mind, and so forth, are held by devotees in many faiths including, of course, the Mahāyānists, for these principles are also stressed again and again in many Mahāyāna scriptures. A few examples are given below.

From the *Laṇkāvatāra Sūtra:* [2]

[Mind] is the measure [of all things]; it is the abode of self-nature, and has nothing to do with causation and the world; it is perfect in its nature, absolutely pure. This is the measure indeed, I say.

Mind is beyond all philosophical views; it is apart from discrimination; it is not attainable, nor is it ever born; I say, there is nothing but Mind.

Suchness, Emptiness, the limit, Nirvāṇa, Dharmadhātu, variety of will-bodies—they are nothing but Mind, I say.

What appears to be external does not exist in reality; it is indeed Mind that is seen as multiplicity; the body, property and abode—all these, I say, are nothing but Mind.

That which can take and that which is taken—all these, I say, are nothing but Mind.

All pairs of subject/object are manifestations of Mind, without a self or self-belonging; the Brahman and the gods—all these, I say, are nothing but Mind. Apart from the Mind, in short, nothing whatsoever exists! [3]

From the *Hwa Yen Sūtra:* [4]

Thereupon, the Bodhisattva Chüeh Lin, blessed by the grace of Buddha, observed the ten directions and gave voice to the following statement:

"Just as a painter mixes and blends the various
Colors [in his paintings], so by the delusory
Projections of Mind are made the various forms

Of all phenomena. Yet the four elements
Indicate no such distinctions.

"No colors in the [four] elements can be
Found, nor the [four] elements in the colors.
The paintings are not found in the Mind,
Nor is there a Mind within the paintings.
Yet without the Mind
No painting can be made.

"The Mind eternally abides in naught,
Being beyond all thoughts and measures!
Yet, It manifests all forms and colors
Without either knowing the other.

"Not knowing his Self-Mind, a painter
Can still draw pictures through It. For
This is the nature of all dharmas.
[Indeed, such is the dharma-nature!]

"The mind is like a skillful painter;
It draws the pictures of all worlds,
Creating all including the five skandhas!

"The Buddha differs not from the Mind,
Nor sentient beings from the Buddhas.
Yet, both Mind and Buddhas are by nature infinite!
He who knows the Mind as the creator of all worlds,
Sees the Buddha and His true essence.

"The Mind abides not in the body,
Nor the body in the Mind. Yet all
Buddha's acts are done with ease and freedom.

"If You want to know all the Buddhas in the past, the present,
And the future, just observe the nature of the universe—
That one's own Mind creates the total and everything!

"All the realms of sentient beings
Are within the three times;
All beings of these times
Subsist on the five skandhas
Which have karmas as their ground;
All karmas are rooted in one's Mind,
Which like all the worlds and universes
Is but a phantom or a magic play!" [5]

From *The Awakening of Faith:* [6]

"The principle is the Mind of sentient beings. This Mind includes in Itself all states of beings in the phenomenal world as well as in the transcendental world. It is on the basis of this Mind that the [entire] meaning of Mahāyāna can be elucidated. Why? Because, this Mind, as the [eternal] Suchness, *is* no other than the essence of Mahāyāna itself; and, as the rise-and-fall of phenomena, *can* demonstrate the essence, form and functions of Mahāyāna. . . .

The principle of this One Mind has two aspects. One is the aspect of Mind as Suchness, and the other is the Mind as the rise-and-fall of phenomena. Each of the two aspects embraces all states of beings. Why? Because they are inseparable or [mutually inclusive]. . . .[7]

This Mind has five different names.[8] The first is called the "karma-mind." This means that by the force of ignorance, the Mind is stirred to move without being aware of it.

The second is called the "evolving mind." This means that [only] by relying on a mind that is constantly moving can one perceive objects [in the phenomenal world].

The third is called "reflecting-mind." This is to say, that just as a bright mirror can reflect all material images instantaneously, so the mind can reflect all objects of phenomena at once, when it confronts the five sense objects. This is because this "reflecting-mind" arises spontaneously at all times when it encounters [any dharma].

The fourth is called the "distinguishing-mind." This means that it can distinguish the differences between the pure and the defiled dharmas.

The fifth is called the "continuing-mind," for it is constantly associated with [all sorts] of *thoughts,* without any interruption. [On the one hand], it preserves and upholds all the good and bad karmas accumulated in the infinite lives of the past, without losing them; and on the other hand, it can also ripen all the present and future karmas, and bring their respective fruits, painful or pleasant, into effect without making any mistake. It can also cause one to recollect things in the past and present and inspire fantasies of things to come in the future. Therefore all [things] in the three worlds are unreal and delusory; they are only projections of the Mind. Apart from the Mind there are no objects of the six consciousnesses. What does this mean? This means that since all dharmas are projected by the Mind and its deluded thoughts, all distinctions are in fact acts of distinguishing one's own mind. But the mind cannot see the Mind, for there is no form whatsoever that can be obtained. Therefore, one should know that all the objects and experiences of this world are sustained only by men's ignorant and deluded minds. Just like the images reflected from a mirror, all things are devoid of a true entity; they are false, delusory, and of Mind-Only, because only when mind arises do all things arise; when mind stops [its function], all things also cease to exist.

From the above quotations, the reader may get a general idea about the Mind-Only doctrine as presented in the Mahāyāna scriptures. Attempts have been made to verify this doctrine throughout the ages, by Mahāyāna thinkers and by those Yogācāra scholars who have undertaken the colossal task of trying to prove that the objective world, "so concrete and so real," is merely a projection, a reflection, a shadow, a portion or a "whatnot" of this insubstantial mind. These thinkers have built around their doctrine an extremely complicated system of radical idealism to challenge one's fanciful imagination and sagacious judgment. Philosophically speaking, Yogācāra may or may not be as important as Mādhyamika, depending on one's personal judgment and predispositions; but with respect to Buddhist doctrine, Yogācāra seems to be more useful in expounding the essential ideas of Mahāyāna, because of its bountiful technical vocabularies (fa hsiang). Its old-fashioned, over-systematized approach may appear to be out of date for the present age, but it has provided an extremely useful tool for a better comprehension of the kaleidoscopic Mahāyāna doctrines up to this time. A highly complicated philosophy of idealism was offered by this School to "verify" the Mind-Only doctrine. But since most philosophical systems are notoriously inconclusive and often unconvincing, it will be of little value to introduce the Yogācāra philosophy here at length. To elaborate in full this highly complex and technical system is obviously beyond the scope of this book and would not serve any important purpose here.

Perhaps a much simpler way of approaching this problem is to attempt to understand why Buddhism claims this idea of Mind-Only, and on what rational grounds its followers accept and interpret it. Despite its vast accumulation of literature, richly abounding in philosophical systems and ideas, Buddhism is primarily a *religion*. Since a religion *always begins with someone's experience,* so does Buddhism and its sub-schools and sects. In contrast to those philosophical systems created purely out of fanciful speculations, nearly every major doctrine found in the various Buddhist schools originated from the direct experience of the founder or founders of that particular school. Nāgārjuna and Asanga of India, Gambopa and Lunchin Rabjhung of Tibet, Tu Shun and Hui Yuan of China, are only a few examples of those influential and significant founders. All were great yogis who had gained profound realizations before they undertook the task of propagating their discoveries. According to tradition, even the pedantic and abstruse Abhidharma Collection is said to be a compilation of works composed by many arhat-scholars in the light of their inner experiences.[9]

The endorsement of the Mind-Only doctrine by most Buddhist sages was, therefore, due primarily to a conviction derived from their experience. This experience, so intimately and repeatedly witnessed, was too overwhelming to neglect or to explain away. It is quite understandable that those who had it would have a great urge to convey it to others. But the difficulty is that those who have not had the experience cannot understand it properly unless the description is given in comprehensible languages and in terms befitting their modes of thought. When descriptions became inadequate, and acclamations unconvincing to the listeners, then the scholar-priests had no other choice but to turn to philosophizing. The doctrine of Mind-Only should therefore not be treated as a mere system of speculative philosophy, but as exposition and arguments whose purpose is to elucidate and rationalize a religious experience and insight. Accounts evidencing the truth of Mind-Only in the yogic experience are bountiful in Buddhist literature. Here are some examples from Zen sources.

From the Autobiography of Master Han Shan: [10]

After some time Miao Fêng [my friend] went to Yeh T'ai, while I remained alone. I fixed my mind upon one thought and spoke to no one. If anyone came to the door I merely looked at him and said nothing. After a while, whenever I looked at people, they appeared like dead logs. My mind entered a state in which I could not recognize a single word. At the start of this meditation, when I heard the howling of the storms and the sound of the ice grinding against the mountains, I felt very disturbed. The tumult seemed as great as that of thousands of soldiers and horses in battle. [Later] I asked Miao Fêng about it. He said, "All feelings and sensations arise from one's own mind; they do not come from outside. Have you heard what the monks in the old days said? 'If one does not allow his mind to stir when he hears the sound of flowing water for thirty years, he will come to the realization of the miraculous understanding of Avalokiteśvara.' "

I then went to sit on a solitary wooden bridge and meditated there every day. At first, I heard the stream flowing very clearly, but as time passed I could hear the sound only if I willed it. If I stirred my mind, I could hear it, but if I kept my mind still I heard nothing. One day, while sitting on the bridge, I suddenly felt that I had no body. It had vanished, together with the sound around me. Since then I have never been disturbed by any sound.

My daily food was a gruel of bran, weeds, and rice water. When I first came to the mountain someone had given me three packs of rice, which lasted for more than six months. One day, after having my gruel, I took a walk. Suddenly I stood still, filled with the realization that I had no body and no mind. All I could see was one great illuminating Whole, omnipresent, perfect, lucid, and serene. *It was like an all-embracing mirror from which the mountains and rivers of the earth were projected as reflections.* When I awoke from this experience, I felt as "clear-and-transparent" as though my body and mind did not exist at all, whereupon I composed the following stanza:

In a flash, the violent mind stood still;
Within, without are both transparent and clear.
After the great somersault
The great Void is broken through.
Oh, how freely come and go
The myriad forms of things!

From then on, both the inward and the outward experience became lucidly clear. Sounds, voices, visions, scenes, forms, and objects were no longer hindrances. All my former doubts dissolved into nothing. When I returned to my kitchen, I found the cauldron covered with dust. Many days had passed during my experience, of which I, being alone, was unaware.

Now let us read an account by another Zen monk, from the *Autobiography of Master Hsüeh Yen:* [11]

[The chief monk, Hsiu, said to me], "You should sit erect on your seat, keep your spine straight, make your whole body and mind become one Hua Tou,[12] and pay no attention to drowsiness or wild thoughts." Working in accord with his instructions, I unknowingly forgot both my body and mind—even their very existence. For three days and three nights my mind stayed so serene and clear that I never closed my eyes for a single moment. On the afternoon of the third day I walked through the three gates of the monastery as if I were sitting. Again I came across Hsiu. "What are you doing here?" he asked. "Working on Tao," I answered. He then said, "What is this you call the Tao?" Not able to answer him, I became more confused and perplexed. With the intention of meditating further I turned back toward the meditation hall. But accidentally I met Hsiu again. He said, "Just open your eyes and see what it is!" After this admonishment I was even more anxious to return to the meditation hall than before. As I was just going to sit down, something broke abruptly before my face as if the ground were sinking away. I wanted to tell how I felt, but I could not express it. Nothing in this world can be used as a simile to describe it. Immediately I went to find Hsiu. As soon as he saw me he said, "Congratulations!" Holding my hand, he led me out of the monastery. We walked along the river dike, which was full of willow trees. I looked up at the sky and down at the earth. [I actually felt] that *all phenomena and manifestations, the things I saw with my eyes and heard with my ears, the things that disgusted me—including the passion-desires and the blindness—all flowed out from my own bright, true, and marvelous Mind.* During the next fortnight no moving phenomena appeared in my mind.

A few more quotations, which give no first-hand account of the experience but provide some illustrations and reasonings of the Mind-Only doctrine, follow. From Asanga's *An Outline of Mahāyāna Doctrine (Mahāyāna-samparigraha-Śāstra)* . vol. II, p. 2: [13]

With what metaphors can we illustrate the principle [of Mind-Only]? With dreams and so forth. This is to say that all dream-[visions] do not truly exist; they are but [manifestations of the] Mind. Although various forms, sounds, smells, tastes, touches, houses, woods, mountains . . . are projected therein, they are not truly existent. With this metaphor one can understand that in all times and places, all things are but the Mind. . . .
Question: When one awakes from the dream, he realizes at once that everything he saw in his dream was but a projection of his

own Mind. If what you have said is true, that *all things at all places and times* are but manifestations of the Mind, then why don't we realize this truth when we awake?

Answer: When [one reaches Enlightenment, or when] the true Wisdom is awakened, he will then come to the realization. This is just the same as when one does not realize the nature of a dream while he is dreaming. By the same token, when one has not yet awakened from the dream of saṁsāra, a full realization of the truth of Mind-Only will not come to him.

From the *Sūtra of Elucidation on the Profound Hidden Meaning:* [14]

The Bodhisattva Maitreya asked the World-Honored One, "Should we say that the visions and images seen by the act of Samādhi are different, or are not different, from the Mind?" Buddha replied, "You should say that they are not different from the Mind. Why? Because these images are, on the one hand, things-perceived-by-the-Mind, and on the other, manifestations of the Mind. Hence they are all of the Mind."

"In that case, my Lord, if the visions and images do not differ from the Mind, why does the Mind grasp the Mind itself?"

"Maitreya, there is not a single dharma that can grasp any other dharma. However, when this Mind arises *in such a manner,* the images will also manifest in such a corresponding manner. For example, when something is used as an object for seeing, one sees this object [and nothing else], but some people [erroneously] claim that what they see is only the image of the object—not the object itself. Likewise, when the Mind arises, the images that appear to be different and apart from the Mind, also arise. . . . When in the Samādhi [of observing impurities] one sees bruises, festers, boils, bones, skeleton, and so forth . . . what he actually sees is but his own Mind and nothing else. For this reason a Bodhisattva should know that in all states of all consciousnesses, [whatever one sees and perceives] is not an objective 'things-perceived' but his own subjective Mind. Again, one should notice the fact that when one sees the bruises, boils, skeletons, and so forth, during Samādhi, it is a direct perceiving at the present moment, unlike the 'object-perceived' seen in memory [and in ratiocinations]. The consciousness of grasping and of memory, that which is established through the medium of words and learning, perceives [mainly] things in the past, [thus *indirectly,*] but even these perceived-objects are obviously manifested by the mind. Therefore, [either by judging the immediate experience, or by judging the intermediate 'object-perceived' in the past,] the truth of the Mind-Only doctrine can be proved with certainty. By these reasonings a Bodhisattva, though he has not yet obtained genuine Wisdom, can infer the truth of Mind-Only without error."

It seems as though anyone who has made a genuine effort to "turn his mind inward" for any length of time, would eventually become an idealist of one kind or another. The farther and deeper he digs into the bottomless Mind within, the more radical an idealist he will become. It is said that the realization of the Mind-Only truth develops gradually, in a stage-by-stage pattern. In the initial stage of realization, the enlightened yogi will notice the fact that the whole universe has always been a reflection of his own mind—hitherto misconceived. The objective external world now becomes unreal, like a mirage—no longer concrete, as it appeared before. In the next stage, the yogi will begin to acquire a partial mastery over his mind and he will be able to abolish, create, or transform all "perceived-objects" at will. If he wishes, he can also enter a state of non-distinction, thus completely obliterating all the different things in the objective world.

When one reaches this state he will inevitably become a radical idealist, for he has now witnessed himself what the Mind-Only doctrine really means. The objective world and its laws now appear as capricious and unreal to him as the self-made visions of a wandering mind.

Finally, the Buddhist tradition claims that when one reaches the last stage, he can even transform his own physical body, as well as the objective world around him, in any way he desires. A great many accounts of demonstrations of such miraculous powers are recorded in Buddhist scriptures; one may relegate them to the level of pure fantasy, but it is noteworthy that this "brave new world" of ours is not very conducive to the production of men with such abilities today.

THE ĀLAYA CONSCIOUSNESS
AND TOTALITY

A few points of the Mind-Only doctrine should be made clear here. The word *mind* used in Hwa Yen as well as in Yogācāra has a very broad meaning. It is at once psychological and metaphysical, ethical and religious. It is the total psyche of man, including both the conscious and unconscious. To simplify the issue, we may ignore the highly complicated analysis and "mapping" of the Eight Consciousnesses [15] as given in the Yogācāra system, and discuss only a few essential points of the most noteworthy issue in the Mind-Only doctrine; namely, the concept of the Ālaya (or Store) Consciousness, which is also called the Karma-Supporting Consciousness, Fundamental Consciousness, the Consciousness of All Seeds, and so forth. The major characteristics and function of this Ālaya Consciousness, as viewed by the Yogācāra system, can be summarized as follows:

1. It functions blindly and autonomously without self-awareness or self-control.[16] It is, therefore, a kind of unconscious beyond the control of the everyday mind in normal circumstances.

2. It is a great reservoir that holds or stores all mental impressions and learning, including those instincts acquired in lives in the remote past in saṁsāra.

3. It is the supporter of all the other seven consciousnesses, and it is the reservoir of karmic forces. The potential power of the Ālaya is inconceivably great, and the extent of its sphere of influence is immeasurably vast.

4. The physical world as we see it, is projected and upheld by the Ālaya Consciousnesses of men, and is comparable to the images reflected from a mirror without self-entity. Although the Ālaya's operation of continuous projection and subsistence of the physical world has been carried on for ages by the collective consciousnesses of men through their common karma, the process is involuntary and "unconscious," out of one's reach and awareness.

5. Under normal circumstances the conscious mind can influence, but cannot directly control the Ālaya at will; the full control of the

total Ālaya is called liberation and the success of making the *total*
content of the unconscious conscious is called Enlightenment.

Now we can see that the Mind-Only doctrine is a form of radical
idealism, similar to the idealism of George Berkeley. But Yogācāra
seems to go even further than Berkeley by asserting that the physical
world, being a projection of the Ālaya, can actually be transformed, if
the Ālaya is transformed. The omnipresent Spirit, or God, who contains and supports the "objective world" of Berkeley clearly reminds
us of Yogācāra's Ālaya. The difference between the two lies, perhaps,
in the accessibility, modifiability, and means of realizing the Universal
Mind.

Now, the outstanding feature of Hwa Yen philosophy is its thorough
totalistic approach. In the Prajñāpāramitā and Mādhyamika literature,
we have learned the basic doctrine of Śūnyatā, but only in Hwa Yen do
we find the totalistic Śūnyatā on a great, grand scale in a completely
new setting. Without the insight of the Hwa Yen Masters, it would be
difficult for a man to imagine the wonders of the Shih-shih Wu-ai
Dharmadhātu, which is no other than the cosmic drama revealed by
the totalistic Emptiness. In Hwa Yen, we not only see the truth of
Emptiness in a different perspective, but every single Buddhist teaching
including the doctrines of karma, of Bodhicitta, and of Mind-Only.
All these doctrines are now revealed in a revolutionary new light. For
example, in the Yogācāra system, the Mind-Only doctrine merely
asserts that the material world is a projection of one's Mind; it has
however, never come to the point of inter-projection of mutual containment as propounded by Hwa Yen. The Mind-Only doctrine of
Hwa Yen is best expressed in a parable given by Ch'êng Kuan in his
A Prologue to Hwa Yen, which we have mentioned before in our discussion of the Ocean-Mirror Samādhi in the last chapter; we repeat it
here for the sake of illustration: [17] (See pp. 124–126.)

A monk is preaching the Dharma to his disciple in a room where
there hangs a mirror. The mirror, the monk, and the disciple symbolize
the True Mind, the Buddha, and Man, respectively. The mirror reflects a picture of two individuals facing each other; one is preaching,
and the other is listening. The mirror can be ascribed either to the
monk or to the disciple, depending on one's choice and stress. To describe the interrelationship of the participants of this phenomenon,
we can either say that the *monk within the mirror of the disciple* is
preaching the Dharma to the *disciple within the mirror of the monk;*

or we can say that the *disciple within the mirror of the monk* is listening to the Dharma preached by the *monk within the mirror of the disciple.* With this illustration, the mutual projection and containment of Buddha's Mind and man's Mind are clearly seen.

When Buddha preaches the Dharma to man, it is not a "two-way" relationship (i.e., one preaches and the other listens), but it is a "four-way" relationship—the Buddha *who is within man's Mind* preaches the Dharma to man *who is within Buddha's Mind,* and the man *who is within Buddha's Mind* listens to the preaching of the Buddha *who is within man's Mind.* It is in this light that the mutual projection and containment of the Mind-Only doctrine of Hwa Yen is clearly understood.

NOTES [Part II, Section 3]

1. Ch'êng Kuan, *A Prologue to Hwa Yen,* Chap. V, pp. 65–66.
2. See the *Laṅkāvatāra Sūtra,* Chap. III. Also see D. T. Suzuki's translation in *A Study of the Laṅkāvatāra Sūtra,* pp. 241–42.
3. *Laṅkāvatāra Sūtra,* Chap. III. *Taisho* 671, p. 618.
4. *Taisho* 279, p. 102. Also the Tibetan *bKah-hGyur.Phal.Chen.Ri,* 62a to 64a (Tokyo-Kyoto: 1957), p. 135.
5. *Taisho* 279, p. 101.
6. See *The Awakening of Faith, Taisho* 1666, p. 575.
7. Ibid., p. 576.
8. Ibid., p. 577.
9. But this simply does not make any sense at all: how can any enlightened being compile a collection of such arid and listless Abhidharmas?
10. See Garma C. C. Chang, *The Practice of Zen* (New York, 1959), pp. 94–95.
11. Ibid., p. 107.
12. Hua Tou: the critical word or point in a Zen koan, upon which the Zen practitioner tries to contemplate and break through.
13. Quoted from *Fa Hsiang T'zu Tien* (*A Dictionary of Fa Hsiang Tsung*), (Shanghai, 1939), p. 1007.
14. Ibid., p. 1008.
15. The Eight Consciousnesses: According to Yogācāra these are: Eye-consciousness, Ear-, Nose-, Tongue-, and Body-consciousnesses; plus the Mind, or the sixth consciousness; the Mana, or Ego-consciousness; and the Ālaya or Store-consciousness.
16. See the *Triṁsikā* of Vasubandhu.
17. Ch'êng Kuan, *A Prologue to Hwa Yen,* Chap. VI, pp. 53–54.

華嚴論典

PART THREE

A SELECTION OF HWA YEN READINGS AND THE BIOGRAPHIES OF THE PATRIARCHS

THE GREAT VOWS OF SAMANTABHADRA

Introduction

It would be extremely difficult, if not impossible, to select one chapter from the voluminous *Hwa Yen Sūtra* that would adequately represent both the deep religious spirit and the vast perspective of infinity portrayed in this work. However, if a choice must be made for this purpose, I would without hesitation choose the chapter on "The Bodhisattva Samantabhadra's Vows." According to the Mahāyāna tradition, there are three great Bodhisattvas—Avalokiteśvara, Mañjuśrī, and Samantabhadra—who represent respectively the great compassion, wisdom, and vows of all Buddhas. In the vows of Samantabhadra we witness the compassionate zeal of the ideal Bodhisattva whose only concern in life is to relieve the pains and burdens of all sentient beings, and to bestow upon them true happiness through the achievement of Buddhahood.

> Again, O noble-minded men, what is meant by making great offerings to the Buddhas? It means that in making such great offerings one should think:
>
> "In the smallest dust-motes of all the worlds, in the three periods of time and the ten directions, throughout the entire realm-of-dharma and the realm-of-space, there dwell Buddhas equal in number to the smallest dust-motes to be found in all the universes. Each and every Buddha is surrounded by an ocean-wide assembly of Bodhisattvas. Through the power of Samantabhadra's vows, and with deep faith and understanding, I see them as though we were face to face. To them all, I offer superb and wondrous oblations, such as clouds of flowers, heavenly music, celestial tapestries, angelic garments, and so many varieties of perfumes. . . . I present them with lighted lamps of various kinds . . . the wick of each lamp will be as huge as Mount Sumeru and the oil as vast as the expanse of the great oceans. To all the Buddhas, I humbly offer these oblations. O noble-minded men, the crown of all these offerings is the Offering of the Dharma, but what does this include? It includes the offering of following all the Buddha's instructions, the offering of benefiting all sentient beings, the offering of embracing and sustaining all sentient be-

ings, the offering of taking upon oneself the sufferings of others, the offering of vigorously fostering the root of merit, the offering of swerving not from the Bodhisattva's duty, and the offering of never departing from the Thought-of-Enlightenment.

I will never abandon, but continue to practice, this vast, great, and supreme offering without cessation. My effort will be ended if the realm-of-beings and the realm-of-space are ended, or if the karmas, sorrows, and passion-desires of beings are ended. But since they are endless, so also will be my offerings, thought succeeding thought without interruption, in bodily, vocal, and mental deeds without weariness. . . .

Here we witness not only the love and aspirations of a Bodhisattva, but more importantly, we see them on an infinite scale. Perhaps what makes Mahāyāna unique and attractive to the modern mind is its spiritual insight, embodied in the vast openness of infinity. After reading this chapter, one can rest content that he has found a spiritual goal and orientation that are most profound and inspiring, for he has caught a glimpse of the universal drama enacted on the stage of Dharmadhātu through Samantabhadra's vows.

On Entering into the Inconceivable Realm of Liberation by the Practice and Vows of Bodhisattva Samantabhadra [1]

Having praised the superb merits and virtues of the Tathāgata, the great Bodhisattva Samantabhadra spoke to Kumara Sudhana and a great company of Bodhisattvas in these words:

"O noble-minded men, the infinite merits and virtues of the Tathāgatas are ineffable. If, by a joint effort, all the Buddhas in the ten directions were to enumerate them through infinite aeons of kalpas equal to the number of the dust-motes in the inconceivable and incalculable Buddha-domains,[2] they could not thereby be exhausted. Those who aspire to the attainment of this high degree of merit should practice the great Tenfold Pāramitās. What are these Pāramitās? They are:

1. To pay homage to all Buddhas.
2. To praise all Buddhas and their virtues.
3. To make great offerings to all Buddhas.
4. To confess and repent one's evil deeds and hindrances.

5. To rejoice at the attainment of merits by others.

6. To entreat Buddha to set in motion 'the Wheel of Dharma.'

7. To beseech Buddha to remain in the world.

8. To be a zealous follower of Buddha's ways at all times.

9. To accommodate all sentient beings for their own benefit.

10. To turn over one's merit to all sentient beings."

Sudhana then said: "O great Sage, pray explain to us what course we should follow from paying homage to the Buddhas to turning over our own merits to all sentient beings?"

The Bodhisattva Samantabhadra replied to Sudhana: "O noble-minded man, in regard to paying homage to all Buddhas, one should think:

" 'With deep faith and understanding, and by the blessed power of Samantabhadra's vows, I see all the Buddhas, as though face to face in the past, present, and future and in all the ten directions throughout the realm-of-dharma and the realm-of-space, [in the infinite universes] equal to the total sum of the dust-motes of the Buddhas' domains. With all the virtue of my body, voice, and mind, I shall pay sincere homage to them without cessation. In each and every Buddha-Land, I shall transform countless bodies, and with each body I shall pay my veneration to incalculable Buddhas throughout the infinite Buddha-Domains, equal to the total number of the dust-motes combined therein. My homage will be ended when the realm-of-space is ended. But since the realm-of-space is boundless, so will be my homage to the Buddhas. Likewise, if the spheres-of-beings are ended, the karmas of beings are ended, and the sorrows and passion-desires of beings are ended, my homage will then be ended. But as these too are endless, so will be my homage to all Buddhas, moment after moment without interruption, in bodily, vocal, and mental acts without weariness.'

"Again, O noble-minded man, how should one praise all Buddhas and their great virtues? To do so, one should think:

" 'In each and every dust-mote of all the worlds in the three periods of time and the ten directions throughout the entire realm-of-dharma and the realm-of-space, there dwell Buddhas equal in number to the small dust-motes of all the worlds, and each Buddha is surrounded by an assembly of Bodhisattvas as wide as the ocean. I shall apply my profound thought and insight to fathom them as if they were before me face to face. To the great assembly I shall sing praise of the Tathāgatas with a tongue more eloquent than those possessed by the maidens of Heaven; each tongue emitting a boundless ocean of voices, each voice emitting a boundless ocean of speeches, all proclaiming the ocean-like merits of all Tathāgatas. Such praise shall continue without cessation throughout the realm-of-dharma in the infinite universes. My praises will be ended when the realm-of-space is ended, the spheres-of-beings are ended, and the karmas, sorrows, and passion-desires of beings are ended, but since the realms-of-space, even to the sorrows of beings, are endless, so will be my praise, thought succeeding thought without interruption, and by bodily, vocal, and mental acts without weariness.'

"Again, O noble-minded man, what is meant by making great offerings to the Buddhas? It means that in making such great offerings one should think:

" 'In the smallest dust-motes of all the worlds, in the three periods of time and the ten directions throughout the entire realm-of-dharma and the realm-of-space, there dwell Buddhas equal in number to the smallest dust-motes to be found in all the universes. Each and every Buddha is surrounded by an ocean-wide assembly of Bodhisattvas. Through the power of Samantabhadra's vows, and with deep faith and understanding, I see them as though we were face to face. To them all, I offer superb and wondrous oblations, such as clouds of flowers,³ and heavenly music, celestial tapestries, angelic garments, and so many varieties of perfumes, scented balms, fragrant incense and powders that the gifts together rise as high as Mount Sumeru. I present them with lighted lamps of various kinds, such as the butter lamp, the oil lamp, and sweetly perfumed lamps; the wick of each lamp shall be as huge as Mount Sumeru and the oil as vast as the expanse of the great oceans. To all the Buddhas I humbly offer these oblations.'

"O noble-minded man, the crown of all these offerings is the *Offering of the Dharma,* but what does this include? It includes: the offering of following all the Buddha's instructions, the offering of benefiting all sentient beings, the offering of embracing and sustaining all sentient beings, the offering of taking upon oneself the sufferings of others, the offering of fostering the root of merit vigorously, the offering of swerving not from the Bodhisattva's duty, and the offering of never departing from the Thought-of-Enlightenment.

"O noble-minded man, truly the merit to be derived from [material] offerings such as those enumerated above are infinite; yet, in comparison with a single thought of the Offerings-of-Dharma, they are not equal to a hundredth part, a thousandth part, a hundred-thousandth part of the latter, nay, not to a millionth part, a billionth part, a trillionth part, a part of inconceivable and incalculable infinities. Why is this so? It is so, because the Dharma is held most dear to all Tathāgatas, and it is the Dharma that gives birth to all Buddhas. If a Bodhisattva practices the Offerings-of-Dharma, he completes the truest offerings and services to all Tathāgatas. One should thus think: 'I will never abandon, but continue to practice this vast, great and supreme offering without cessation. My effort will be ended if the realm-of-beings and the realm-of-space are ended, or the karmas, sorrows, and passion-desires of beings are ended. But since they are endless, so also will be my offerings, thought succeeding thought without interruption, in bodily, vocal, and mental deeds without weariness.'

"Again, O noble-minded man, how should one confess and repent one's evil deeds? To repent one's sins and transgressions one should think:

" 'From the very no-beginning of time, in infinite aeons of kalpas, I have committed, through lust, hatred, and ignorance, boundless sinful deeds with my body, tongue, and mind. If such deeds were in corporeal form, the cosmic space, illimitable as it is, could not contain them. With deepest sincerity and by pure deeds of body, speech, and thought, I now confess and repent them before all the Buddhas and Bodhisattvas throughout the universe, and I pledge myself never to commit them again. I will observe all the pure and meritorious precepts. I will continue to practice this penitence until the realm-of-space is ended, the realm-of-being is ended, and the karma and passion-desires of beings are ended. Since all these things, from the realm-of-space to the passion-desires of beings are endless, this penitence of mine will also be endless, thought succeeding thought without interruption in bodily, vocal, and mental deeds without weariness.'

"Again, O noble-minded man, how should one rejoice at the merits and virtues of others? To do so one should think:

" 'In all the realm-of-dharma and the realm-of-space in the ten directions there are infinite Buddhas equal to the amount of infinite dust-motes throughout the Buddha domains in past, present, and future. From the very first moment when they brought forth the Thought-of-Enlightenment and set their minds to the attainment of the All-Knowing Wisdom of Buddhahood, they have diligently practiced all spiritual deeds through aeons of kalpas equal to the amount of infinite dust-motes throughout the Buddha-domains. In each and every kalpa they have sacrificed an infinitude of heads, eyes, hands, and feet in fulfillment of the altruism of a Bodhisattva. They have performed all these arduous acts, fulfilled all the requirements of the different Pāramitās, realized the various stages of a Bodhisattvas' Wisdoms, accomplished the Supreme Enlightenment of Buddhahood and, eventually, have entered into Parinirvāṇa with the [subsequent significant] acts of distributing relics. In all these great acts of merit I will emulate them and rejoice. Nay, I will rejoice at the merit or virtue, even though it be infinitesimal as a single grain of dust that may be possessed by any being in any realm of the six divisions, four births,[4] or any kind of existence in the ten directions throughout the universes. Again, all the Śrāvakas, the Pratyeka Buddhas, the Thoroughly-Learned Ones and the Partly-Learned Ones, with all such saints in the ten directions in the past, present, and future, I rejoice at whatever merit they may possess. The infinitely vast merits of Bodhisattvas, their self-sacrifice and their courage in carrying through the most difficult act-of-Bodhi, their determination and perseverance in pursuing the supreme Enlightenment . . . in all these immense merits I will rejoice. My rejoicing at these merits will cease when the realm-of-space is ended, or the karma, sorrows, and passion-desires of beings are ended, but since these are endless, so also is my rejoicing endless, thought succeeding thought without interruption, in bodily, vocal, and mental deeds without weariness.'

"Again, O noble-minded man, how should one beseech Buddhas to set in motion the Wheel-of-Dharma? To do so, one should think:

" 'In each and every one of the smallest dust-motes of all the worlds in the three periods of time and the ten directions throughout the entire realm-of-dharma and the realm-of-space, there exist inconceivable and incalculable vast domains of the Buddhas equal to the number of the smallest dust-motes. In each Buddha's domain countless [Bohisattvas] are now reaching the state of perfect Buddhahood every moment, surrounded by an ocean-wide assembly of other Bodhisattvas. I will employ my body, mouth, and mind in different manners and different actions to beseech these Buddhas to set in motion the wondrous Wheel-of-Dharma. This request will not cease *even* when the realm-of-space and the realm-of-beings are ended, or the karmas, sorrows, and passion-desires of beings are ended, thought following thought without interruption, in bodily, oral, and mental deeds without weariness.'

"Again, O noble-minded man, how should one beseech the Buddhas to remain in the world? To do so, one should think:

" 'In all the Buddhas' domains throughout the realm-of-dharma and the realm-of-space, in the ten directions of past, present, and future, infinite Buddhas, equal to the number of the smallest dust-motes, are about to make the gesture of entering into Parinirvāṇa. These and all the infinite Bodhisattvas, Śrāvakas, and Pratyeka Buddhas, Wholly-Learned Ones, Partly-Learned Ones, and all the spiritual friends and good men, who are about to enter into Nirvāṇa, I shall entreat not to depart but to remain in the world [in order to remain in touch with all sentient beings]. For the sake of benefiting all living beings, I will continue this entreaty without cessation in the infinite kalpas to come. My entreaty will not be ended till the realm-of-space and the realm-of-beings are ended, or the karmas and sorrows and passion-desires of beings are ended, thought following thought without interruption, in bodily, vocal, and mental deeds without weariness.'

"Again, O noble-minded man, how should one be an ever-zealous follower of Buddha's ways? To do so, one should think:

" 'The Tathāgata Vairocana of this Sahā-World, who from the outset when he made the vow to attain Buddhahood exerted Himself in practicing the Bodhisattva's acts. For alms-giving He sacrificed countless bodies and lives; to learn the Dharma, he stripped off His own skin for parchment, used His own blood as ink and split His bones to make a pen with which to write the Sūtras and scriptures which amount to a bulk as great as that of Mount Sumeru. In appreciation and reverence to the Dharma, He disregarded His own body and life; how much less did he regard the throne, the palace, the gardens, the towns, and all his other worldly possessions? He spared no energy in His ascetic deeds, self-sacrifice, and spiritual endeavors until He attained the Supreme Enlightenment under the Bodhi-tree. Thereupon He displayed many miracles and wondrous conjurations and presided over numerous assemblies, such as the assembly of the great Bodhisattvas, of the Śrāvakas and Pratyeka Buddhas, of the great kings, rājas, Kshatriyas, Brahmins; elders and laymen; and of gods, nāgas,[5] spirits, men and non-men groups. At these numerous assemblies, He spoke in a voice of thunder to the audience, in accordance with the occasions and their needs, ripening them with resourcefulness and ingenious instructions. In these ways, he led sentient beings to the accomplishment of Buddhahood, until He made a gesture towards entering into Nirvāṇa. I will follow not only these examples of Vairocana, the World-Honored One of the present time, but also those of all the Tathāgatas in the infinite dust-motes of the Buddha-domains, in the ten directions and three periods of time throughout the realm-of-dharma and the realm-of-space. In each and every moment, I will follow their examples for my devotion. This practice of *imitation-of-Buddha* will never cease till the realm-of-space is ended, the realm-of-beings is ended, the karmas, sorrows, and passion-desires are ended, thought following upon thought without interruption and in bodily, vocal, and mental deeds without weariness.'

"Again, O noble-minded man, in what manner should one accommodate and serve sentient beings? To do so, one should think:

" 'Throughout the realm-of-dharma and the realm-of-space, in the ocean-like cosmoses in the ten directions, there are infinite kinds of sentient beings; some are born of eggs; some are born of the womb, of wetness, or of metamorphosis. . . . Some live by earth, some by water, fire, wind, space, trees, or flowers. . . . O countless are their kinds, and infinite are their forms, shapes, bodies, faces, longevities, races, names, dispositions, views, knowledge, desires, inclinations, manners, costumes, and diets. They abide in numerous kinds of dwellings: in towns, villages, cities, and palaces. They comprise the devas, the nāgas, the eight-groups,[6] men, non-men, the beings without feet, the beings with two, four, or many feet; some are with form, some are without form, some with or without thoughts, or neither with nor without thoughts. To all these infinite kinds of beings, I will render my service, and accommodate them in whatever way is beneficial to them. I will provide them with all they need and serve them as though serving my parents, teachers, or even Arhats and Tathāgatas, all equally without discrimination. To the sick, I will be a good physician; to those who have lost their way, I will show them the right path; to the wanderers in darkness I will light the light; and to the poor and needy I will show the treasury.'

"It is in these ways that a Bodhisattva should benefit all sentient beings without discrimination. Why? Because, if a Bodhisattva accommodates sentient beings as such, he is then making sincere offerings to all Buddhas. If he respects and serves sentient beings, he is paying respect and giving service to all Tathāgatas. If he makes sentient beings happy, he is making all Tathāgatas happy. Why? Because the essence of Buddhahood consists in great compassion. Because of sentient beings, a great compassion is aroused; because of the great compassion, the Thought-of-Enlightenment is aroused; because of the Thought-of Enlightenment, Supreme Buddhahood is achieved. This is like unto a great tree in the wilderness of a desert; if its roots are well-watered, it will flourish in full foliage, blossom and bear plentiful fruit. So it is also with the great Tree-of-Bodhi . . . all sentient beings are its roots, and all the Bodhisattvas and Tathāgatas are its flowers and fruits. If a [Bodhisattva] applies the water of compassion to help sentient beings, the Bodhi-tree will bear the fruit of Tathāgata's wisdom. Why is this so? Because if a Bodhisattva can benefit man with the water of compassion, he will most assuredly attain the Supreme Enlightenment. Therefore, Bodhi belongs to sentient beings, without them no Bodhisattva can achieve the Supreme Buddhahood.

"O noble-minded man, if you can help all sentient beings equally without discrimination, you will then consummate the full and perfect compassion, with which, if you accommodate sentient beings, you can then make all Tathāgatas happy and satisfied. In this manner a Bodhisattva should accommodate and embrace all sentient beings. This compassionate embracing will not cease till the realm-of-space is ended, the realm-of-beings is ended, the karmas, sorrows, and passion-desires are ended, thought succeeding thought without interruption, with bodily, oral, and mental deeds without weariness.

"Again, O noble-minded man, how should one turn over one's merits to all? To do so, one should think:

" 'All the merits I have acquired from the commencement of paying homage to the serving of all sentient beings, I will turn over to each and every living being throughout the entire Dharmadhātu in the infinite realm-of-space. [By the power of my merits,] I wish them to be always happy and free from all ills and sorrows; [by the power of my merits,] I wish all their evil plans to fail, and all their virtuous undertakings to succeed. Let all the doors that lead to evil and misery be closed, and let the broad paths that lead to heaven and Nirvāṇa [7] be open! Let me take upon myself the burdens and sufferings of all sentient beings, lest they suffer the heavy afflictions of retribution. In this manner, I will continue to turn over my merits to all until the realm-of-space is exhausted, the sphere-of-beings is ended and the karmas, sorrows, and passion-desires of beings are ended, thought following upon thought without interruption, with bodily, oral, and mental deeds without weariness.'

"O noble-minded man, these are the full and complete ten great vows and acts of all Bodhisattvas and Mahasattvas. Those who follow these great vows will be able to ripen all sentient beings and enter into the Supreme Enlightenment of Tathāgatahood."

A COMMENTARY ON THE HEART SŪTRA

Introduction

In China, the Hwa Yen School of Buddhism is also called Hsien Shou Tsung (the School of Hsien Shou). Hsien Shou is another given name of Master Fa Tsang who was generally regarded as the most important master of this school. It was Fa Tsang who firmly established the foundation of Hwa Yen Buddhism through his multifarious writings on the Doctrine. I have selected two of his famous essays for our study here. The first is his exegesis of the *Heart Sūtra,* and the second, his famous work *On The Golden Lion.*

Among the multiple different exegeses and commentaries on the *Heart Sūtra,* Fa Tsang's work is not only outstanding in its clarity and penetrating insight, but also unique in its presentation of Prajñā-pāramitā in the light of the totalistic perspective. It is through this work, we note, that a bridge between Prajñāpāramitā and Hwa Yen was built by Fa Tsang. A preliminary understanding of this exegesis will greatly facilitate the reading of other important Hwa Yen works, such as *On the Meditation of Dharmadhātu* and *On The Golden Lion.*

An Excerpt from the Commentary on the *Heart Sūtra*[8] by Master Fa Tsang

The Prologue

In the exposition of the *Prajñāpāramitā Hridaya Sūtra* five accounts are given: first, the motivation for preaching the Sūtra; second, the category of the Sūtra; third, the tenets and aim of the Sūtra; fourth, the interpretation of the title; fifth, the exegesis of the text.

FIRST ACCOUNT: The Motivation for Preaching the Sūtra.

It is for a number of reasons that this Sūtra was preached:

1. To refute heretical views.
2. To convert the followers of Hīnayāna to Mahāyāna.

3. To protect the novice-Bodhisattva from misunderstanding the truth of Śūnyatā [Voidness].

4. To give a correct understanding of the Two Truths and of the doctrine of the Middle Way.

5. To illustrate the superior merits of Buddhahood, thus promoting the pure faith among men.

6. To inspire people to raise the great Thought-of-Enlightenment.

7. To encourage people to practice the deep and vast deeds of the Bodhisattva.

8. To dispell all hindrances.

9. To bestow the fruit of Bodhi-Nirvāṇa.

10. To transmit this message to posterity for their benefit.

SECOND ACCOUNT: The Category of the Sūtra.

Among the Tripiṭakas [the three Canons—Sūtra, Śāstra, and Vinaya], this Sūtra belongs to the Canon of the Sūtras. Between the Two Baskets [of the Disciples and of the Bodhisattvas], it belongs to the Basket of the Bodhisattvas. Between the Expedient and the True Doctrines, it belongs to the True Doctrine.

> [Comment: It is significant to note here that Fa Tsang regards the *Heart-Sūtra,* a work of Prajñāpāramitā, as being of the Ultimate or True Doctrine (liao i), not of the Expedient Doctrine (pu liao i). This seems to be clear evidence that he was not primarily a Mind-Only or Yogācāra-oriented philosopher, one who usually regards the Mind-Only doctrine to be the only ultimate or true doctrine. From this and other evidence—for example, the predominant role which the meditation on True Voidness has in *Fa Chieh Kuan (On the Meditation of Dharmadhātu)*—we can clearly see that Hwa Yen Buddhism does not rest entirely on the Mind-Only doctrine, as is generally believed. On the contrary, the doctrine of Voidness seems to play quite an important role in the formation of Hwa Yen Philosophy.]

THIRD ACCOUNT: The Tenets and Aim of the Sūtra.

[What is the meaning of *tenets* and *aim* here?] That which is indicated by words represents the tenets, and that which is pursued represents the aim. Generally speaking, the tenets of this Sūtra can be said to include the main teachings of the three Prajñāpāramitās; namely, the

Prajñāpāramitā of Reality: the real-nature under observation [the object]; the Prajñāpāramitā of Observation: the wondrous intuitive wisdom [the subject]; the Prajñāpāramitā of Words: the interpretations of the first two Prajñāpāramitā through symbols. . . .

> [Comment: With the division of these three Prajñāpāramitās, the entire issue of Prajñāpāramitā becomes transparently clear. In the study of Prajñāpāramitā, one must know first that everything said in the Prajñāpāramitā Sūtras is no more than the Prañāpāramitā of Words (Wên Tzu Po Jo). Its function is to present or interpret two subjects: the Reality or Suchness under observation; and the intuitive wisdom, or that which observes the Suchness. The former is called here the Prajñāpāramitā of Reality (Shih Hsiang Po Jo), and the latter the Prajñāpāramitā of Observation (Kuan Chao Po Jo). The bulk of Prajñāpāramitā literature covers no more than these two subjects. With these three headings, one can avoid the various misconceptions arising from the study of the teaching of Prajñāpāramitā.]

FOURTH ACCOUNT: An Interpretation of the Title of the Sūtra.

The word *Prajñāpāramitā* means ["The Perfection of Wisdom" or] "Reaching-the-Other-Shore-Through-Wisdom," and the word *Hridaya* means "the heart," "the gist," or "the essence." The *Prajñāpāramitā Hridaya Sūtra* is, therefore, a Sūtra that expounds the essence of the Prajñā truth. The word *Prajñāpāramitā* can also be interpreted in another manner. *Prajña*, Wisdom, indicates that which embodies the reality; *pāramitā*, reaching-the-other-shore, indicates the approaching or reaching of the reality [This is a free and abridged translation.]

FIFTH ACCOUNT: The Exegesis of the Text.

Text: *At the time when Bodhisattva Avalokiteśvara was coursing in the deep Prajñāpāramitā. . . .*

Exegesis: *Deep* Prajñāpāramitā indicates the difference between the Prajñā truth realized by the Mahāyāna and the Prajñā truth realized by the Hīnayāna. The former includes the Voidness of all dharmas; whereas the latter confines Voidness in the self [or pudgala].

Text: *He saw that all the five skandhas are empty, thus he overcame all sufferings and ills.*

Exegesis: Because of the realization of Voidness, all sufferings are overcome, and saṁsāra is exhausted.

Text: *O Śāriputra, form is not different from the Voidness and the Voidness is not different from form; form is the Voidness, and the Voidness is form, so are the feelings, notions, emotions, and consciousnesses.*

Exegesis: To elaborate the meaning of this passage, five steps are taken: first, to dispel the doubts of outsiders; second, to illustrate the teaching of Dharma; third, to point out that which is to be relinquished; fourth, to pin down that which is to be obtained; fifth, to conclude and praise the superior function [of Prajñāpāramitā].

THE FIRST STEP: TO DISPEL THE DOUBTS OF OUTSIDERS.

This again can be divided into four headings: I. to dispel the doubts of the Hīnayāna followers; II. to dispel the doubts of the Mahāyāna followers; III. to illustrate the correct meaning of the text; IV. to expound the text in the light of contemplation.

I. *To dispel the doubts of the Hīnayāna followers.* Śāriputra was an outsider, so this passage was addressed to him. The word, *Śāriputra*, literally means "the Son of the Eagle." *Śāri* means "eagle"—a nickname of Śāriputra's mother who was extremely intelligent, and whose wit was as quick as an eagle's eyes. Śāriputra was also known to possess the supreme intelligence [among the Hīnayāna disciples]. This was the very reason that *he* was selected as the addressee. The doubt that remained in his mind was [supposedly] this:

> Question: According to our Hīnayāna teaching, those who have attained the Nirvāṇa-With-Residues would only see the existence of skandhas, but not of a self or individual ego. This should also be called the Voidness-of-dharma. If so, what difference is there between [the Voidness of Mahāyāna and of Hīnayāna]?
> Answer: Your doctrine of the Voidness of skandhas says that *there is no self existing in the skandhas,* but it does not say that the skandhas are also empty in themselves; hence, the skandhas are different from Voidness. But here, [the Voidness of Prajñāpāramitā] declares that all skandhas are void by their own nature. The two are therefore quite different, and that is why this Sūtra stresses the point that form is not different from Voidness.[9]
> Question: According to our Hīnayāna teaching, those who have obtained the Nirvāṇa-Without-Residues have exhausted all physi-

cal forms and mental functions. To them there are no forms [and
no feelings, and so forth]. What difference is there then?
Answer: Your doctrine says that Voidness is something that comes
into being *after* the extinction of forms, and does not say that the
forms are void by themselves. But here, [the Prajñāpāramitā] de-
clares that form is Voidness *per se,* and this is quite different from
the Voidness of extinction of forms.

The doubts raised by the Hīnayānist usually are of those two kinds—
namely, a misconception of Śūnyatā as Voidness of absence, or as Voidness of extinction.

II. *To dispel the doubts of the Mahāyāna followers.* This exposition
can also dispel the doubts of some Bodhisattvas. According to *Ut-
taratantra Śāstra,* there are three possible kinds of doubts within the
mind of a Bodhisattva who does not know Śūnyatā correctly.

One, he regards Voidness as different from form [rūpa] and thinks that
Voidness exists outside of form. Now, to correct this misunderstanding,
the Sūtra points out that forms are not different from Voidness.

Two, he regards Voidness as that which negates or destroys forms and
accepts Voidness as annihilation. To correct this misunderstanding, the
Sūtra points out that form is Voidness *per se* and that Voidness is not
[something which appears] after the extinction of forms.

Three, he considers Voidness as a "thing" and regards it as in some
manner existing [Yu]. To dispel this doubt, the Sūtra points out that
Voidness is form *per se* and excludes the idea of taking Voidness as an
[existing Voidness].

When these three doubts are dispelled, the true Voidness will be
manifest.

III. *To illustrate the correct meaning of the text.* When form and
Voidness are set facing each other, three principles will become evident.

One, the Principle of Contradiction. [This principle is witnessed in
the text:] "Therefore, in Voidness there is no form, [no feelings, no
conception]. . . ." [This is an observation of] Voidness negating form.
Hence, this principle also implies that in form there is no Voidness.
Following the same reason, form should also negate Voidness. Thus,
if both exist together, a mutual negation and destruction will result.

[Comment: Man's Svabhāva way of thinking, which is innate and pervasive, conditions him to regard being and non-being, form and emptiness and all antithetical entities, as mutually exclusive or negating. As long as he stands on this *Svabhāva side* of the fence, he cannot truly think non-dualistically. Therefore, he is unable to keep in tune with the mystical insight such as "form is Emptiness and Emptiness is form." As a result, when one deals with the problem of the Non-Dual, a reflection of the dualistic conflict always emerges. Although Hwa Yen Totality is a realm of complete mergence and harmony (yüan-t'ung wu-ai), when it is viewed from the Svabhāva side, a conflicting picture will unavoidably come into view. On the other hand, all Svabhāva beings simply do not exist when viewed from the other or transcendental side. This truth of non-existence, when expressed in our language, is called "negation," or the Principle of Contradiction. When Avalokiteśvara was coursing in the deep Prajñāpāramitā, He saw that all five skandhas were empty; only after this deep experience of the thorough negation of beings, was he able to proclaim the teaching that form is Emptiness and Emptiness is form. From an ontological viewpoint, perhaps no negation of form is ever needed, because forms are Voidness itself from the very outset. However, from the experiential and soteriological viewpoint, a thorough negation of all beings is necessary to cross over this barrier. Hence, we have here the so-called Principle of Contradiction.]

Two, the Principle of Non-Contradiction or Non-Obstruction. This principle says that since forms are illusory and insubstantial, they cannot contradict or obstruct the Voidness. Likewise, if the Voidness is true and genuine it must not contradict or obstruct the illusory forms. But if [a Voidness] contradicts forms, it cannot be other than a *Voidness of annihilation* [or obstruction]. By the same token, if a form contradicts or obstructs the Voidness, it cannot be other than a substantial [Svabhāva] form and not an illusory Form.

Three, the Principle of Collaboration. This says that if forms are not completely void, [or if forms do possess an iota of own-being], they can never be considered to be illusory. It is just because forms *are* void by themselves that the existence of forms is made possible. The *Mahā-Prajñāpāramitā Sūtra* says:

If all dharmas are not empty
There will be no Path and no Fruits.

Mādhyamika-Kārikās [*Chung Lun*] says:

> Because of Śūnyatā all
> Beings can be established.

True Voidness should be understood in this way. [With the foregoing reasoning,] we may now deduce four meanings or viewpoints of True Voidness. I. The viewpoint of negating this [Voidness] and affirming that [form].[10] This is witnessed in the statement "Voidness is form" which stresses the disclosure of forms but the concealment of Voidness. 2. The viewpoint of negating that [form] and affirming this [Voidness]. This is witnessed in the statement "form is Voidness" which stresses the exhaustion of forms and the disclosure of Voidness. 3. The viewpoint of the co-existence of this and that. True Voidness is the non-differentiation of the disclosed and the concealed. When we say that forms are not different from Voidness, we imply that they are illusory. In this sense forms do exist. When we say that Voidness is not different from forms we illustrate True Voidness. Here, Voidness is disclosed. Since this and that do not obstruct each other, they can co-exist with each other. 4. The viewpoint of mutual-annihilation of this and that. This means that since forms and Voidness are *completely* identical, [the identity of] both this and that is utterly obliterated—a state that transcends all dichotomies.

Following the above reasoning, we can also make four observations from the viewpoint of forms: 1. to disclose that [form] and conceal this [Voidness]; 2. to disclose this and conceal that; 3. to illustrate the co-existence of this and that; 4. to illustrate the mutual-annihilation of this and that. Thus, illusory forms can exist or not exist without the slightest obstruction, and true Voidness can appear or be concealed in utmost freedom. When both [form and Voidness] are merged into one, the characteristic of this [wondrous] state is said to be *round-and-through without abiding.*

> [Comment: This section is the pinnacle of the essay. Fa Tsang's Totalistic interpretation of the key sentence of the *Heart Sūtra* ("form is Voidness and Voidness is form"), is clearly presented. He reasoned that setting form and Voidness facing each other, three principles become evident: (1) the Principle of Contradiction; (2) the Principle of Non-Contradiction; (3) the Principle of Collaboration. From the Totalistic viewpoint, none of these three principles can be excluded, because each plays its indispensable

role in the formation of Totality, which is described by the Hwa Yen vocabulary as the Non-Obstructive Dharmadhātu, the Harmoniously-Merging Sphere, the Realm of Non-Abiding Freedom, and so forth as seen in the all-inclusive Round Doctrine.

Because of this Totalistic approach, the meaning of True Voidness can be given from at least four different frames of reference: (1) negating this (Voidness) and affirming that (form); (2) negating that and affirming this; (3) the co-existence of this and that; and (4) the mutual-annihilation of this and that. This is an exact equivalent of the principle of the *Non-Obstruction of concealment and disclosure* in the ten mysteries. In the light of this principle, all philosophical controversies are simply disputes blindly fought over a matter of "concealing this or disclosing that"!]

IV. Interpretation of the text in the light of meditation and contemplation [śamatha and vipaśyanā]. This can be discussed in three headings:

One, to observe form as Voidness, thus, the practice of meditation [śamatha or Dhyāna] is established; or to observe Voidness as form, thus, the practice of contemplation [vipaśyanā] is established. When in a split second [one suddenly realizes the non-differentiation of Voidness and form], it is then the practice of simultaneous meditation-and-contemplation [śamatha-vipaśyanā], and only this can be considered as the ultimate [practice].

Two, when one sees that form is Voidness, he accomplishes the great Wisdom, and he abides no more in saṁsāra. When one sees that the Voidness is form, he attains the great compassion and will no more remain in Nirvāṇa. Because form and Voidness, Wisdom and compassion, have all become non-differentiated, he is able to practice the non-abiding acts.

Three, the great Master Chih I proposed the so-called Three Observations within one Mind based on the *Ying Lao Sūtra.* They are:

1. The observation by reducing illusory forms [Māyā] to Voidness, that is, form is Voidness.

2. The observation by reducing the Voidness into illusory forms [Māyā], that is, Voidness is form.

3. The observation of the equality of Māyā and Voidness; this is to say that form and Voidness are not different.

Now let us examine the second of the five steps mentioned on page 200.

THE SECOND STEP: TO ILLUSTRATE THE TEACHING OF THE DHARMA.

Text. *Śāriputra, the marks of the Voidness of all dharmas [are not arising, not ceasing, not pure, not defiled, not increasing and not decreasing].* . . .

Exegesis: In "The marks of the Voidness of all dharmas," *all dharmas* here means the various skandhas, and *marks* [lakshaṇa] means the qualities or the characteristics. The marks of Voidness, according to the *Treatise On the Distinction of the Middle and the Extremes,* imply that the nature of Voidness is essentially non-dual; that is, the non-existence of subject and object. [A free and abbreviated translation.]

Text: *Not arising, not ceasing, not defiled, not pure, not increasing, not decreasing.* . . .

Exegesis: It is to be noted here that this passage contains three pairs and six negations. Three different explanations of them are given as follows.

I. *An explanation given in the light of the stages in the Path.* "Not arising and not ceasing": this means that before the stage of Enlightenment [or the first Bhūmi] an ordinary being must go through the process of birth and death and ever wander in the long-lasting saṁsāra. This is the stage of birth and death, or the stage of arising and ceasing. But the True Voidness is far from this; therefore, it is said to be "not arising, and not ceasing."

"Not defiled, not pure": this indicates that the different stages in the Bodhisattva's Path are marked with both purity and defilement. This is because these Bodhisattvas have attained a certain degree of Enlightenment but have not yet completely eradicated all avidyas [ignorance] and hindrances.[11] This is the stage of purity-and-defilement. True Voidness is far from this; therefore, it is said to be "not defiled, not pure."

"Not increasing, and not decreasing": when the final phase of the Path is over, and Buddhahood is obtained, all ignorance and hindrances of saṁsāra formerly not cleared are now cleared. This is called "decreasing." Through spiritual cultivation, the infinite merits formerly not attained are now securely attained. This is called "increasing." But True Voidness is far from this; therefore, it is said to be "not increasing and not decreasing."

Again, in the *Śāstra of Buddha-Nature,* the names of three Buddha-Natures are given.

One, before the initial Enlightenment of the Path, the [Buddha-Nature] is called the Buddha-Nature by Itself, [or the Immanent Buddha-Nature].

Two, [during the various stages of Enlightenment in the Path,] it is called the Disclosed Buddha-Nature.

Three, after the Path, it is then called the Buddha-Nature of Perfect Fruit.

Actually there is only one Buddha-Nature, but in accordance with the stages of the Path, it is divided here into three. It should also be kept in mind therefore that True Voidness [by itself] has no divisions whatsoever, but merely for the sake of understanding, it is divided here according to the stages in the Path.

II. *An explanation in the light of Dharma* [i.e., the absolute or transcendental aspect of Voidness]. Although this True Voidness is identical with forms and so on, forms are produced through dependent-arising, but the True Voidness is never produced. [This means that it never comes into being.] Likewise, forms are extinguished through dependent-arising, but True Voidness is never extinguished. It is not defiled when involved in saṁsāra, nor pure when hindrances are all cleared; it is neither decreasing nor increasing when in or out of passion-desires. For all these—arising, extinction, decreasing or increasing, and so forth—are the marks of conditioned beings [saṁskṛta dharmas]. Only by negating them all is the "mark" [lakshana] of True Voidness revealed. This is what the "marks of Voidness" means in the Sūtra. . . .

ON THE MEDITATION OF DHARMADHĀTU

Introduction

The most original and important piece of work in the literature of Hwa Yen Philosophy is no doubt Tu Shun's *Fa Chieh Kuan, On the Meditation of Dharmadhātu.* The germinal thoughts and characteristic approach of Hwa Yen Philosophy are clearly visible in this essay. The four famous masters subsequent to Tu Shun—Chih Yen, Fa Tsang, Ch'êng Kuan, and Tsung Mi—all gained their inspiration from this essay and wrote their works following the principles and arguments laid down therein. With regard to philosophy, this treatise is no doubt the most important piece of work of Hwa Yen Buddhism. The main theme is the development of a philosophy of the all-embracing Totality of Shih-shih Wu-ai. This is done by elaborating in sequence three philosophical observations.

1. Meditation on True Voidness.

2. Meditation on the Non-Obstruction of Li and Shih.

3. Meditation on the All-Embracing Totality.

From the sequence and development of these three Meditations, we can clearly see that the foundation of Hwa Yen Philosophy is the Philosophy of Voidness rather than of Mind-Only as generally believed.

Readers of this text may wonder why the author, instead of speaking plainly and simply, has chosen to express his ideas in such an abstruse fashion. For instance, in the Meditation on True Voidness the sentence, "form is not void because it is void" is repeated three times, although each repetition denotes a different idea. The reason for such vagueness may be that this work was not intended to serve as a full-fledged philosophical treatise but as a manual of meditation. It is modeled, therefore, after the compendious style and laconic expression of the *Heart Sūtra,* based upon the belief that only in this manner can the richness of meaning contained in such pithy statements as "form is Voidness and Voidness is form" be fully appreciated.

Tu Shun's arguments might have been simpler and his work more readable had he not been obsessed by the "auspiciousness" of the number ten. His belief in the significance of this number led him to adopt a procrustean approach, dividing every discussion into ten categories. This artificiality is indeed most unfortunate, and it is perhaps the only blemish we can find in this remarkable work. The repetitions of the same or similar arguments, which the readers will undoubtedly detect in this essay, can be explained again by the fact that this is a manual of meditation whose primary function is to provide a guide for appropriate contemplations. From this point of view, the repetitious and parallel observations are not only helpful but even necessary.

Since the Meditation on the Non-Obstruction of Li and Shih has been explained before in the section of the Philosophy of Totality in Part Two, no additional comments are given here. Comments are kept to a minimum to preserve the style and flavor of the text itself. If preferred, the reader may skip this section and read the next meditation, *Meditation on the All-Embracing Totality,* p. 218.

On The Meditation of Dharmadhātu [12] by Master Tu Shun

The Meditation observes: The practice of viewing the great Dharmadhātu in the vast Buddha realm contains three branches of Meditations: Meditation on the True Voidness; Meditation on the Non-Obstruction of Li [noumenon] against Shih [phenomenon]; Meditation on the All-Embracing Totality.

I. Meditation on the True Voidness.
The Meditation observes: To illustrate our first topic, Meditation on the True Voidness, four observations in ten principles are to be considered. The four observations are: the observation of reducing form into Voidness; the observation of identifying Voidness with form; the observation of the Non-Obstruction of form and Voidness; the observation of absolute dissolution and non-attachment.

A. *The observation of reducing form into Voidness.*
The Meditation observes: [13] To explain the first, the observation of reducing form [or matter] into Voidness, four reasonings are given.

1. *Form is not void because it is void.* What does this mean? [14] It means that to say form is not Void is to stress the fact that form is not a void-of-annihilation, but a true void in its total essence.

2. *Form is not void because it is void.* What does this mean? It means that inasmuch as neither yellow nor green is *exactly* the principle of Voidness, we say that form is not void. However, [from the viewpoint

of Transcendental Truth,] the yellow or the green have no substance—
they are nothing but Voidness; therefore we say [again] that they are
Voidness. [On the other hand, one should also notice] that the Voidness
of the yellow and green is different from the yellow and green themselves; therefore we say they are not exactly the Voidness.

3. *Form is not void because it is void.* What does this mean? It means
that inasmuch as there is no form that can be traced in the [Absolute]
Voidness, we say that it is not void. [However, from the viewpoint
that] form is reduced into Voidness, we say that it is void. When form
is reduced into Voidness, no form whatsoever will exist in the Voidness; [under this condition,] it simply makes no sense to speak of the
identity or difference of form and Voidness. That is why we say here
that since form is void [when it is reduced into the Voidness], form is
not void—[because no mutual identity is possible in this case.]

COMMENT: Ch'êng Kuan comments on the above arguments.[15]
    Since there is no form in the [Absolute] Voidness, form can-
not be the Voidness itself, yet apart from form, there is no other
truth; hence, the Voidness cannot be apart from the form. True
Voidness is, therefore, neither identical nor different from form.
. . . But there are men who cherish the idea that Voidness exists
outside of form and is essentially different from it . . . so it is
pointed out here that since there is no trace of form whatsoever
existing in the [True] Voidness, how can there be a Voidness that
exists face to face with form? Again, when form is reduced [into
the Voidness], no substance is seen; therefore, we say, it is void.
How would it be possible then to envision a Voidness that exists
outside of form [making up a contrasting pair]? This is why the
sages of ancient times said:

> When Form has gone
> No Void is left.
> Voidness has no edge
> And no abiding.

4. *Form is void.* Why? Because all forms should, on no account, be different from True Voidness. Since all forms are without substance [or
Selfhood], they are all void. If form [*rūpa*] is void, so are all the other
dharmas. Contemplate on this.

B. *The observation of identifying Voidness with form.*
Now, to explain the second of the four observations, that of identifying Voidness with form. This again has four headings.

1. *Voidness is not form because Voidness is form.* What does this mean?
It means that the voidness-of-annihilation is not form; therefore we
say [Voidness] is not form. Nevertheless, the True Voidness should on
no account be different from form; therefore we say Voidness is form.
Because the True Voidness is identical with form, the voidness-of-
annihilation cannot be identical with form.

2. *Voidness is not form because Voidness is form.* What does this mean?
It means that [from a certain viewpoint] since the principle of Voidness as such is not the green or the yellow themselves, we say Voidness
is not form. However, the True Voidness of non-green and non-yellow
should on no account be different from the green and the yellow;
therefore we say Voidness is form. In short, we either claim that Voidness is form, or is not form on the basis of that which is not different
from or not identical with the green and the yellow.

3. *Voidness is not form because Voidness is form.* What does this mean?
This means that Voidness is not that which acts [neng i] but that which
is to be acted upon [so i]. In this sense we say that Voidness is not form.
[However, from the viewpoint that] Voidness *must function* [as the
ground upon which] form acts [and thus form and Voidness are always
co-existing and mutually-identical] we say that Voidness is form. In
other words, Voidness *is not* form, because it is the object [so i], and
Voidness *is* form, also because it is the object [so i] when viewed as a
function. This is why we say that because Voidness is not form, therefore Voidness is form.

> [*Comment:* Insofar as the Voidness is devoid of all attributes, it
> cannot be said to be identical with form or matter. Voidness can-
> not act by itself; nevertheless, it can serve as the universal ground
> upon which all forms or matter act. In this passive sense, Void-
> ness can be considered to be only a neutral ground to be acted
> upon (so i), but not the subject or the actor (neng i). This is why
> Voidness (as so i) cannot be regarded as form (which is neng i).
> On the other hand, since Voidness *must* function as the ground
> upon which all forms act, it is not only inseparable from forms,
> but, because of the principle of dependent-arising, it is identical
> with all forms. This conclusion is deduced from the reasoning of
> the basic śūnyatā doctrine: Form/Voidness = dependent-arising =
> Māyā = True Voidness.]

4. *Voidness is form.* Why? Because True Voidness should on no account be different from form, and this truth of the selflessness-of-

dharmas [dharmanairātmya] is not annihilatory; therefore we say that
Voidness is form. If form/Voidness is so, all other dharmas should also
be so. Contemplate on this.

C. *The observation of the Non-Obstruction of form and Voidness.*
Now, the third observation, that of the Non-Obstruction of form and
Voidness. The entire body of form is not different from Voidness—it is
actually the form-exhaustion Voidness. Without abolishing form as
such, the Voidness appears. The Voidness per se is not different from
form—it is actually the Void-exhaustion form. Although form and
Voidness are exactly identical, the Voidness does not, on account of
this fact, hide itself from appearing. Therefore, when a Bodhisattva
observes form, he sees Voidness, and when he observes Voidness, he
sees the form. This is the Dharma-At-Onement, which is without the
slightest hindrance or obstruction. Contemplate on this and you will
understand.

> [*Comment:* Tsung Mi comments on this paragraph.[16]
>
> Although the term *form/Voidness* is used here, the author's
> original intention was [to stress the point of] reducing forms into
> the Voidness. Because all forms are without a speck of substance,
> both their appearances and names are delusory. The practice of
> this Meditation ought to be focused on this direction. This is
> witnessed in the first and second sentences in the text where form
> is used as the subject: ". . . it is actually the form-exhaustion
> Voidness. Without abolishing form as such, *the Voidness appears.*"
> But in the next sentence where Voidness is used as the subject,
> there is no parallel proclaiming that form appears. Instead, the
> assertion is that "Although form and Voidness are exactly identi-
> cal, *the Voidness does not, on account of this fact, hide itself from
> appearing.*" Therefore, the focus of this Meditation is on the True
> Voidness. It could not be called "The Meditation on the True
> Voidness and Illusory forms."]

D. *The observation of absolute dissolution and non-attachment.*
Now, the fourth and last observation, that of absolute dissolution and
non-attachment. The True Voidness under [correct] observation cannot be said to be identical with or different from form. Nor can it be
said to be identical with or different from the Void. Nothing is accepted
here, nor is this non-acceptance accepted; even this statement itself is
not accepted. This absolute negation and non-attachment [of the be-
yond] is beyond words and understanding. It is a "realm of experience

and realization." Why? Because if any ideas or thoughts should arise, they would violate the Dharma nature and thus go astray.

> [Comment: This is a very good description of Absolute Voidness (Pi Chin K'ung). Here we seem to be reading a typical passage in a Zen book.
>
> In reviewing these four observations, it is noted that the first two, together with their eight reasonings, are all given to disperse erroneous ideas and to reveal the correct understanding. The third observation (i.e., that of the Non-Obstruction of form and Voidness) is given to end this very understanding, in order to enter the actual practice; and the fourth is given to achieve the realization of the practice. The rationale behind this sequence is that if an understanding is not established first, there will be no way for one to follow the practice. On the other hand, if one does not know that this practice transcends the conceptual understanding, he cannot achieve a genuine understanding. Again, if one clings to the view and does not let go of it, he can never enter the right practice. In short, practice can only begin with understanding, and understanding will end when practice actually starts.

Tsung Mi comments on this: [17]

> By practicing these four observations, four defects can be avoided.
>
> The first observation of reducing all forms into Voidness [can] free [us] from the defect of accretion. [That is to say, when all forms are reduced into the Voidness, there is no possibility of making any unneeded or extraneous addition to the self-sufficient Reality.]
>
> The second observation of identifying Voidness with form [can] free [us] from the defects of both accretion and reduction. [That is to say, when form and Voidness are seen as one, the unity of Māyā-Śūnyatā is realized which goes beyond the extremes of being and non-being, but is inclusive of both.]
>
> The third observation of the Non-Obstruction of form and Voidness stresses the negation of both being and non-being, thus it [can] free [us] from the defect of all playwords.
>
> In the fourth observation of absolute dissolution and non-attachment, even the concept of the unity of both form and Voidness is negated, thus it can free [us] from the defect of all contradictions.
>
> When these four defects are eschewed, the hundred flaws and

mistakes will [automatically] disappear. This is indeed the essence
of the eight collections of Prajñāpāramitā scriptures and the consummation of all teachings in the Great Vehicle.]

II. *Meditation on the Non-Obstruction of Li [Noumenon] against
Shih [Phenomenon].*

Ten principles are set forth here to elucidate both the fusion and dissolving of Li and Shih, their *co-existence* and *extinction, co-operation*
and *conflict.*

[Comment: Ch'êng Kuan comments on this: [18]
    In the previous Meditation, on the Voidness of all forms,
Voidness represents the Li and form represents the Shih. Why is
it not then called the Meditation on the Non-Obstruction of Li
and Shih? There are four reasons for this.

First, in the previous Meditation, although the fact of form, or
Shih, is dealt with, the stress is on establishing the principle [Li]
of Voidness, and the Non-Obstruction between form and Voidness.
It is therefore [primarily] a Meditation on the True Voidness.

Second, in the previous Meditation, the aspect of the Voidness is
explained, but the aspect of the wondrous dynamic becoming [yu]
of Tathatā is not discussed.

Third, [the Meditation] of [absolute] dissolution and non-attachment negates both Shih and Li.

Fourth, the previous Meditation does not reveal the sphere of
Non-Obstruction which evinces the action of non-action, form
without form, all "Shihs" and "Lis" simultaneously open to view
without hindrances, a realm of fusion of all antitheses.
    Because of these four reasons, the previous Meditation cannot
be called the Non-Obstruction of Shih and Li. . . .
    Ten principles are set forth here to unite Shih and Li into
one [inseparable whole]. Just as a large furnace can melt all metals
and transform them into the shapes of various images, Li can also
dissolve all Shihs. The harmonious fusion of Li and Shih brings
into the open a double non-duality. All ten principles set forth
here are meant to elucidate this principle of Non-Obstruction. . . .
    The co-existence of Li and Shih is elucidated in principles
nine and ten, because they assert the fact that the true Li is not

Shih, and Shih is not Li. Here both Li and Shih maintain their [independent] existences.

The extinguishment of Li and Shih is elucidated by principles seven and eight. They both assert that Shih is Li and Li is Shih. This obliteration of self for the fusion with others simultaneously dissolves both Li and Shih.

The conflict between Li and Shih is elucidated in principles five and six. When the true Li annuls Shih, we see the fact that Li contradicts Shih, and when Shih conceals Li, we see that Shih also contradicts Li.

The co-operation between Li and Shih is elucidated by principles three and four. Here we see that it is based on Li that all Shihs are established. This emphasizes the fact that Li accommodates or co-operates with Shih. On the other hand, the Shih can reflect or demonstrate Li, this is the evidence that Shih also co-operates with Li. These two observations actually contain the gist of all ten principles. The doctrine of the Non-Obstruction of Li and Shih is therefore established.]

1. *The principle that Li [must] embrace Shih.* Li, the law that extends everywhere, has no boundaries or limitations, but Shih, the objects that are embraced [by Li], has boundaries and limitations. In each and every Shih, the Li spreads all over without omission or deficiency. Why? Because the truth of Li is indivisible. Thus, each and every minute atom absorbs and embraces the infinite truth of Li in a perfect and complete manner.

2. *The principle that Shih [must] embrace Li.* Shih, the matter [or event] that embraces, has boundaries and limitations, and Li, the truth that is embraced [by things], has no boundaries or limitations. *Yet this limited Shih is completely identical, not partially identical, with Li.* Why? Because the Shih has no substance—it is the selfsame Li. Therefore, without causing the slightest damage to itself, an atom can embrace the whole universe. If one atom is so, all other dharmas should also be so. Contemplate on this.

This all-embracing principle is beyond [the comprehension of] the ordinary mind and is difficult to understand. It cannot be depicted [properly] by means of any metaphor of this world. [But being compelled now to illustrate the subject, the following metaphor is used.]

The entire ocean is [embodied] in one wave, yet the ocean does not shrink. A small wave includes the great ocean, and yet the wave does not expand. Though the ocean simultaneously extends itself to all waves, it does not by this fact diversify itself; and though all waves simultaneously include the great ocean, they are not one. When the great ocean embraces one wave, nothing hinders it from embracing all other waves with its *whole* body. When one wave includes the great ocean, all other waves also include the ocean in its entirety. There is no obstruction whatsoever between them. Contemplate on this.

[At this juncture] one raises [the following] question: "If the Li embraces an atom with its *total* body, why then is it not small? If the Li does not reduce itself to the same size as the atom, how can you say that its *total* body embraces the atom? Furthermore, when an atom includes the nature of Li, why is it not large? If the atom does not equal Li and thus become great and vast, how can it embrace the nature of Li? This reasoning is self-contradictory and unreasonable."

Answer: Setting Li and Shih face to face, they are neither identical nor different; thus they can [each] totally include [the other], yet not impair their respective positions.

First, to see Shih from the position of Li, four principles are found. *a.* Because the reality of Li does not differ from Shih, its totality dwells in each Shih. *b.* Because the reality of Li and Shih are not identical, the principle of Li always stretches to infinity. *c.* Because the non-identity is the non-difference itself, boundless Li is completely included in an atom. *d.* Because the non-difference is the non-identity itself, the one atom's Li is boundless and without division.

Second, to see Li from the position of Shih, four principles are also found. *a.* Because Shih and Li are not different, an atom includes the nature of Li in full. *b.* Because Shih and Li are not identical, an atom is not impaired. *c.* Because the non-identity is the selfsame non-difference, a small atom embraces the infinite reality of Li. *d.* Because the non-difference is the selfsame non-identity, an atom is not expanded when it includes the boundless reality of Li. Contemplate on this.

[Here one may raise an objection by asking,] "When boundless Li embraces an atom, do we find, or not find, the reality of Li in other atoms [at the same time]? If we do, then it means that Li exists outside the atom, hence Li is not totally [engaged in] embracing an atom. On the other hand, if the reality of Li is not found outside the atom, then you cannot say that Li embraces all things. Hence, your argument is self-contradictory."

Answer: Because the nature of Li is omnipresent, harmonious, and fusing,[19] and because innumerable things [Shih] are [mutually] non-obstructive, therefore the [truth of Totality] exists both inside and outside [of Li and Shih] without obstruction or impediment. [To elaborate on this,] four reasons are given [from the viewpoint of both inside and outside of Li and Shih].

First, from the standpoint of Li: *a.* While Li embraces all things with its total body, it by no means impedes the existence of this total body in one atom. Therefore, to be outside is to be inside. *b.* While the total body [of Li] exists in one atom, it does not impede the existence of this total body in other things. Therefore, to be inside is to be outside. *c.* The nature of non-duality is omnipresent; therefore it is outside and it is also inside. *d.* The nature of non-duality is "beyond all;" therefore it is neither outside nor inside.

The first three reasons are given to illustrate the non-difference of Li from all Shih, the last to illustrate Li's non-identity with Shih. It is because Li is neither identical nor different from Shih, that outside and inside are seen without obstructions.

Second, from the standpoint of Shih: *a.* When one thing [Shih] includes Li with its total body, it does not impede all other things from including Li in its entirety. *b.* When all things embrace Li, they do not impede one atom from embracing [Li] in full. Therefore, to exist outside is to exist inside. *c.* Because all things embrace [Li] simultaneously in each and every manner, therefore all things are completely inside (Li) and at the same time outside (Li), without any obstruction. *d.* Because all different things do not impair one another, by setting one against the other, it is neither within nor without. Contemplate on this.

3. *The production of Shih must rely on Li.* This means that Shih has no other essence [than Li]; it is because of Li that Shih can be established, for all causations are devoid of self-nature (niḥsvabhāva). It is also because of this No-Selfhood that all things come into being. The waves push the water and make it move, and owing to the contrast of water and wave, motion is produced. By the same token, it is because of the Buddha-matrix [Tathāgata-garbha] that all dharmas can come into being. Contemplate on this.

4. *Through Shih the Li is illustrated.* When Shih grasps Li, Shih is emptied and Li is substantiated; and because the Shih is emptied, the Li that "dwells" in the total Shih vividly manifests itself, as when the *form* of a wave is annulled, the body of the water appears naked. Contemplate on this.

5. *Through Li the Shih is annulled.* When Shih grasps Li and makes Li emerge, the form of Shih is annulled, and the only thing that clearly and equally appears is the sole and true Li. Beyond the true Li, not a single piece of Shih can be found. When the water annuls the waves, not one wave remains. [In other words, the reasoning here is] to keep the water in order to exhaust the waves [or, to disclose the water and conceal the waves].

6. *The Shih can hide the Li.* The True Li follows and establishes causal events. However, since these causal events are against Li, the result is that only the events appear, but the Li does not appear. Similarly, when water becomes waves, the aspect of motion appears while the aspect of stillness does not appear at all. The Sūtra says, "The Dharmakāya that circles and wanders in the five lokas is called a sentient being." Hence, whenever a sentient being appears, the Dharmakāya always [follows] but does not [necessarily] manifest itself.

7. *The True Li is Shih itself.* If a Li is true, it should never be outside of Shih. There are two reasons for this. First, because of the principle of dharmanairātmya [the emptiness-of-selfhood-of-all-things]. Second, because Shih must depend on Li, [Shih] itself is but hollow without any substance. Therefore, only if the Li is identical with Shih through and through can it be considered to be the True Li. [Taking again the parable of water and waves:] since the water is the waves themselves, no motion can be excluded from wetness. This is why we say that the water itself is the waves. Contemplate on this.

8. *Things and events [Shih Fa] themselves are Li.* All things and events of dependent-arising are devoid of Selfhood, hence they are identical with reality [Li] through and through. Therefore, a sentient being is Suchness per se without [going through] annihilation. Similarly, when the waves are in motion they are exactly identical with water at the same time, and there is no difference between them whatsoever.

9. *The True Li is not Shih.* The Li that is identical with Shih is not Shih as such. This is because the true Li is different from the illusory,

and the real is different from the unreal; also that which is depended upon [object, so i] is different from that which depends [subject, neng i]. Likewise, the water that is identical with waves is not waves as such, for motion and wetness are different.

10. *Things and events [Shih Fa] are not Li.* The Shih—that which is embodied in the total Li—is not always the Li as such, because its form and nature are different, and because that which depends is not that which is depended upon. Although the total body of [Shih] is in the Li, things and events can also vividly appear. Likewise, the waves— that which is totally embodied in water—are not always the water, for the meaning of motion is different from that of wetness.

The above ten principles all consist in dependent-arising. To see Shih from the standpoint of Li, we find forming [cheng] as well as annulling [huai], unification [ho] as well as separation [li]. To see Li from the standpoint of Shih, we find revealing [hsien] as well as concealing [yin], one as well as many. [In the great Totality, therefore,] contradiction and agreement all become harmonious with no impediment and no obstruction, and all in all arise simultaneously. One should meditate on this deeply to let the "view" clearly appear. This is called the Meditation of the Harmony and Non-Obstruction of Li and Shih.

> [Comment: The principle of dependent-arising (pratītya-samut-pāda) is basic and essential to all Hīnayāna and Mahāyāna doctrines. The interpretation and understanding of this basic principle, however, differs greatly among the various schools. In the Hwa Yen Doctrine, dependent-arising is more than just a principle that denotes merely the interdependence of various factors in cause-effect relationships. It now becomes the great harmony of interpenetration of Li and Shih in the Dharmadhātu. Here is the Totality in its true sense, not only because of its vastness, but also because of its unique quality of universal harmony. Everything becomes consistent here, even "contradiction and agreement all become harmonious!" No wonder this is a realm "without impediment or obstruction, and all in all arise simultaneously."]

III. *Meditation on the All-Embracing Totality.* [This is also the wondrous Shih-shih Wu-ai Dharmadhātu.]

Because Shih is identical with the fusing Li, it embraces all without obstructions and penetrates into and interfuses with all in a natural and spontaneous manner. To illustrate this point, ten principles are set forth as follows.

1. *The principle that Li equals Shih.* Since Shih is vacuous, all its forms come to exhaustion; and since the essence of Li is real, the body of Li completely comes into view. Therefore, Shih is not a Shih other than the total Li. For this reason, when a Bodhisattva sees Shih, he also sees Li. However, [in this principle] the Shih should not be considered to be the Li per se.

> [Comment: The stress of this principle is on the simultaneous identity of the disclosed and the hidden. When a Bodhisattva sees Shih, he also sees Li at the same time. However, in this principle the Shih should not be considered to be the Li per se as in the Dharmadhātu of Li. The two-in-one identity of Li and Shih requires the presence of both elements; whereas, in the Dharmadhātu of Li, only Li is observed.]

2. *The principle that Shih equals Li.* Since Shih is not different from Li, it "follows" Li and is omnipresent in all places. As a result, one atom is able to embrace the entire universe. [Again,] when the total body of the universe is omnipresent in all dharmas, this one atom, like Li, is also omnipresent in all dharmas. If one atom is so, all other dharmas should also be so.

3. *The principle that Shih includes the truth of the Non-Obstruction of Li and Shih.* Since Shih Fa and Li are not one, the Shih remains as it is, and yet embraces all. For an example, the form of one atom does not expand, and yet it can embrace the infinite universes. This is because all the cosmoses are not separate [or different] from the Dharmadhātu, so they can all appear within one atom. If one atom is so, all the dharmas should also be so, since in their harmonious fusing Shih and Li are neither identical nor different. This truth of the fusing of Li and Shih contains four principles:

First, one in one.
Second, all in one.
Third, one in all.
Fourth, all in all.

Each of these principles is supported by different and sufficient reasons. Contemplate on this.

> [Comment: This is no doubt the key statement of this Meditation, and the core of the entire essay: "Since Shih Fa and Li are not

one, the Shih remains as it is and embraces all." Here we see a big jump from the reasoning of the Li-shih Wu-ai (the Non-Obstruction of Li and Shih) to that of Shih-shih Wu-ai (the Non-Obstruction of Shih and Shih). We have now reached the climax of the Hwa Yen philosophy of the Non-Obstruction of Events Against Events. In the previous argument of the Non-Obstruction of Li and Shih, a Shih is "made" to embrace all by reducing itself to the omnipresent and non-differentiated Li. Shih has to lose its own identity to fuse with Li first, to be "enabled" to embrace all. But now, the observation goes one step further by asserting that *"the Shih remains as it is and yet embraces all . . .* the form of one atom does not expand and yet it can embrace the infinite universes. . . . Shih Fa departs not from its position and yet it extends to all atoms." Here no reduction into Li on the part of Shih is needed; all particularity and individuality of Shih is kept intact, and yet each and every Shih, in all dimensions of Dharma-dhātu, interpenetrates and embraces every other Shih simultaneously, without the slightest strain! If a man wants to comprehend the realm of Shih-shih Wu-ai forever, stepping stones of contemplation, the principles of Li-shih Wu-ai (the Non-Obstruction of Li and Shih), are absolutely necessary. As far as intellectual understanding is concerned, there is simply no other way to approach Shih-shih Wu-ai conceptually except by way of Li-shih Wu-ai. Here we must not forget the basic premise that Shih-shih Wu-ai is by no means an abstract principle to be "understood" through conceptualization, nor is it something to be approached through mental cleverness. Shih-shih Wu-ai is a realm of direct realization; no intellection is needed and all philosophies become redundant and useless here! Shih-shih Wu-ai is simply so and always remains so. The problem here is not a matter of understanding or verification, but how to grasp the realization through direct and concrete experience.]

4. *The principle of the Non-Obstruction of the universal-whole and the local-spot.* Since the non-identity of all Shih Fa and Li is the selfsame non-difference of all Shih Fa and Li, a Shih Fa departs not from its position and yet it extends into all atoms. [Again,] because identical-ness is the difference itself, [an atom] stretches in all the ten directions, yet it does not move away from its local position. So it is far and also near, stretching and also remaining; there is no obstruction and no hindrance whatsoever.

5. *The principle of the Non-Obstruction of the vast and the small.* Since the non-identity of all Shih Fa and Li is the selfsame non-difference of all Shih Fa and Li, an atom is not impaired and yet it contains all the oceanlike universes in the ten directions. [Again,] because the *identity is the difference* itself, when an atom contains all the vast universes in the ten directions, it does not expand. This is to say that an atom is wide and also narrow, large and also small. There is no obstruction and no impediment.

> [Comment: These fourth and fifth principles are almost exactly like the third principle. "[Again,] because identity is the difference itself, [an atom] stretches in all the ten directions, yet it does not move away from its local position. . . . When an atom contains all the vast universes in the ten directions, it does not expand . . . an atom is wide and narrow, large and also small. There is no obstruction and no impediment." The main argument of these three principles is focused, I believe, on the basic principle of Svabhāva-Śūnyatā. The identity is the selfsame difference; that is to say, even identicalness and difference have no Selfhood. If an atom must move away from its local spot in order to stretch over in all ten directions, or if an atom must expand itself to contain the vast universe, *then it would be the Svabhāva form of operation confined within the realm of finity and obstructions.* If there is a realm of infinity and Totality at all, it must be this "wondrous Non-Obstruction" depicted here in the Shih-shih Wu-ai Dharma-dhātu.]

6. *The principle of the Non-Obstruction of [all] spreading and [all] containing.* Because all-spreading is the selfsame all-containing, when an atom is set against all [universes] and spreads over all, it simultaneously contains all dharmas and includes them *within* its own [shell]. Again, because the all-containing is the selfsame all-spreading, an atom, while containing all, spreads over all the different dharmas it contains. Thus, one atom spreading over all is the all spreading over one; it can contain and also enter; it simultaneously embraces all dharmas without any obstruction. Contemplate on this.

7. *The principle of the Non-Obstruction of entering and including.* Because entering the other dharma is the selfsame including the other dharma, when all dharmas are set against one dharma, the total entering-into-one on the part of all, enables the one, at the same time, to

"return" to its own realm which includes all without any obstruction. Again, because including the other is the selfsame entering the other, when one dharma abides in all, it also enables all dharmas to remain in one simultaneously without any obstruction.

> [Comment: The statements of the sixth and seventh principles are the natural conclusions derived from the principle of thorough Non-Differentiation which is expressed in Hwa Yen literature in a number of ways. The central idea of this principle is the unity or fusion of all antitheses, such as form and Voidness, man and Buddha, cause and effect, difference and identity, the finite and the infinite, the small and the large, the spreading and the containment, the entering and the including, and all the rest. Once this two-in-one postulate is affirmed, nothing is impossible and everything becomes non-obstructive.]

8. *The principle of the Non-Obstruction of interpenetration.* When one dharma is set against all, it has the including aspect as well as the entering aspect. This can be summarized under four headings:

First, one includes all and enters all.

Second, all includes one and enters one.

Third, one includes one and enters one.

Fourth, all includes all and enters all.

They interpenetrate one another without any obstruction.

9. *The principle of the Non-Obstruction of mutual existing.* Setting all dharmas against one, there are both the containing and the entering aspects. This again, has four headings:

First, [all] contain one to enter one.

Second, [all] contain all to enter one.

Third, [all] contain one to enter all.

Fourth, [all] contain all to enter all.

They simultaneously interpenetrate one another without obstruction or hindrance.

10. *The principle of the Non-Obstruction of universal fusing.* This is to say that all and one are simultaneous. Setting both against each other, each has the two-fold headings and four sentences just introduced. They fuse into each other in a total manner without any obstruction as seen in other aforementioned principles.

Those who practice this Meditation should make an effort to bring forth the round and illuminating insight in accordance with the practice and experience of [the great Hwa Yen Dharmadhātu] without obstruction or impediment. They should contemplate this in depth until this wondrous vision comes into view.

ON THE GOLDEN LION

Introduction

Fa Tsang's treatise, *On The Golden Lion,* is a very significant—and the most popular—work of Hwa Yen Philosophy. There are two excellent English translations of it, one by Professor Derk Bodde, and one by Professor Wing-Tsit Chan. The present translation is done with grateful recognition of the aid given by these two previous works.

In the *Biographies of Outstanding Monks,* the Sung version,[20] we read:

> Fa Tsang expounded the new translation of the *Hwa Yen Sūtra* for the Empress [Wu] Tsê-T'ien, but when he came to the doctrines of the ten mysteries, of Indra's net, the Ocean-Seal Samādhi, the convergence of the six forms and the realm of the universal perception, which constitute the general and specific principles and teachings in the various chapters of the Sūtra, the Empress became puzzled and uncertain. Thereupon, Fa Tsang pointed to the golden lion guarding the palace hall and used it as a metaphor to illustrate the teachings. The doctrines were thereby made extremely clear and easy to understand, and the Empress quickly came to a full comprehension of the essence of the teaching. [This lecture was later written in prose] with ten principles to elaborate the general and specific theories, and it was called the *Treatise On The Golden Lion.*

Treatise On The Golden Lion [21] Narrated by Monk Fa Tsang

[Ten observations are given here to illustrate the Hwa Yen Doctrine through the medium of the golden lion in Her Majesty's palace.]

1. To understand the principle of dependent-arising.
2. To distinguish form and Emptiness.
3. To summarize the three characters.
4. To reveal the non-existence of forms.
5. To explain the truth of the unborn.
6. To discuss the five doctrines.

7. To master the ten mysteries.

8. To embrace the six forms.

9. To achieve the perfect Wisdom of Bodhi.

10. To enter into Nirvāṇa.

1. *To understand the principle of dependent-arising.* This is to say that gold has no inherent nature of its own [i.e., no Svabhāva]. It is owing to the artistry of the skillful craftsman that the form of the lion arises. This arising is the result solely of the cause-conditioning; therefore it is called the arising through dependent-arising.

> [Comment: Here we witness Fa Tsang's conviction that dependent-arising is the *first* principle which sustains the entire doctrine of Hwa Yen Buddhism. Because gold (noumenon) has no Selfhood, numerous forms (phenomena) can be brought into being through dependent-causation. The implication here is that if noumenon had any Self-existence (Svabhāva) at all, the phenomenal world would have never come into being.]

2. *To distinguish form and Emptiness.* This means that the form of the lion is unreal; what is real is the gold. Because the lion is not existent, and the body of the gold is not non-existent, they are called form/Emptiness. Furthermore, Emptiness does not have any mark of its own; it is through forms that [Emptiness] is revealed. This fact that Emptiness does not impede the illusory existence of forms is called form/Emptiness [sê-k'ung].

3. *To summarize the three characters.* Because of men's delusory perceptions, the lion [seems to] exist [in a concrete manner]; this is called the character of universal imagination [parikalpita]. The [manifestation] of the lion *appears* to be existing, this is called the character of dependency on others [paratantra]. The nature of gold never changes, this is called the character of perfect reality [pariniṣpanna].

> [Comment: These three characters are proclaimed by the Yogācāra School to be the basic criteria by which the problem of being and non-being should be decided. Men's karmic and fictitious projections of the external world are like the rope which a viewer mistakes for a snake. This kind of existence is, in reality, non-existent, although it appears to be existent. This is the character of universal imagination (parikalpita) . The phenomenal world, however, seen as a projection of one's mind, cannot be said to be

non-existent if we understand the fact that it has no independent existence apart from one's own mind. This manifestation of Mind brought into play through dependent-arising (in the Yogācāra sense) cannot be said to be completely non-existent. This is the character of dependency-upon-others (paratantra). The essence of Mind is free from all karmas and delusions. It is intrinsically devoid of subjective-objective dichotomies. This ultimately real Mind testifies the character of perfect reality (pariniṣpanna) .

The all-inclusive approach of Hwa Yen could not afford to ignore this important doctrine of Yogācāra, so Fa Hsang felt obliged to include it here to make up his cherished, "auspicious" ten principles in full.]

4. *To reveal the non-existence of forms.* This is to say that when the gold completely takes in the lion, there is no form of lion to be found. This is called the non-existence of forms.

[Comment: This is to reduce Shih into Li. In the Dharmadhātu of Li no form whatsoever exists.]

5. *To explain the truth of the unborn.* This means that at the very moment when [we see] the lion come into existence, it is actually the gold that comes into existence. There is nothing apart from the gold. Although the lion may come into and go out of existence, the substance of gold [in fact] never increases or decreases. This is called the truth of the unborn.

[Comment: This is a simple description of the Dharmadhātu of Li.]

6. *To discuss the five doctrines.* The first: although the lion is a dharma produced through dependent-arising, it undergoes generation and destruction in each and every moment. [Since nothing in the phenomenal world endures,] no form of the lion can ever be found. This is called the teaching for the ignorant Śrāvakas [Hīnayāna].

The second: all things, being the product of dependent-arising, are devoid of Selfhood [Svabhāva], and in the final analysis, are nothing but Emptiness. This is called the preliminary teaching of Mahāyāna.

The third: although all things are Emptiness through and through, this does not impede the vivid appearance of the Māyā/becoming. All that which is of dependent-arising is fictitiously existent [and therefore it is truly void.] This co-existence of both being and non-being is called the final teaching of Mahāyāna.

The fourth: inasmuch as these two characters [that of Emptiness and that of form] mutually annul each other, they are both abolished. Here, no imaginings or false presuppositions exist; neither the concept of Emptiness nor the idea of existence retains any influence. [This is the sphere in which] the ideas of both being and non-being vanish. It is a realm that names and speech cannot reach. Here the mind rests without any attachment. This is called the instantaneous teaching of Mahāyāna.

The fifth: when all false feelings and wrong ideas are eliminated, and the true substance is revealed, everything becomes merged into one great mass. Great functions then arise in abundance, and whatever arises is absolutely true. The myriad manifestations, despite their variety, interpenetrate without confusion or disarray. The all is the one, for both are empty in substance. The one is the all, for cause and effect clearly manifest themselves [without fail]. In their power and functions [the one and the all] embrace each other. They spread out and roll up in utter freedom. This is called the Round Doctrine of the One Vehicle.

> [Comment: The wide variety of doctrines of different Buddhist schools imported into China from the third to the eighth centuries (and thereafter) must have caused great uneasiness in the minds of the Chinese Buddhists, for these doctrines not only were divergent, but often contradicted each other despite the fact that they all claimed to speak for the central teaching of genuine Buddhism. To solve this unbearable situation, a comprehensive evaluation of all the doctrines of the various schools was needed. Consequently, a "scholastic" activity called P'an Chiao, passing judgment on the various doctrines, gained momentum in the Sui and T'ang Dynasties, notably in the T'ien Tai and Hwa Yen Schools. The P'an Chiao of the Hwa Yen School came to the conclusion that there are altogether five major doctrines in the great family of Buddha's Dharma. They are listed in order of depth and importance as follows.
>
> *The Small Doctrine.* This includes all the Hīnayāna teachings provided in the Āgamas and Abhidharma scriptures. The stress here is on the teaching of the non-existence of self.
>
> *The Preliminary Doctrine (of Mahāyāna).* This includes the basic teachings of the Mādhyamika and Yogācāra systems. Un-

fortunately, the bulk of the Prajñāpāramitā literature was also ascribed to this group. The emphasis here is supposedly on the Thorough Emptiness of all dharmas.

The Final Doctrine. This is the "higher" or "final" teaching of Mahāyāna. Typical examples of this group are seen in Sūtras such as the *Vimalakīrti Sūtra, Tathāgata-garbha Sūtra, Mahānirvāṇa Sūtra,* and so forth. This group stresses the importance of the potential Buddha-nature (Tathāgata-garbha) in all sentient beings.

The Instantaneous Doctrine. This is the teaching of Zen Buddhism. Direct and instantaneous realization of one's own Buddha Mind is stressed.

The Round Doctrine. This is the teaching of the Non-Obstruction of Totality given in the various Hwa Yen Sūtras. It explains the spiritual experience and realization of Buddhahood and Bodhisattvahood in all dimensions. The stress is on absolute freedom, or Non-Obstruction, in the all-embracing infinity of Dharmadhātu.]

7. *Mastering the ten mysteries.* The first: the gold and the lion are simultaneously established, all-perfect and complete. This is called the principle of simultaneous completeness.

The second: if the eyes of the lion take in the complete lion, then the all [the whole lion] is the eyes. If the ears take in the complete lion, then the all is the ears. If all the organs simultaneously take in the whole lion and all are complete in their possession, then each and every organ is "mixed" [involving others] as well as "pure" [being itself]. This is called the principle of full possession of the purity and mixture by the various storehouses.

The third: the gold and the lion both establish and include each other in harmony. There is no obstruction between one and many. [In this complete mutual inclusion,] the Li and the Shih, the one and the many, remain in their own positions. This is called the mutual inclusion and differentiation of one and many.

The fourth: all the parts of the lion, down to the tip of each and every hair, take in the whole lion in so far as they are all gold. Each and every one of them permeates the eyes of the lion. The eyes are the ears, the ears are the nose, the nose is the tongue, the tongue is the body. They all exist in total freedom without obstruction or impediment. This is called the mutual identity of all dharmas in freedom.

The fifth: if we look at the lion [as a lion], there is only lion and no gold. This is the disclosure of the lion but the concealment of the gold. If we look at the gold [as gold], there is only gold and no lion. This is the disclosure of the gold but the concealment of the lion. If we look at both simultaneously, they are both manifest or hidden. Being hidden they are secret, being manifest they are revealed. This is called the simultaneous establishment of disclosure and concealment in secrecy.

The sixth: the gold and the lion may be manifest or hidden, one or many, pure or mixed, powerful or powerless. The one is the other. The principal and the companion interchange their radiance. Both Li and Shih simultaneously come into view. Being mutually compatible, they do not impede one another's existence. This is true even in the case of the minute and the subtle aspects and is called the peaceful co-existence of the minute and the subtle.

The seventh: in each of the lion's eyes, in its ears, limbs, and so forth, down to each and every single hair, there is a golden lion. All the lions embraced by each and every hair simultaneously and instantaneously enter into one single hair. Thus in each and every hair there are an infinite number of lions. Furthermore, each and every hair containing infinite lions returns again to a single hair. The progression is infinite, like the jewels of Celestial Lord Indra's net; a realm-embracing-realm ad infinitum is thus established, and it is called the realm of Indra's net.

The eighth: the lion is spoken of in order to indicate men's ignorance; the gold is spoken of in order to reveal the true nature. By jointly discussing Li and Shih the Ālaya Consciousness is described so that a correct understanding [of the doctrine] may be reached. This is called the creation of understanding by revealing the Dharma through facts.

The ninth: the lion is a transient and conditioned thing [samskṛta dharma]; it arises and fades away at every moment, and each moment can be divided into past, present, and future. Each of these three periods again contains three sections of past, present, and future; therefore, altogether there are three-times-three units, thus forming the nine ages; grouping them together we have a total gate to the Dharma-truth. Although there are nine ages, each is different from the other, and yet their existences are established because of one another. They are harmoniously merged without the slightest obstruction in one identical [eternal] moment. This is called the different formation of separated dharmas in ten ages.

The tenth: the gold and the lion may be manifest or hidden, one or many, but they are both devoid of a Self-being [Svabhāva]. They manifest in various forms in accordance with the turning and transforming of the Mind. Whether we speak of them as Li or Shih, there is [the Mind] by which they are formed and exist. This is called the universal accomplishment through the projection of Mind-Only.

8. *To embrace the Six Forms.* The lion represents the character of wholeness, and the five organs, being various and different, represent diversity. The fact that they are all of one dependent-arising represents the character of universality. The eyes, ears, and so on remain in their own places and do not interfere with one another; this represents the character of particularity. The combination and convergence of the various organs makes up the lion; this represents the character of formation. The fact that each organ remains at its own position represents the character of disintegration.

9. *To achieve the perfect Wisdom of Bodhi.* "Bodhi," in the Chinese language, means the Way [Tao] or Enlightenment. This is to say that when we look at the lion, we see at once that all conditioned things, without going through the process of disintegration, are from the beginning in a state of quiescent non-existence. By being free from both clinging and detachment, one can follow this path into the ocean of omniscience [sarvajña]; therefore it is called the Way. To comprehend the fact that from the very no-beginning all illusions are in reality nonexistent is called Enlightenment.

10. *To enter into Nirvāṇa.* When we look at the lion and the gold, the marks of both are exhausted. At this point, the passion-desires no longer arise even though beauty and ugliness are displayed before one's eyes. The mind is tranquil like the sea; all disturbing and delusory thoughts are extinguished, and there are no compulsions. One emerges from bondage and is free from all hindrances. The source of all suffering is forever cut off, and this is called entering into Nirvāṇa.

THE BIOGRAPHIES OF THE PATRIARCHS

Time and the nature of this work have not allowed me to present a critical review of the historical development of the Hwa Yen School. I shall therefore speak briefly about the life stories of the four Hwa Yen masters in order to give the reader a general idea of what part they played in the formation of this school.

Tu Shun (558–640)

Traditionally Tu Shun, or Fa Shun (558–640), the author of *On the Meditation of Dharmadhātu,* was considered to be the first patriarch and was no doubt the most original and creative thinker of this school. His Dharma name was Shih Fa Shun; because his surname was Tu, he was also called Tu Shun. Born in the second year of Yung Tin of the Ch'êng Dynasty, Tu Shun appears to have been extremely pious even as a child. He often acted as a monk and pretended to give sermons to his playmates in the neighborhood. When he was fifteen, he joined the army doing such menial labor as carrying water and gathering firewood.

At the age of eighteen, he was ordained by the Ch'an master Tao Chên and received from him the instructions of meditation. After concentrating on meditation practice for some time, he could perform miracles, and he demonstrated great healing power wherever he went. He cured all sorts of diseases helping even the deaf and the dumb. It was said that the Emperor T'ai Tsung of the T'ang Dynasty was once very ill and asked him for help. Tu Shun's advice was to grant a universal amnesty to the nation; soon after this was done the Emperor regained his health. With gratitude the Emperor bestowed upon him the honorary title the Holy One of the Imperial Heart, and because of his miraculous power, people called him the Bodhisattva of Tun Huang. According to one of many legends, he once hung a pair of boots on the gate of a bazaar, and for three days nobody stole them. When people asked him how this was possible, he said, "From the infinite kalpas in the past till now I have never stolen even a penny from men; how can anyone steal anything from me?" Many thieves were greatly moved by his personality and reformed.

Tu Shun did not have a permanent teacher; he concentrated his study on Hwa Yen and lived as a hermit on the Chung Nan Mountain for many years. Based upon the teachings of the *Hwa Yen Sūtra,* he wrote the essay *On the Meditation of Dharmadhātu.* When the work was done, he threw the manuscript into the fire and prayed, "If what I have said in this paper is in accordance with Buddha's teaching, then not a single word should be destroyed by this fire." The fire burned out, but the manuscript was left intact.

Tu Shun once wrote a bit of verse called *The Stanza of Dharma-Nature,* which reads:

> A cow in Chia Chou [Eastern China] consumes the grass
> But the horse in I Chou [Western China] is satiated.
> [Instead of] seeking a good physician
> [You should] cauterize the left arm of a pig.

This stanza was very popular among the Zen Buddhists and has been used as a koan. On the 25*th* day of the eleventh moon in the year of 640, Tu Shun assembled all his followers in the temple and bade farewell to them. Then he went to the palace and said goodbye to the Emperor. Returning to his temple, he soon passed away without any sign of illness.[22]

Two more legendary accounts of Tu Shun are available in the Chinese canon; unfortunately, like other Chinese biographies, these accounts do not provide detailed information about his life. More disappointingly, they fail to furnish any information concerning the development of his philosophical thought even though he was an excellent Buddhist thinker. Thirteen hundred years after his time Tu Shun appears to us now more as a philosopher than a saint-magician. But his contemporaries seemed to hold a different opinion about him; to them he was more of a saint than a philosopher. The legends appearing in the Chinese canon translated here reflect this view.

(from Taisho 1868, pp. 512–13)

Master Tu Shun had a monk-disciple who attended him for more than thirty years. For many years, the disciple wanted to make a pilgrimage to Mount Wu T'ai to worship Bodhisattva Mañjuśrī. One day he begged permission to make this journey. The master tried to dissuade him, to no avail. Finally, he gave in and said, "You may go, but be sure to return soon. I shall wait for you."

After a ten-day's journey, the monk reached Wu T'ai and paid homage to the holy place. Then he saw an old man approaching who asked him, "From whence have you come?"

"I came from Chung Nan Mountain."

"Why did you come here?"

"I came to pay homage to the Bodhisattva Mañjuśrī."

"But the Bodhisattva Mañjuśrī is not here."

"Where is he?"

"He is now at Chung Nan Mountain, assuming the form of a Ch'an master named Tu Shun."

"But Tu Shun is my master, whom I have attended for more than thirty years!"

"Although you have served him for so long, you did not recognize him. You should rush home at once. If you hurry back without delay, you can see him; if you delay for but one night, you will never see him again."

The monk turned homeward at once, but when he reached the Western Capital it was still quite early in the day, so he paid some visits to his good friends in the city. When he heard the drum sound [for the closing of the gate], he rushed to the city gate but arrived there too late; the gate was already closed for the day, so he had to remain in the town that night. The next morning, when he returned home, he found that Master Tu Shun had passed away. In great distress, he then realized that his own master had been none other than the Bodhisattva Mañjuśrī Himself.[23]

(from Taisho 2064, p. 984)

The original surname of Shih Fa Shun was Tu. He was a native of Wan Nien county in Yung Chou. Shih Fa Shun was naturally good tempered and virtuous; at eighteen he renounced the world and became a monk. At one time, when Zen master [Tao] Chên was giving public instruction in meditation, Tu Shun went to the vicinity of Ch'in Chou for alms. He secured a patron who volunteered to provide food for five hundred people. However, when the time came, more than a thousand people showed up. The patron was greatly worried, but Tu Shun said, "Do not be afraid—just give all you have, and do not give less than the offering should be." The festival then went on, and all the thousand guests were filled. . . .

Once, during the summer Tu Shun led many monks to Li Mountain for meditation. But the place was full of insects and ants, and they could not plant any vegetables without hurting them. Tu Shun then [drew some landmarks on the ground and] ordered the ants to move beyond these boundaries. Before long all the ants and insects had moved away.

Tu Shun always had some festering boils on his body with the pus oozing out continuously. Seeing them, people avoided him; but when some people [out of kindness] cleansed the pus off with a cloth, the boils healed up immediately. The pus that had been wiped away gave off a very fragrant odor, and even the cloth smelled good for days. In San Yüan county a man called T'ien Sa To was born deaf, and another called Chang Su was born dumb. Tu Shun sent for them and cured their afflictions in an instant by ordering them to talk. A monk of the county of Wu Kung was possessed by a vicious dragon. People brought the monk to Tu Shun. As they sat face to face, the dragon said, "Since your Reverence, the great Ch'an Master, has now come here, I shall leave at once. Please forgive any annoyance that I may have brought to you. . . ." From far and near, people with all kinds of sicknesses came to him for help. By merely sitting face to face with the sick, he cured them all without any medication. At one time Tu Shun journeyed to the southern part of the countryside and arrived at the shores of the Yellow River while it was in flood. He tried to cross but fell into the flood waters from the steep and slippery bank. He climbed out, but fell once more. Then the flood began to subside, allowing him to walk across through the river bed and reach the other shore. Immediately after, the flood resumed its course as before. . . . In the fourteenth year of Cheng Kuan (640 A.D.), Tu Shun exhorted his disciples and gave his final instructions to them. Then, without any illness, he sat upright as if engaging in Samādhi, and passed away in the suburb south of I Shan Monastery.[24]

Chih Yen (602–668)

Chih Yen, the successor of Tu Shun, was regarded as the second patriarch of this school. His important writings include *The Ten Mysteries in One Vehicle of Hwa Yen (Taisho 1868)*, *The Fifty Questions and Answers of the Hwa Yen Doctrine (Taisho 1869)*, *Notes and Commentaries on the Various Chapters of Hwa Yen Sūtra (Taisho 1870)*, and *A Search for the Profound Mysteries of Hwa Yen Sūtra (Hwa Yen Chin Sou Hsüan Chi)*. Perhaps the most important contribution of

Chih Yen was his proposal of the ten mysteries. Though most of the content of these mysteries was included in the Shih-shih Wu-ai Dharma-dhātu of *Fa Chieh Kuan,* this concept of the "balanced" ten mysteries was indeed novel and refreshing from the viewpoint of the literature of his time. In *The Biography of Hwa Yen Sūtra,*[25] we read a brief account of Chih Yen.

> Shih Chih Yen's surname was Chao. He was a native of T'ien Shui. . . . At the time when his mother was about to conceive him, she dreamed that an Indian monk, holding a staff, came to her and said, "You should at once wash your body and cleanse your mind, observe the precepts and fast." She woke in awe. The room was filled with wondrous fragrance, and she then conceived. Chih Yen showed a superior intelligence when he was only a few years old. He often played games by erecting stupas with bricks and making canopies of flowers. At times he played the part of a preacher and let the other children take the parts of his listeners— a clear indication that he was a talented and well-destined person. When Chih Yen was twelve years old, the divine monk Tu Shun came to his house. Tu Shun laid his hand upon the child's head, and said to his father, "This is my son; you should return him to me." Chih Yen's parents knew that Tu Shun was an outstanding monk; they gladly granted his request. Tu Shun then entrusted Chih Yen to his chief disciple Ta for care and education. The boy was taught to study the Scriptures day and night without burden-ing the care of [Tu Shun]. Some years later, two Indian monks came to visit the Chih Hsiang Monastery. Witnessing Chih Yen's outstanding intelligence, they taught him Sanskrit. Chih Yen mastered the lessons in a very short time. Later the Indian monks told people in the monastery that this child would some day be-come a great preacher. Chih Yen wore the black rope [becoming a monk] as early as the age of fourteen.
>
> At that time, the fortunes of the Sui Dynasty were declining, and people were suffering from hunger. Although Chih Yen was very young, he showed great will power and endurance during this hard time. Later, he studied Asanga's *The Outlines of Mahāyāna* [*Mahāyāna-samparigraha*] under Master Ch'ang, and within a few years he had [fully mastered many scriptures] and was able to render subtle and penetrating interpretations on them. Master Ch'ang often let him speak among the many great scholars who assembled in the monastery for conference. . . .
>
> After receiving his ordination, Chih Yen studied the Vinayas,

Abhidharmas, Satyasiddhi, Daśabhūmi, Ti-Ch'ih, and Mahānir-vāṇa Sūtras and Śāstras. Then he studied extensively under Master Lin, probing into the profound and subtle doctrines, and he received great credit. Chih Yen had always been troubled by the voluminosity and complexity of the Buddhist scriptures. He often thought, "Among the vast and deep, ocean-like Buddhist teachings, which one should I rely upon?" He then stood before the Three Canons and made obeisance to them. He made a wish with a prayer, then he picked up one book at random out of the Canons which happened to be the first volume of the *Hwa Yen Sūtra*. He then attended Master Chih Cheng's lecture on Hwa Yen, but all that he could obtain from this class were outworn explanations. In his mind he mulled over many new thoughts on the Hwa Yen Doctrine. He determined to clear his doubts by exploiting new interpretations; thereupon, he read the complete Canon and studied all the available commentaries, but not until he read the Exegesis by the Vinaya master Kuang T'ung were his doubts slightly cleared. Through this work he began to understand the gist of the infinite dependent-arising as endorsed by the *One Vehicle Special Doctrine*.

Sometime later, a strange monk came to him and said, "If you want to understand the meaning of the One Vehicle Doctrine, you should not neglect to study the *Theory of Six Forms,* as given in the [chapter of the] Ten Bhūmis. You should spend one or two months in seclusion and contemplate on it—then you will be able to understand." After saying this, the monk suddenly disappeared. In astonishment, Chih Yen wondered at these words for a long time. Because of this revelation, he began to study in depth and before long had fully mastered the Doctrine; he was then only twenty-seven years old. After this he meditated for seven days and nights, and prayed for guidance in discriminating right from wrong. One night, he dreamed that a celestial youth came and showed approval of his understanding. Nevertheless, he did not make himself known among his contemporaries at that time, but lived inconspicuously with the common people. Not until he was quite old did he begin to preach the Doctrine in public. At the time when the Royal Prince came to bestow a title on the Lord of Pei, Chih Yen preached for the prince who [deeply impressed by his preaching] ordered the local government to provide him with an ample allowance and supplies so that he could preach continuously without interruption. Chih Yen was a very versatile man, talented in many fields. Once he painted a picture of the

Lotus-Treasury World which was a masterpiece unprecedented in skill and scope in the East of the Tsung River [China proper?]. . . . In the first year of Tsung Chang [668 A.D.], he dreamed the Altar-of-Wisdom in the monastery suddenly collapsed. His disciple Hui Hsiao dreamed of a huge canopy hanging high above touching the sky. On top of the canopy there was a great jewel radiating beams of light as bright as the sun. The canopy gradually moved nearer and nearer, and when it reached the capital, it fell down. Chih Yen himself was also aware that the time had come for his departure. One day he said to his disciples, "This physical body of mine is made through dependent-causations and has no permanent substance. Now I am leaving temporarily for the Pure Land; then I shall visit the [Hwa Yen] Lotus-Treasury World. I hope you will all follow in my footsteps and make the same wish." On the night of the 27*th* of the twelfth moon [668 A.D.], without visible change of countenance, Chih Yen lay down on his side and passed away. . . .

Fa Tsang (643–712)

Among the four Hwa Yen masters, the most prolific writer was Fa Tsang. It was said that he wrote one hundred volumes (chüan) of books and essays. Because of his indefatigable efforts in preaching and writing on the Hwa Yen Doctrine, the teaching of Hwa Yen gained high regard and distinction. He was therefore regarded by many as the actual founder of this school. Out of great respect and admiration for him, people called him Hsien Shou (Head of the Wise). The Chinese Emperor also gave him an honorary title: the Dharma-Teacher Kuo-I (One in the State). Fa Tsang's surname was K'ang. His family was originally from Samarkand, and his father was a high officer in the Chinese government. In the year 643 A.D. his mother had a dream. She dreamed that she swallowed the entire bodies of the sun and the moon and then she became pregnant.

When Fa Tsang was sixteen years old, he burned one finger as an offering to Buddha's relic in a stupa. At the age of seventeen, he traveled everywhere to seek a good teacher, but none of the contemporary scholars could satisfy him. Then he left home and stayed in a hermitage on the T'ai Pei Mountain, sustained by weeds, living an ascetic life for a number of years, and only because of his parents' illness did Fa Tsang once return home. At that time Master Chih Yen was preaching the *Hwa Yen Sūtra* in the Yün Hwa Monastery in the capital. One night Fa Tsang dreamed that beams of celestial light shone from heaven illuminating his entire house; he thought, "There must be some person who is preaching the great Dharma." The next morning he called upon Master Chih Yen. Greatly impressed by his preaching, Fa Tsang became Chih Yen's disciple.

Fa Tsang was still a layman when he was twenty-five years old, and Chih Yen was anxious to get him ordained. At the time when he was twenty-eight, Empress Wu Tsê-T'ien, in memory of Madame Jung Kuo, built a new monastery called T'ai Yuan and appointed Fa Tsang to be the abbot. He was then formally ordained. At the request of the Empress Wu, Fa Tsang gave numerous lectures on various Sūtras. During his lifetime, Fa Tsang expounded the entire *Hwa Yen Sūtra* more than thirty times! It was said that many miraculous signs also appeared during his preachings. Once, in the Yün Hwa Monastery, people saw streams of light emanate from his mouth and rise up to the sky forming a huge canopy. Another time when Fa Tsang was expounding the topic of the "shaking of the Hwa Yen Ocean," the earth also shook during the sermon as a heavenly and auspicious omen. Once he assisted Hsüan-Tsang in the latter's work of translation; however, because of "different viewpoints," Fa Tsang left Hsüan-Tsang. Fa Tsang wrote many important essays and commentaries; among them the most popular of his time was the *Commentary on the Heart Sūtra*. It was widely studied by all ranks of people in the entire nation. When he died at the age of seventy, an extravagant state funeral was held in his honor.[26]

Ch'êng Kuan (738–840)

Ch'êng Kuan's surname was Hsia-Hou; he was a native of Yueh Chou. He became a monk when he was fourteen years old. For a time he studied the Three Śāstras of the Mādhyamika School under Master Hsuan Pi of Chin Ling. The thriving success of the San Lun School in the Yangtze valleys was said to be partly due to his efforts. There seems to be some confusion about Ch'êng Kuan's birth date and the exact year he died. In one version, according to Sung Kao Shêng Chuan, Ch'êng Kuan died when he was seventy some years old in the era of Yuan Ho—which could vary from 806 to 820. Takakusu gave the years of his life, as 760–820.[27] But according to tradition, which we have no compelling reason to doubt, Ch'êng Kuan was born in 738 and died in 840. He lived, therefore, for one hundred and two years and was well known to be the Imperial Master of six successive T'ang Emperors (Te Tsung, Shun Tsung, Hsien Tsung, Mou Tsung, Chin Tsung, and Wen Tsung). He studied under many famous scholars and outstanding Zen masters.

One day he observed himself and said, "The Bodhisattvas of the Fifth Stage are able to realize the Tathatā and absorb their minds in the sphere of Buddha-nature. However, in the After-Śamatha State [Hou Te Chih Wei], they would all undertake the task of mastering the mundane skills and learnings in order to benefit sentient beings and deepen their own insight. I should also follow their steps to study the various sciences and disciplines." Thereupon Ch'êng Kuan studied broadly and acquired for himself knowledge of all branches of learning, including such disciplines as the Chinese classics, histories, literature, philology, Sanskrit, pagan doctrines, spells, magic, rhetoric, logic, medicine, and handicrafts of various kinds. He seemed to be an extremely versatile and well-learned person. In his celebrated work, *A Prologue to Hwa Yen,* we may witness his comprehensive knowledge covering almost all the branches of learning of his time.

He lived for many years in the great Hwa Yen monastery on the Wu T'ai Mountain, and there he completed his magnum opus, *The Great Exegesis of the Hwa Yen Sūtra,* which contains close to a million words; *A Prologue to Hwa Yen* was written as an introduction to *The Great Exegesis.* It was said that when Ch'êng Kuan was about to commence this gigantic undertaking, he prayed hard for several days and petitioned Buddha to give him a sign. Then he had a dream that a golden man stood erect in radiance like a mountain standing before the sun. He welcomed the golden man and embraced him, then he started to swallow the golden man until its entire body was swallowed down. When he awoke, Ch'êng Kuan was delighted, This *Great Exegesis* took him five full years to complete. At the time of completion, he offered food to one thousand monks as a token of thanks to the Buddhas; it was also said that auspicious signs often appeared when Ch'êng Kuan preached the Sūtras to the public. He had more than a hundred disciples who were capable of transmitting the Dharma, and more than a thousand students who could expound the Sūtras.

Ch'êng Kuan once proposed the following vows:

1. I will always live in a monastery and keep only three pieces of clothing as a bhikṣu.
2. I will renounce all worldly gains and fame as if they were wastes.
3. I will never look at a woman.

4. My shadow will never linger upon a household.

5. I will always recite the *Lotus Sūtra* till I have cleansed all my clingings.

6. I will always read the Mahāyāna Sūtras to benefit all sentient beings.

7. I will continuously expound the *Hwa Yen Sūtra* to all walks of life.

8. I will never lie down in my life, regardless of day or night.

9. I will never, for the sake of self-glory or pride, confuse others.

10. I will never withdraw from the great compassion and kindness towards all sentient beings in the universe, but will strive for their salvation and benefit.

It was said that Ch'êng Kuan truly kept these vows and acted accordingly all his life.[28]

Although Ch'êng Kuan, who was born twenty-seven years after Fa Tsang's death, could never have studied under Fa Tsang (the third patriarch), he was nevertheless considered by the "orthodox" Hwa Yen Buddhists to be the fourth patriarch of the Hwa Yen School. The reason for this strange succession was that Ch'êng Kuan was looked upon as a true orthodox who *restored* Fa Tsang's original teachings after the latter's disciple Hui Yuan had misinterpreted them by inserting some of his own "heretical" views. Ch'êng Kuan was therefore considered the "indirect heir" of Fa Tsang who truly understood and could speak for Fa Tsang. But I am of the opinion that Ch'êng Kuan and Hui Yuan's differences on Hwa Yen Doctrine, especially on the ten mysteries, are rather minor and no outstanding significance should be attached to this claim.

Tsung Mi (780–841), the alleged fifth patriarch, was both a Hwa Yen and a Zen scholar, but since his contribution to Hwa Yen was not on a par with those of the other four patriarchs, his life story is omitted here.

NOTES [Part III]

1. This chapter was translated by Miss Pi-Cheng Lu in the nineteen thirties and appeared in her book *The Two Buddhist Books in Mahāyāna*. The present translation was done with the aid of Miss Lu's translation; the author ac-

knowledges his gratitude to Miss Lu's work. The text was based upon *Taisho* 293, pp. 844–46.

2. Buddha's Domain: see the Prologue and Notes.

3. Here the phrase *clouds of flowers* (or clouds of offerings) is only an expression of bountifulness or great quantity; it has no other special significance or meaning.

4. The six divisions—or the six lokas, i.e. the six types of living beings in the cosmos: devas or heavenly beings, men, asuras, animals, hungry ghosts, and those of purgatory or "hell." The four births: those who are born from wombs, from eggs, from water, and from metamorphosis.

5. Nāgas: mythical semi-divine beings, having a human face with the tail of a serpent and the expanded neck of the cobra. The word means "snake" or "dragon." The nāgas are also a people now residing in the mountainous regions of India, Burma, and Indo-China. Some believe that they were a Scythic race and probably obtained their name from worshipping serpents or holding them in awe and reverence.

6. Eight groups: these are the various mythical beings often mentioned in Buddhist literature; they include devas, nāgas, yakṣas, gandhrvas, asuras, garuḍas, kinnaras, and mahoraga.

7. Literally, "Let the correct paths that lead to man, heaven (deva), and Nirvāṇa be open!"

8. *Taisho* 1712, pp. 552–53. After careful consideration, I have concluded that it would not be profitable to translate this exegesis literally because of its highly punctilious and archaic style. A literal translation would only cloud the issue and obscure the philosophical thought which the author has attempted to present. Less important portions of the essay are therefore omitted and in a number of places the translation is quite free.

9. This contention is probably directed against the Sarvastivādins and other Hīnayāna schools who believe in the true existence of all dharmas, though they accept the Emptiness of a Self or pudgala.

10. Here "this" implies Voidness and "that" implies form.

11. See and compare the Bodhisattva's ten stages in Part I.

12. *Taisho* 1883, pp. 684–92.

13. In the beginning of every paragraph, the text reads: "The Meditation observes" (kuan yüeh), which is not only unnecessary but also confusing. Therefore, it is deleted in the translation after this point.

14. Literally, "What are the reasons?" or "Why?" but judging from the context, it should be translated as "What does this mean?"

15. *Taisho* 1883, p. 673.

16. *Taisho* 1884, p. 686.

17. *Taisho* 1884, p. 687.

18. *Taisho* 1883, p. 676.

19. See Note 12 in Part II, Section 2.

20. *Taisho* 2061, p. 732.

21. *Taisho* 1880, pp. 663–666.

22. This is based on Nan Ting's *A History of Hwa Yen Tsung* (Taipei, 1956), pp. 347–84; and Fo Tsu T'ung Chi, *Taisho* 2035, pp. 292–93.

23. *Taisho* 1868, pp. 512–13.

24. *Taisho* 2064, p. 984.

25. *Taisho* 2073, pp. 163–64.

26. The material for this passage is from *The Biography of Monk Fa Tsang* by T'sui Chih Yuan, *Taisho* 2054.

27. See *The Essentials of Buddhist Philosophy*, p. 112.

28. The material for this passage is from Sung Kao Shêng Chuan, *Taisho* 2061, p. 737.

EPILOGUE

In the foregoing pages, I have tried to present the gist of the Hwa Yen philosophy by introducing the three essential elements of that system—namely, the Philosophy of Emptiness, the Philosophy of Totality, and the Doctrine of Mind-Only—for the absence of any one would render the Hwa Yen thought incomplete and even misleading. The prologue and the first part of this book, *The Realm of Totality*, were given to provide a necessary background for the comprehension of such a philosophical system. Also, they may serve to present the basic Mahāyāna view on the cosmos, life, the various stages of Enlightenment, and the inconceivable realm of Buddhahood as it appears in the *Hwa Yen Sūtra*. The Chinese Buddhists are fond of calling the *Hwa Yen Sūtra* "the King of All Sūtras." This acclamation is quite understandable to those who have read this remarkable work, for they cannot help but catch a glimpse of an awe-inspiring panorama of totality in which the vastness and depth of Buddha's insight, His perspective, and His love and acts are revealed in lively freshness. To one who is interested in Zen Buddhism, the Ten Stages of a Bodhisattva's Enlightenment may be extremely useful, for he can now gauge his Zen experience against those described in the Sūtra and see how far or how little he has progressed in the Path.

So far as *philosophy* is concerned, I believe that the great majority of significant principles and arguments from the Hwa Yen doctrine have been included in the last two parts of this work. The all-important essay *Fa Chieh Kuan, On the Meditation of Dharmadhātu*, by Tu Shun was introduced in full with commentaries by different thinkers. Although another important essay of his, *Wu Chiao Chih Kuan*, the *Śamatha-Vipaśyana Practice of the Five Doctrines*, was not translated in full, a number of its important passages are included in the discussions of Totality and the Round Doctrine.

It is obvious that all I have said in this book can serve as no more than a fragmentary introduction to the *Hwa Yen Sūtra*. A thorough understanding of its teaching calls for a complete study—hence a translation—of the voluminous text itself. It is my sincerest hope that before long some courageous student of Hwa Yen will undertake this highly significant enterprise.

LIST OF CHINESE TERMS

Chao Chou 趙州

ch'e 車

cheng 證

ch'eng 成

ch'eng-hsiang 成相

Ch'eng Kuan 澄觀

Chi Tsang 吉藏

chi-wu tzu-hsing 極無自性

ch'i-ch'e 汽車

chiao-t'a-ch'e 腳踏車

Chih Cheng 智正

Chih I 智顗

chih-kuan 止觀

Chin-shih-tzu chang 金獅子章

Ching Tsung 敬宗

Ch'ing Chou 青州

chu 主

ch'üan-li 全理

Chüeh Lin 覺林

Chung-lun　中論

ch'ung-ch'ung wu-chin　重重無盡

Fa Ch'ang　法常

Fa-chieh　法界

Fa-chieh-kuan　法界觀

Fa-hsiang　法相

Fa Hui　法慧

Fa Tsang　法藏

Feng Yu Lan　馮友蘭

Fu Ta Shih　傅大士

hai-ching san-mei　海鏡三昧

hai-yin san-mei　海印三昧

Han Shan　憨山

ho　合

hou-te-chih wei　後得智位

Hsia-hou　夏侯　(surname of Ch'eng Kuan)

hsien　顯

Hsien Shou Tsung　賢首宗

Hsien Tsung　憲宗

Hsüan Pi　玄璧

hsüeh-ch'e　雪車

Hsüeh Yen 雪巖

hu chi 互卽

hua-t'ou 話頭

huai 壞

Hui Hsiao 慧曉

Hui Yüan 慧遠

hu ju 互入

Hung Chou 洪州

huo-ch'e 火車

Hwa-yen-ching 華嚴經

Hwa-yen-ching chih-kuei 華嚴經指歸

Hwa-yen i-hai pai-men 華嚴義海百門

I Chou 益州

i-hsiang 異相

i-hsin 一心

jung 融

Jung Kuo Fu Jen 榮國夫人

Kao Tsung 高宗

kuan-chao po-jo 觀照般若

Kuang T'ung 光統

k'ung 空

Li 理

li 離

liao-i 了義

li-shih wu-ai 理事無碍

lu-hsiang 六相

lu-hsiang-i 六相義

lu-hsiang yüan-jung 六相圓融

Ma Tsu 馬祖

Miao Feng 妙峯

Monk Shao (or Monk Chao) 僧肇

Mu Tsung 穆宗

p'an-chiao 判教

pi-ching-k'ung 畢竟空

pieh-hsiang 別相

pin 賓

pu-liao-i 不了義

se-hsin erh-fa 色心二法

se-k'ung 色空

sheng-hsing 聖性

Shih 事

shih-chih 十智

Shih Chih Yen　釋智儼

shih-fa　事法

shih-hsiang po-jo　實相般若

shih-hsüan　十玄

shih-shih wu-ai　事事無碍

shih-shih wu-ai fa-chieh 事事無碍法界

shih-p'ien-ju　十遍入

Shun Tsung　順宗

Sung-kao-seng-chuan　宋高僧傳

Sung　宋

T'ai Tsung　太宗　(T'ang Dynasty)

Tao　道

Tao Chen　道珍

ta-tzu-tsai　大自在

Te Tsung　德宗

Ti Ch'ih　地持

T'ien T'ai　天台

t'ung-shih tun-ch'i　同時頓起

t'ou-t'o　透脫

Tsung-chin-lu　宗鏡錄

tsung-hsiang　總相

Tsung Mi　宗密

Tun Huang　敦煌

t'ung-hsiang　同相

t'ung-shih hu-she　同時互攝

Tu Shun (or Fa Shun) 杜順（或法順）

t'ung-shih chü-ch'i　同時俱起

t'ung-shih wu-ai　同時無碍

Wen Tsung　文宗

wen-tzu po-jo　文字般若

wu　無

wu-ai　無碍

wu-chih　無執

Wu-chiao chih-kuan　五教止觀

wu-chu　無住

wu-shih　無始

wu-wo　無我

Wu Tse T'ien　武則天

yin　隱

Yin Shun　印順

Ying-lao-ching　纓絡經

yu　有

yüan-ch'eng-i　圓成一

yüan-chiao　圓敎

yüan-chiao-chien　圓敎見

yüan-t'ung wu-ai　圓通無碍

Yüng Ming　永明

Yüng Ting　永定

Yü T'ien　于闐

GLOSSARY

Abhidharma. A collection of early Buddhist philosophical theses, stressing the analysis of the composite elements of body, mind, and matter in order to reach an understanding of the doctrine of no-self (anātman).

Advaita-Vedānta. The Vedānta School that stresses the non-dual nature of Brahman, or Godhead. The outstanding philosopher of this School was Śankarācārya of the early ninth century. Vedānta is perhaps the most influential School of Hinduism today.

Ālaya Consciousness. The fundamental consciousness of all sentient beings, proposed by the Yogācāra School. Ālaya means the "store-house," implying that this consciousness contains and preserves all the potential psychic energy within its fold. It is the reservoir of all ideas, memories, and desires, and is also the fundamental cause of both saṁsāra and Nirvāṇa.

anātman. The Buddhist doctrine of no-self.

anumāna-pramāṇa. Chinese: pi-liang. According to Indian tradition there are two major sources of valid knowledge. One is the direct perception, pratyakṣa-pramāṇa, and the other is inference or reasoning, anumāna-pramāṇa. The former is a direct and the latter an indirect source of valid knowledge.

Arhat. The perfect saint who has eliminated all passions and desires, who is forever freed from the bindings of saṁsāra, and who has reached the fourth or last stage of Hīnayāna Enlightenment. In contrast to the four stages of the Hīnayāna version of Enlightenment, Mahāyāna proclaims the ten successive Enlightenment stages of a Bodhisattva.

Ārya. The superior person; often used in the Buddhist sense to denote the various stages of Enlightened beings.

asaṁkhya. Innumerable, infinite.

asaṁskṛta. The unconditioned dharmas, or things.

Asanga. The founder of the Yogācāra school, an extremely important philosopher of Mahāyāna Buddhism in the fifth century.

asura. In the Buddhist mythology, a kind of jealous and ferocious spirit or demi-god. They are always jealous of the heavenly angels or devas and fight the devas continually.

ātman. Self, ego, or individual personality.

Atyanta-Śūnyatā. The Voidness that is beyond all limits, including the "limit of itself," the Absolute or Thorough Voidness.

Avalokiteśvara. Perhaps the most important Bodhisattva in Mahāyāna Buddhism; he is supposed to be the embodiment of the compassion of all Buddhas, depicted in female forms in China and Japan. In China this Bodhisattva is known as Kuan-Yin, in Japan as Kannon.

Avataṁsaka Sūtra. The Garland Sūtra, Chinese: Hwa Yen Ching. Traditionally, this Sūtra is believed to have been delivered by Buddha while he was in deep Samādhi immediately after his Enlightenment, under the Bo tree in Bodhigāya. To the human eye, Gautama Buddha was in deep meditation alone, but to the eyes of the devas or angels, an infinite Universe (Dharmadhātu) was opened up by Buddha's miraculous power and grace. The dramas and preachings which took place in the Garland Sūtra were revealed in this all-embracing Dharmadhātu.

avidyā. Ignorance, not knowing, the fundamental ignorance of the truth of no-self which causes the self-perpetuating reincarnations of saṁsāra.

ayuta. A large number, probably a million.

bhāva. Being, existence, becoming.

bhikṣu. The fully ordained Buddhist monk.

bhūmi. Earth, or a stage. In the Garland Sūtra it denotes the ten successive Enlightenment stages of a Bodhisattva.

Bhūtatathatā. Reality, the suchness of reality, the ultimate.

binbara. A large number, probably a hundred million.

Bodhi. The state or "fruit" of the supreme Enlightenment of Buddhahood.

Bodhicitta. The Thought-of-Enlightenment, -on-Enlightenment, or -in-Enlightenment. Generally it refers to the initial motivation of a Mahāyāna Buddhist who aspires to the attainment of Buddhahood for the benefit of all sentient beings. As soon as one arouses this aspiration, or the Thought-of-Enlightenment, and makes a formal vow of carrying through the Bodhisattva's acts, he is considered to be a Bodhisattva.

The meaning and implications of this term are extremely broad and far-reaching. It represents the essence of Mahāyāna Buddhism. In the Garland Sūtra, Bodhicitta not only denotes the initial Thought-of-Enlightenment, but also the Enlightened Mind of the Ten Stages. Bodhicitta is translated sometimes as Mind-for-Bodhi, Bodhi-Mind, Heart-for-Bodhi, and so forth.

Bodhidharma. The founder of Ch'an or Zen Buddhism in China. He is considered the first patriarch of Zen Buddhism.

Bodhisattva. The practitioner of Mahāyāna Buddhism. He who aspires to the attainment of Enlightenment for the sake of all living beings. The one who has brought forth the Thought-of-Enlightenment (Bodhicitta), and made a formal vow to practice Mahāyāna Buddhism and to do all possible altruistic deeds. There are many different stages in the Bodhisattva's path, but both the beginner and the enlightened saint can be regarded as Bodhisattvas.

bodhyangas. A general term for the thirty-seven practices and principles that are conducive to the attainment of Enlightenment and its merits, which include the practice of the four mindfulnesses, the four proper lines of exertion, the four steps towards supernatural power, the five spiritual faculties, the five powers, the seven degrees of enlightenment, and the eight-fold noble path. These include almost the entire teaching of Buddhism as a whole. See Har Dayal, *The Bodhisattva Doctrine in Buddhist Sanskrit Literature,* Chapter IV (London: Kegan and Paul, 1932).

Brahmā. The Hindu God, who considers himself to be the creator of the Universe. In Buddhism his status is greatly demoted; he is only as one of the gods, or devas, who often appears in the Buddhist congregations to beseech Buddha to give a sermon and perform certain services for the assembly.

Brahman. The Godhead, the Absolute, the Ultimate Substratum of all things.

Buddha. The Enlightened One, or He who has attained the Supreme Enlightenment. The historical Buddha is the religious teacher Gautama Śākyamuni (563–483), who founded the religion generally known in the West as "Buddhism," but the Divine Buddha, envisioned by the Mahāyāna Buddhists, is more than a historical figure and teacher. He is practically regarded as the supreme "God," the embodiment of all virtues and perfections. To reveal the infinity of Buddha's

Realm and virtues is said to be the main concern of Hwa Yen Buddhism.

Candrakīrti. An important Mādhyamika philosopher of the sixth century.

Ch'an. The Chinese word for Dhyāna, or meditation. It usually denotes either the Ch'an Sect founded by Bodhidarma, which is generally known as Zen Buddhism, or the meditation practice and its various stages.

clinging-to-ego. Chinese: wo-chih. The innate tendency of man to hold on to the identity and existence of self or ego.

dependent-arising. Sunskrit: pratītya-samutpāda. Translated also as dependent-arising or dependent-origination, or conditioned co-production, implying a basic principle of Buddhism that all things have no independent existence. They are brought to pass by a combination of factors and conditions other than themselves. Hence nothing has a selfhood, or true being; it exists only conditionally and momentarily. This term is said to represent at the same time the doctrine of Śūnyatā.

deva. A god, angel, or benevolent celestial being.

Dharma. Buddhist doctrine or teachings; that which is true and good. Dharma can also be used to indicate Buddhism as an organized religion.

dharma. Things, events, becoming, matter, phenomena. Certain authors claim that dharma does not mean 'things,' but this is only a partial interpretation; dharma simply means things or events, as is seen in numerous Buddhist texts, especially in the Mahāyāna scriptures.

Dharma-Body of Buddha. Sanskrit: Dharmakāya. The ultimate or true body of Buddha, which is beyond all forms, attributes, and limits.

Dharmadhātu. Chinese: Fa-chieh. Literally, "the realm-of-dharmas." In the Hwa Yen literature it denotes the all-embracing Totality of the infinite universes revealed before the Bodhisattva's eyes by the grace of Buddha. It can be roughly understood to mean the Infinity and Totality of Buddha's Domain. The Tibetan scholars translated this word as Chos.Kyis.dByins, suggesting strongly not only the *extent* or expanse of Infinity but also its deepest nature, or essence (dByins is equivalent to the Chinese word Hsin), which is of course in agreement with the over all Hwa Yen doctrine.

Dharmakāya. See DHARMA-BODY OF BUDDHA.

dharmanairātmya. The principle that all things have no selfhood; the absence of a self-being of all dharmas.

dharmatā. Dharma-nature; the nature, or self-so, of all beings, which is not other than Emptiness or Śūnyatā.

Dhyāna. Meditation; often referring to a state of perfect concentration. A synonym of Samādhi in Buddhism.

Diamond Sūtra. Sanskrit: Vajracchedikā-prajñāpāramitā; Chinese: Chin Kang Ching. One of the most popular and important chapters in the Prajñāpāramitā literature, it is even recited as a daily prayer by the Chinese, Japanese, and Tibetan Buddhists.

dust-mote. Sanskrit: paramāṇu or aṇu. The infinitesimal portion, or atom, Chinese translation renders it as "wei ch'en"—tiny dust-mote.

Emptiness. Sanskrit: Śūnyatā; Chinese: K'ung Hsin. Voidness or the Void; a paramount facet of the Hwa Yen doctrine.

Enlightenment. The intuitive awareness or cognition of the dharma-nature; the realization of ultimate reality. The outcome of this realization is the elimination of passion-desires and the clinging-to-ego, and the liberation from saṁsāra.

End. Extreme, or limit (Sanskrit: anta). Anta, in the Buddhist sense, means the extreme or one-sided view, the opposite of Middle-Way. This can be either nihilism or realism, in various forms.

Four Noble Truths. The four basic principles of Buddhism preached by Buddha in his first sermon: 1. that in the final analysis life is suffering; 2. that the causes of suffering are passion-desires; 3. that there is a state of peace and joy called Nirvāṇa which is beyond all sufferings and passions; and 4. that the way (the Path) which leads to Nirvāṇa includes the practice of discipline, meditation, and intuitive wisdom.

Gambopa. An outstanding Yogi-scholar of Tibet (1079–1153). He was the disciple of Milarepa; it was through him that the Khagyupa School became widespread. He wrote many books, including *The Jewel Ornament of Liberation,* translated by Herbert Guenther. Also, see *The Hundred Thousand Songs of Milarepa,* Story 41, translated by Garma C. C. Chang.

Hīnayāna Buddhism. The Small Vehicle, a derogatory appellation given by the Mahāyānists to denote the Śrāvaka Schools, including the present Theravadins in Southeast Asian Countries.

Indra. A Hindu god; he plays a rather important role in various Sūtras as a protector of Buddhism.

Indra's net. The innumerable decorative jewels or pearls covering Indra's celestial palace forming an extensive "net"; these jewels mutually reflect one another, forming a "realms-embracing-realms-net" within each pearl. This is used as a metaphor to illustrate the mutual penetration and containment of Totality of the Hwa Yen Dharma-dhātu.

Jātaka stories. A collection of 550 stories of the former lives of the Buddha Gautama. They are of great value to folklore and Buddhist mythology reflecting Buddhist moral principles in the framework of the doctrine of karma.

kalpa. An aeon, or, according to the Hindu tradition, a kalpa is a day and a night of Brahmā; 4,320,000,000 years.

karma. Action, causation, the binding force of the universe which enforces the law of "like cause produces like effect." Karma applies not only to the natural phenomena but—more important—it also applies to moral events. It is therefore a metaphysical principle that explains the overall phenomenon of man's world.

karunā. Compassion (karunā) and Wisdom (prajñā) are two cardinal virtues of a Bodhisattva, who should cultivate them to perfection.

Karunā-Prajñā. Compassion and Wisdom as not only inseparable virtues, but merged into an indivisible whole in the advanced stages of Enlightenment.

kleśa. Passion-desires, defilement; the innate drive to possess and to act, which in turn propels the wheel of saṁsāra.

koan. A Zen story, a Zen problem, a technique of Zen practice.

koṭi. Ten million.

kṣana. A split second, an instant, the shortest moment of time.

kṣanti. Patience, tolerance, maturity (of the realization of Śūnyatā).

Kṣatrīya. The warrior class of India.

Kumārajīva. A great translator who came to China in 401 A.D. and translated many important Buddhist texts from Sanskrit into Chinese. His contribution to Chinese Buddhism is inestimable.

Li. Not to be confused with the other li—the ritual or propriety. This

Li denotes the principles, laws that underlie things and events in the phenomenal world. It also means "noumena," "rules," "theory," "absolute reality" "universals," and so forth.

Lunchin Rabjhung. Tibetan: Kloṅ.Cheṅ. Rab.Byams.Pa. The most important philosopher of the Ningmapa School of Tibetan Buddhism in the latter period, who wrote many books on all subjects of Buddhism, including the *Seven Treasuries of Lunchin* (Kloṅ.Chen. bDsod.bDun). He was probably a man of the fourteenth century.

Mādhyamika. The Middle-Way philosophy founded by Nāgārjuna. It stresses the doctrine of Śūnyatā. This school is considered to be the leading exponent of the Prajñāpāramitā literature.

Mādhyamika-Kārikās. The Middle-Way Stanzas, the original text of Mādhyamika written by Nāgārjuna, which is generally considered to be the most important text of this school.

Mahāsattva. A Great Bodhisattva who has reached the advanced stage of Enlightenment.

Mahāyāna. The school of the Great Vehicle, or generally called the Northern Buddhism, now barely existing in such countries as Tibet, Mongolia, and China, but still quite prevalent in Korea, Japan, and a part of Indo-China. This school grew out of the original Hīnayāna (or Śrāvakayāna) approximately in the second and third centuries. Its teachings are quite different from the Hīnayāna school; it stresses faith, devotion, compassion, positive altruistic activities, and so forth.

Maitreya. An advanced Bodhisattva who is destined to be the Buddha-to-come.

Mañjuśrī. The Bodhisattva who is considered to be the embodiment of all the Buddhas' wisdom.

mantra. A spell, an incantation.

Māra. The king of all devils, the Buddhist version of Satan.

Māyā. Cosmic delusion.

meditation and contemplation. Sanskrit: śamatha-vipaśyanā. Śamatha is a synonym of Dhyāna, and vipaśyanā a synonym of Prajñā. By the practice of śamatha one calms his mind and reaches the state of perfect concentration, and by the practice of vipaśyanā, one eliminates the clinging-of-ego and realizes the Suchness (Tathatā) of reality.

Mind-Only. In Mahāyāna Buddhism of the latter period, the belief that the phenomenal world is but the projection of one's own mind. Buddhist philosophers, notably Asanga and Vasubandu, systematized this doctrine into a highly complex philosophy of subjective idealism, generally known as the Yogācāra School.

mokṣa. Liberation from *saṁsāra* and all its pains; the aim of both Buddhism and Hinduism.

Mother Tārā. The embodiment of both the Compassion and the Wisdom of all Buddhas, witnessed in a female deity, the Mother Tārā of Tibetan Tantrism. She is also considered to be the manifestation of Avalokiteśvara.

mTha. Las. hDas.Pahi.sToṅ.Pa.Nyid. Sanskrit: Atyanta-Śūnyatā. The Emptiness that is beyond all limits or "ends," the Absolute or Thorough, transcending, Emptiness.

mutual entering. Chinese: hu-ju. One of the two basic concepts of Hwa Yen Buddhism, stressing the principle that all things and principles are mutually dependent and interpenetrate one another. It may be called a principle of mutual immanence.

mutual identity. Another basic concept of Hwa Yen Buddhism which claims that all things are identical on a transcendent plane.

nāga. A mythical snake-man. See footnote 5 of Part 3.

Nāgārjuna. The famous Buddhist philosopher of the second century; according to tradition, he discovered many new Mahāyāna texts and thus founded the Mahāyāna School of Buddhism almost single-handedly. He also developed the Mādhyamika philosophy.

neti, neti. Or "na iti, na iti." Not so, not so (quoted from *Brd.Upa.*-3.9.6.) ; indicates the inconceivability of the absolute Brahman.

niyuta. A large number, a trillion (?) .

niḥsvabhāva. The absence of self-being or self-hood; the emptiness of any entity that considers itself to be independent, self-subsistent, or eternally unchanging.

Nirmāṇakāya. The Transformation Body of Buddha, the Body-of-Form of all Buddhas which are displayed, or manifested for the sake of men who cannot yet approach the Dharmakāya: the formless True Body of Buddhahood.

Nirvāṇa. The stopping or cessation of all passion-desires, the state of liberation. In Mahāyāna, the state of perfection that is exclusively of Buddhahood, which is also called the Non-Abiding Nirvāṇa.

Nirvāṇa with residues. Implies those enlightened beings who have not yet completely rid themselves of their saṁsāric burdens of skandhas.

Paramārtha-satya. The Absolute or Transcendental Truth, the truth of the ultimate or the beyond.

pāramitā. The basic Mahāyāna practices which a Bodhisattva must follow. They usually include six major practices or pāramitās: charity, discipline, vigor, patience, meditation, and intuitive wisdom; but in the Hwa Yen Sūtra, the pāramitā-practices are divided into ten, to correspond with the Ten Stages. Pāramitā can either be translated as "perfection" or as "reaching the other shore." Both the Chinese and Tibetan scholars seem to think the latter a better translation.

paratantra. The nature of "depending-on-others-to-arise." This is the Yogācārin version of dependent-arising, that all things are manifestations of mind, and mind is a group of consciousnesses mutually dependent for their continuous existence and functions.

parikalpita. The erroneous idea of considering the phenomenal world to be truly existent and outside of one's mind, the great delusion (e.g., seeing a rope and regarding it as a snake).

parinirvāṇa. The complete Nirvāṇa, the Nirvāṇa attained at the moment of death which forever relinquishes the burdens of saṁsāric skandhas.

pariniṣpanna. The absolute reality, the "perfect-real nature"; the Yogācārin term for transcendental reality.

Prajñā. Wisdom; or transcendental wisdom, which is basically non-dual and non-discriminative.

prajñā-pāramitā. The perfection of Wisdom, the paramount practice and virtue of a Bodhisattva. A synonym for the intuitive knowledge of Śūnyatā.

prakṛti. The Sāṁkhya philosophy proposing that there are two basic and irreducible elements in the universe. One is puruṣa, the cosmic soul or spirit; and the other prakṛti, the cosmic matter. The evolution of the universe is spurred by the interplay between these two elements.

pratītya-samutpāda. The principle of dependent-arising advocated by the Mādhyamika philosophy. It is a synonym for Śūnyatā.

pratyeka Buddhas. Buddhism admits that there are men who can reach Enlightenment by themselves without a teacher, without even knowing the Buddha's teachings. By observing the nature of dependent-arising, they can reach Enlightenment by themselves. These men are called pratyeka Buddhas.

pratyakṣa-pramāṇa. The direct perceptions, one of the two valid sources of human knowledge. See ANUMĀNA-PRAMĀṆA.

pudgala. The empirical individual, ego, self.

rūpa. In a narrow sense, form, shape, color; but in a wider sense, matter.

Sagāra. The name of a dragon-king in Buddhist mythology.

Saha (world). Our world or the earth—that which can bear the great burden.

Śākyamuni. The sage of the Śākya tribe, another name of Gautama Buddha.

Samādhi. A synonym for Dhyāna, indicating the state of perfect concentration. However, in the Mahāyāna Sūtras, this term is not used only to refer to the state of perfect concentration, it seems also to suggest the dynamic state of the Enlightened mind, possessing infinite varieties of faculties and powers.

Samantabhadra. A great Bodhistattva who is the embodiment of the vows or will of all Buddhas. He is also the leading figure in the drama of The Garland Sūtra.

śamantha. A synonym for Dhyāna.

Sambhoga-kāya. The Divine Body, Pure Body, or Body-of-Enjoyment of Buddha. The Body-of-Form (Rūpakāya) of Buddha can be divided in two categories, the Transformation-Body (Nirmaṇakāya) and the Body-of-Enjoyment (Sambhoga-kāya) ; since the former can manifest itself in various forms in order to accommodate different sentient beings' karmas, therefore it can be pure as well as impure. However, the Divine-Body, or the perfect Body-of-Enjoyment (Tibetan: Lon.sPyod.rDsod.Pahi.sKu.) manifests only in the pure form; it is a divine or "celestial body," invisible to common eyes. This Body can only be seen by the advanced Bodhisattvas. The Dharmadhātu revealed in the Hwa Yen Sūtra is the realm of the Sambhoga-kāya.

Saṁgha. The Buddhist monk community; the assembly of monks.

Saṁjñā-vedayita-nirodha. The last Samādhi in which the Arhat engages before he enters into the parinirvāṇa. In this Samādhi, all thoughts and feelings are said to have been completely uprooted.

saṁsāra. The continuous rebirth in the phenomenal world, which is considered by both Buddhism and Hinduism to be a burden with great pains.

samskṛta. The conditioned things.

saṁvṛti-satya. The conventional or mundane truth; in contrast to the Transcendental or Absolute Truth (Paramārtha-satya). This is the relative truth conditioned by the various frames of reference in the empirical world.

Śankara. An outstanding philosopher of the Vedānta School, see AD-VAITA-VEDĀNTA.

Śāriputra. An outstanding disciple of Buddha; he was supposed to be the most intelligent disciple among the śrāvakas.

Sarvajñā. The all-knowing wisdom of Buddha.

Śāstra. Commentaries or independent essays on Buddhist teachings.

śāśvata-vāda. Eternalism, the theory that the real is changeless and permanent.

Sat. Being or existence.

satkāya-dṛṣṭi. The dogmatic views which cling to the true existence of substance or self (ātman).

Satyasiddhi. Chinese: Ch'en Shih Lun. A philosophical work of Hīnayāna Buddhism.

Shih. Things, events, particulars, phenomena, matter, the concrete, and so forth.

Shih-shih Wu-ai. The Dharmadhātu of events against events. When all events interpenetrate one another simultaneously in the Dharmadhātu, it reveals the mystery of all in all, the harmonious Totality of the all-embracing Buddha's Realm. This is the highest realm of Dharmadhātu.

Śīla Pāramitā. The Perfection of Discipline, the second pāramitā.

skandhas. Aggregates or heaps; implies that the so-called human body and mind are but a collection of aggregates of various elements, and therefore there is no eternal self within.

skillful-means. Sanskrit: upāya. The ingenious and extremely flexible ways devised by a Bodhisattva to help sentient beings. In order to help various types of living beings, a Bodhisattva should be extremely skillful in his approach to accommodate them.

Smṛti-upasthana. The meditation of Mindfulness, which is the fundamental or most important meditation instruction given by Buddha. In essence, it is a device to be constantly aware of the function of one's body and mind; and as the awareness is sharpened, the realization of the truth of no-self (anātman) will also grow.

Śrāvaka. The disciples of Buddha, or one who hears and follows the teaching of Buddha. This term is used by the Mahāyānists to refer to the Hīnayāna Buddhists and their doctrines.

Suchness. Sanskrit: Tathatā. The absolute reality beyond all designations; the only appropriate description is to call it "suchness."

śūnya. Empty, void, relative.

Śūnyatā. Voidness or Emptiness; the central philosophy of Buddhism. Śūnyatā, though translated as Voidness, does not mean nothingness or annihilation. See Part Two, the section on the Philosophy of Voidness.

Sūtras. The holy scriptures of Buddhism; all Sūtras were supposedly preached by Buddha Himself.

Svabhāva. Self-being, self-existence, Selfhood, that which does not depend on others for its existence; the definite, irreducible and self-subsisting entity that is "being" itself. The concept of Svabhāva is completely rejected by the philosophy of Śūnyatā.

Svabhāva-graha. The clinging to Selfhood.

Tathāgata. Thus-Come, a title of the Buddha (derivation doubtful). It perhaps means "He who has come and gone as former Buddhas"— that is, teaching the same truths and following the same Paths to the same goal.

Tathāgata-garbha. The Buddha nature that is within every man.

Tathatā. See SUCHNESS.

Thought-of-Enlightenment. See BODHICITTA.

The Three Precious Ones. Sanskrit: Triratna. The three sacred "objects" all Buddhists should worship: the Buddha—who is the founder of Buddhism; the Dharma—the teachings of Buddha; and Saṁgha—

the Buddhist monk community, which exemplifies the Buddhist practice and life.

three times. Past, present, and future.

Trikāya. The Three Bodies of Buddhahood: the Body of Truth (Dharmakāya), the Body of Enjoyment (Sambhoga-kāya), and the Body of Transformation (Nirmanakāya).

Tripiṭakas. Sūtra, Śāstra, and Vinaya; the Three Baskets, or the three canons of Buddhism.

two baskets. In Fa Tsang's commentary on the Heart Sūtra, the canons of Hīnayāna and Mahāyāna.

upādhi. Addition, fraud, that which is put in place of another thing, a substitute, a wrong superimposition upon the true Spirit; a synonym for Māyā.

Upanishads. A class of philosophical treatises attached to the Brahmāna portion of the Vedas. So far as philosophy is concerned, the Upanishads are perhaps the most important scriptures of Hinduism.

Vairocana Buddha. The Buddha of Great-Illumination. This is the True-Body-of-Form of Buddha Gautama Śākyamuni. It is through the blessing of Vairocana Buddha that the Hwa Yen Dharmadhātu was revealed.

Vajra. Diamond.

Vasubandu. A great philosopher of the Mind-Only doctrine in the fifth century (420–500). He and his brother, Asanga, jointly founded the Yogācāra School.

Vedānta. The concluding part of the Vedas, the name of a very influencial school of Hinduism. See ADVAITA-VEDĀNTA.

Vedic. That of the Vedas—the holy scriptures of Hinduism.

vijñāna. Consciousness.

Vimalakīrti. A legendary layman Buddhist in India, depicted as the model of the ideal Bodhisattva.

Vinayas. The canon of precepts for monks.

vipaśyanā. The intuitive observation taking place during deep meditation; a synonym for prajñā. See ŚAMANTA-VIPAŚYANĀ.

Wheel of Dharma. A symbolic term for Buddha's sermons.

Wisdom of Ingenuity. Chinese: Fang Pien Hui. A synonym for upāya, the ingenious ways of a Bodhisattva to accommodate men. See SKILL-FUL-MEANS.

yakṣa. A mythical being.

Yogācāra. The Doctrine of Mind Only, established by Asanga and Vasubandu.

Yogi. One who practices yoga.

INDEX